HOLISTIC LEADERSHIP

THRIVING SCHOOLS

*Twelve Lenses to Balance Priorities
and Serve the Whole Student*

JANE A. G. KISE

Solution Tree | Press

555 North Morton Street
Bloomington, IN 47404
800.733.6786 (toll free) / 812.336.7700
FAX: 812.336.7790
email: info@SolutionTree.com
SolutionTree.com
Visit **go.SolutionTree.com/leadership** to download the free reproducibles in this book.

Printed in the United States of America

Library of Congress Cataloging-in-Publication Data

Names: Kise, Jane A. G., author.
Title: Holistic leadership, thriving schools : twelve lenses to balance
    priorities and serve the whole student / Jane A. G. Kise.
Description: Bloomington, IN : Solution Tree Press, [2019] | Includes
    bibliographical references and index.
Identifiers: LCCN 2018050406 | ISBN 9781945349935 (perfect bound)
Subjects: LCSH: Educational leadership--United States. | Student-centered
    learning--United States. | Child development.
Classification: LCC LB2805 .K525 2019 | DDC 371.2--dc23 LC record available at https://lccn.loc
    .gov/2018050406

Solution Tree
Jeffrey C. Jones, CEO
Edmund M. Ackerman, President

Solution Tree Press
President and Publisher: Douglas M. Rife
Associate Publisher: Sarah Payne-Mills
Art Director: Rian Anderson
Managing Production Editor: Kendra Slayton
Senior Production Editor: Todd Brakke
Content Development Specialist: Amy Rubenstein
Copy Editor: Kate St. Ives
Proofreader: Elisabeth Abrams
Text and Cover Designer: Abby Bowen
Editorial Assistant: Sarah Ludwig

For Wendy Behrens

An education leader who not only knows how
to look both ways but also keeps setting me up
to learn and grow as an educator

Acknowledgments

Since 2000, scores of school leaders have invited me into their learning communities as we partnered on professional development. They shared their thoughts and ideas and fears as we worked to foster true collaboration and productive change. Thank you!

Beth Russell in particular allowed me to join her on initiative after initiative. I learned from both her example and from the work we did together on systemic change. Once again, she generously allowed me to share our story in these pages. Other leaders also gave up some of their precious time to talk with me about their successes in leveraging the interdependencies of leadership. A special thanks to Jennifer Abrams, John Alberts, Tim Brown, and Patrick Duffy for their time, their stories, their insights, and their review of how I presented their ideas.

Barry Johnson, founder of Polarity Partnerships (www.polaritypartnerships.com), introduced me to the power of both–and thinking, which helped me reframe the differentiated coaching model. He generously shared ideas, exercises, diagrams, and most of all, wisdom. Other associates of Polarity Partnerships, including Susan Dupre, Leslie DePol, and Cliff Kayser continue to answer questions, share their discoveries, and in other ways engage in the insightful and generous learning community. Wendy Behrens, director of Gifted Education for Minnesota, brainstormed with me early on about how to make this book practical and meaningful. Dozens of other school leaders have also given me information and advice to improve the content. Thanks to all!

Solution Tree Press would like to thank the following reviewers:

Anthony Bridgeman
Principal
West Islip High School
West Islip, New York

Donna DeSiato
Superintendent
East Syracuse Minoa Central
    School District
East Syracuse, New York

Robert Horn
Principal
Etowah High School
Woodstock, Georgia

Clay McDonald
Assistant Principal
Yukon High School
Yukon, Oklahoma

Cody Mothershead
Principal
White River High School
Buckley, Washington

Julie Nickerson
Principal
Morse Street School
Freeport, Maine

Vicki Wilson
Principal
Monroe Elementary School
Wyandotte, Michigan

Visit **go.SolutionTree.com/leadership** to download
the free reproducibles in this book.

Table of Contents

About the Author . . . . *xi*

Introduction *1*

    About This Book 4

CHAPTER 1
Developing Leadership for Whole-Child Schools *9*

    Five Essential Components for Effective Leadership Development 11

    The Whole-Child Leadership Development Process 13

    Reflection and Next Steps 21

CHAPTER 2
Thinking in Terms of Both and And: A Core Leadership Competency *23*

    Polarities 24

    Polarity Identification Instead of Unsolvable Problems 28

    Polarities, Priorities, and Emotional Intelligence 29

    Three Ways to Improve Your Use of Both–And Thinking 30

CHAPTER 3
Understanding Emotional Intelligence and Leading for the Whole Child . . *33*

    The Top Five Truths About EQ 34

    Your EQ Focus 37

    The EQ Skills Most Relevant to You 44

    Three Ways to Improve Your Emotional Intelligence 46

CHAPTER 4

Leading Toward a Common Vision and *Guiding Others in Leading Themselves* *49*

An Example of Leading While Listening 50

Leadership Priorities, Listening Priorities 52

The EQ Connection 55

Priorities Inherent in the Leadership *and* Listening Lens 56

CHAPTER 5

Implementing Initiatives and *Making Them Meaningful* *61*

Initiative Fatigue and How to Overcome It 62

The Breadth You Need With the Necessary Depth 66

The EQ Connection 69

Priorities Inherent in the Breadth *and* Depth Lens 70

CHAPTER 6

Building a Collaborative Learning Community and *Ensuring That Individuals Have Autonomy* *75*

The Dilemma of Community and Individual 76

Your Personal Collaboration Meter 79

The EQ Connection 81

Priorities Inherent in the Community *and* Individual Lens 83

CHAPTER 7

Taking Reality Into Account and *Pursuing a Vision* *87*

When Vision Meets Reality 88

The Need to Bring Vision to Reality 90

The EQ Connection 94

Priorities Inherent in the Reality *and* Vision Lens 95

CHAPTER 8

Building on Current Success and *Changing to Meet the Future* *101*

The Difference Between Resistance and Fear 102

Deliberate Continuity, Constant Change 105

The EQ Connection 108

Priorities Inherent in the Continuity *and* Change Lens 110

CHAPTER 9

Moving Ahead Quickly **and** *Moving Ahead for the Long Haul* **115**

A Focus on Tomorrow While Thinking Five Years Ahead 116

The Long and Short of Planning in Schools 120

The EQ Connection 123

Priorities Inherent in the Short-Term *and* Long-Term Lens 124

CHAPTER 10

Balancing Logical Objectivity **and** *Valuable Subjectivity* **129**

The Interdependency Between Logic *and* Values 130

A Real World of Rules With Exceptions 131

The EQ Connection 135

Priorities Inherent in the Logic *and* Values Lens 136

CHAPTER 11

Getting Results **and** *Building Trust* **143**

Real Results From Real Teams 144

The Measure of Outcomes and People 146

The EQ Connection 149

Priorities Inherent in the Outcomes *and* People Lens 150

CHAPTER 12

Effectively Using Positional Power **and** *Sharing Power* **155**

The Importance of Knowledge From the Ground and From Above 156

Real Results From Real Teams 158

The EQ Connection 162

Priorities Inherent in the Power To *and* Power With Lens 163

CHAPTER 13

Having Clarity on What and Why **and** *Having Flexibility on How* **167**

When Successful Ideas Aren't Universal 168

Flexible, Yet Not Fuzzy, Clarity 169

The EQ Connection 174

Priorities Inherent in the Clarity *and* Flexibility Lens 175

CHAPTER 14

Planning for the Predictable and *Embracing the Possible*. *179*

The Possible and the Probable 180

Effective Plans for a Complex, Unpredictable World 185

The EQ Connection 188

Priorities Inherent in the Predictability *and* Possibility Lens 189

CHAPTER 15

Making Measurable Whole-Child Achievement Progress
and Finding Purpose *195*

Of Campfires and Pressure Cookers. 196

Engaging Journeys and Goal-Oriented Destinations. 197

A Key Neuroscience Truth. 199

Priorities Inherent in the Goal Orientation *and* Engagement Lens 206

CHAPTER 16

Focusing on Your Priorities *209*

A Goal That Guides Development. 209

The Beginning of the End of the Beginning of the Journey. 214

APPENDIX

Personality Type and the Lenses of Leadership *215*

References and Resources. *219*

Index *225*

About the Author

Jane A. G. Kise, EdD, is the author of more than twenty-five books and an organizational consultant with extensive experience in leadership development and executive coaching, instructional coaching, and differentiated instruction. She is considered a worldwide expert in Jungian type and its impact on leadership and education. She works with schools and businesses, facilitating the creation of environments where everyone—leaders, teachers, and students—can flourish.

Jane trains educators around the world on coaching, collaborative practices, effective change processes, and differentiated instruction, especially in mathematics. A frequent conference keynote speaker, she has spoken at education conferences and type conferences across the United States and in Europe, Saudi Arabia, Australia, and New Zealand. Jane has also written articles for several magazines and has received awards for her differentiated coaching research.

Jane teaches doctoral courses in educational leadership at the University of St. Thomas and is a past faculty member of the Center for Applications of Psychological Type. She also served as president of the Association for Psychological Type International (APTi).

Jane holds a master of business administration from the Carlson School of Management and a doctorate in educational leadership from the University of St. Thomas. She is certified in neuroscience and Jungian personality; is qualified to use Myers–Briggs Type Indicator® (MBTI®) Steps I, II, and III as an MBTI Master Practitioner; and is certified in emotional intelligence instruments, Hogan assessments, and Leadership 360° tools.

To learn more about Jane's work, visit her website (www.janekise.com).

To book Jane A. G. Kise for professional development, contact pd@SolutionTree.com.

Introduction

You're leading, or aspiring to lead, a complex system—not just a team or even a professional learning community (PLC), but a broad scope *learning community* of students, teachers, staff, parents, and even local businesses and other stakeholders— and you're doing it in what leadership experts are now calling a VUCA world—a volatile, uncertain, complex, and ambiguous world.

In systems, if you push too hard on one place, something else gets out of whack. If you pay too much attention to A, B starts acting up out of neglect. Particularly as a school leader, when you implement a solution, you just may see a dozen other problems pop up as unintended consequences. So, what can a leader do to navigate this complexity?

Part of it is being able to see the whole of a system, but it also requires you to look two ways at once, learning to see the value in both A and B. If you're truly going to lead a school that meets the needs of the whole child—physically, mentally, emotionally, and spiritually—then recognizing and working with ongoing paradigms, rather than searching for a magic bullet, becomes your number one, ongoing, always-evolving priority for leadership development. It's about leading holistically so that your school thrives.

It's easy to default to a checklist when we think about whole-child learning. Physical education? Check. Academics? Check. Anti-bullying and social-emotional learning curriculum? Check. But to me, whole-child learning is a much bigger concept. Move away from buzz words like *full potential* and *21st century skills* and *global citizen* and really think about both a child's holistic experience of school *and* the holistic experience of the adults in the building. Do they get out of bed with a sense of purpose? Do they feel part of a family—a condition necessary for collective efficacy? Are they working on something each and every day that puts to use their skills and involves their interests? Are they growing not just in knowledge but in the wisdom that helps people see both their own needs and the needs of others? Are they able to navigate creating a meaningful life while making a living and to learning that fosters their own goals and growth that also fits with community goals? In other words, are they holistically thriving? This can only happen if the leaders take a holistic, wise approach to both the day-to-day decisions and long-term choices that affect both students and staff.

If it sounds easy, know that most adults never really learn to hold such tensions well, navigating that holistic view from 30,000 feet up and all of the details that go into leadership (Berger, 2012). This book will help you see and work with the whole system through a series of twelve core leadership paradigms represented in this book as lenses. It will help you recognize which one or two of them are at play in a given decision or initiative, and then target what you need to know and do so that you don't lose sight of one set of a paradigm's values or the other.

For a warm-up, try this: think through a current decision you are facing through the lens of adult educators *and* the lens of the students in your charge.

Were you ever a child? I ask this because sometimes I hear people arguing over learning strategies or school rules or education policies when they could answer disputes by considering, "How would each of us have reacted to this as a child?"

I was once a child. I loved school, and I want all students to end their secondary education experience with the same enthusiasm they had when they finally got to board that kindergarten bus, their backpack awaiting the treasures of learning. Granted, I was wired for school—my favorite T-shirt reads, "A day without reading is like . . . . Actually, I have no idea."

I honestly don't think I've gone a day without reading for pleasure since that moment in September of first grade when I asked my teacher, Miss Witzigrueter (it took us a week to learn how to say her name), what *s-i-t* spelled and the magical world of books opened up for me. I remember field trips to the fossil beds by the Mississippi and experimenting with mystery powders (flour, sugar, and baking soda) in science class. I remember pick-up games of kickball at recess and playing in the band and learning to make pie crust and figuring out a tough geometry proof while sprawled out on the floor in front of the television.

Of course, not every moment was pleasant. I also remember cringing when teachers weren't fair. I can still see little Susie crying when two girls told her they wouldn't play with her anymore. My stomach flips when I recall getting in trouble for—well, let's let that stay a secret!

I hope you noted that my memories are a mix of academics and all the other things that make up a school day. Do you remember how your whole self came to school and not just your brain? Do you remember how it felt to try to sit still when you could hear the birds singing outside, or how much easier it was to dig into a tough assignment for a teacher who had somehow shown you respect than, for example, the eighth-grade teacher who told me I positively lacked any talent for writing?

Remembering what it is like to be a child (and a student) is as important to education decisions as other data in deciding what our schools should be like—remember, memories are a form of empirical data.

"I don't remember at all," some educators tell me. I refrain from retorting that it shows in their unrealistic expectations of six-year-olds, and instead say, "I do. I loved learning, but I couldn't sit still for more than thirty minutes at a stretch. In middle school, my favorite classes were band and cooking, not mathematics or English—and I'm an English major with an MBA in finance!"

Or, I might relay the story of an eleven-year-old I was tutoring for mathematics. When I started to fill out her hall pass, she said she was headed to tutoring for reading. That meant she had six straight hours of academic courses in her day.

"Wow, that's a tough schedule," I said.

"Yeah, I don't get to do anything fun. Not even Spanish," she mourned.

Would you, like me, have lost a love of school in that kind of environment? If you can't remember, spend some time reflecting on any artifacts you have—report cards, class pictures, programs from assemblies, yearbooks, and so on. What might jar your memory and help you think like a child? Doing so doesn't mean you're putting students in charge of things they're too immature to grasp but rather that you're including the natural knee-jerk reactions, needs, aspirations, feelings, and frustrations of those *for whom schools exist*. You aren't letting go of adult wisdom but are instead moving toward *and*-based thinking—how adult *and* child mindsets can work together to inform decisions and planning.

Holistically leading thriving schools isn't just about adding social-emotional learning for students to an already-packed curriculum. Instead, it means recognizing:

- ◆ One's own ongoing need for development; most experts recognize at least five stages of adult development (Berger, 2012) and believe that few adults reach the top two stages (think of that education leader you seek out for wisdom and advice).

- The need to be constantly on the lookout for one's own biases and blind spots, understanding that every strength comes with a blind spot and, when overdone, becomes a weakness

- The value of power with—leading collaboratively to multiply what can be accomplished—and power to—leading others toward a vision worthy of the students in your charge (McFarland, 2006)

- That if we over-focus on academics, students' other needs go unmet; holistic leaders know the value of learning to look in two directions at the same time.

The era of standardized testing that the No Child Left Behind Act (2002) ushered in is an example of looking in just one direction—of implementing a solution in a system and seeing a dozen other problems pop up as unintended consequences. The Association for Supervision and Curriculum Development (ASCD) worked to call attention to this one-way thinking by launching its Whole Child Initiative in 2007, stating, "Each child, in each school, in each of our communities deserves to be healthy, safe, engaged, supported, and challenged. That's what a whole-child approach to learning, teaching, and community engagement really is" (ASCD, 2014, p. 9).

But leading a whole-child school, one that truly embraces meeting these varied needs, means you're constantly making trade-offs, doesn't it? Time for academics or time for recess and responsive classrooms and antibullying initiatives and extra tutoring and . . . the list goes on. Add in the efficiencies of top-down leadership versus the richness of shared leadership, the need for teachers to do the work and prepare to do the work, the role of the school and the role of families and communities . . . the lists of these interdependencies go on and on, too, don't they?

Again, you're leading a complex system in a VUCA world.

About This Book

If you're looking for a practical guide to school leadership, this is it. But you may not recognize it as such right away because it doesn't have a definitive list of what you need to do to succeed. Why not? Because lists are linear, and you aren't leading a linear organization.

Instead of a list of characteristics or responsibilities or essential tasks—although I mention many of these in this book—I'm offering tools for identifying where you should focus given who you are, who you are leading, and what you are trying to accomplish, all within a framework that helps you see when competing priorities are at play. It's a framework that will help you set aside the human tendency to think in terms of *either–or* and instead embrace the necessity of *both–and* thinking in which you can recognize the tension between two competing, yet interdependent, priorities and understand how to benefit from the valuable contributions of both.

This book is designed around twelve such interdependencies, or as I call them, the *Twelve Lenses of Leadership*, to help you identify when you're at risk of engaging in either–or thinking instead of both–and thinking. The following are the lenses you will learn about.

1. Leadership *and* listening
2. Breadth *and* depth
3. Community *and* individual
4. Reality *and* vision
5. Continuity *and* change
6. Short term *and* long term
7. Logic *and* values
8. Outcomes *and* people
9. Power to *and* power with
10. Clarity *and* flexibility
11. Predictability *and* possibility
12. Goal orientation *and* engagement

Each of these lenses comes from research on effective leaders (Coyle, 2018; Kouzes & Pozner, 2010), but recognize that choosing one lens to focus on still requires you to be savvy about how it intertwines with other lenses. Priorities inherent in each lens are interdependent with things that might not even seem important in the moment but will come to be so.

With this book, I will help you to recognize how to engage both–and thinking to accomplish the following.

◆ Improve your ability to create an environment where collaborative teacher efficacy exists in an atmosphere of trust—the number-one predictor of student achievement (DeWitt, 2017).

◆ Hone your skills at inspiring and empowering others for the long haul of change.

◆ Ensure that you, the other adults in the building, and the students, are energized, efficient, empowered, and engaged for the tough, tough work of becoming thinking, creative contributors.

Go back to my question of, "Were you ever a child?" Think for a moment about the kind of school you would like to attend if you were seven, or eleven, or sixteen years old again. What would keep you engaged, foster your curiosity, encourage you to persevere, help you learn to ask good questions, and trust that your efforts will bring about results? Are you seeing the answers to these questions reflected in the schools around you?

A vision of such a school, supported by research on what truly works, should be the most motivating force for a school leader. Leadership expert Margaret Wheatley (2017) states:

> What are the values, intentions, principles for behavior that describe who we want to be? Once established, are these common knowledge, known by all? As we work together, do we refer to our identity to make decisions? How do we respond when something goes wrong? Do we each feel accountable for maintaining the integrity of this identity? . . . Only the leader is in the position to see the whole of the organization. No matter how willing people might be, everyone is overwhelmed and consumed with their own work. Sane leadership is developing the capacity to observe what's going on in the whole system and then either reflect that back or bring people together to consider where we are now. (pp. 232–233)

Because a leader is the one person best positioned to see the whole of a learning community, I designed these pages to help you see that whole, even as you set goals for yourself and for other parts of it. To get the most out of *Holistic Leadership, Thriving Schools*, please don't just read these pages. Instead, commit to the following process.

- ◆ **Work on real goals for your development:** Chapter 1 highlights the five essential components of effective leadership development and offers guidance for choosing the right kinds of goals and priorities using the Twelve Lenses of Leadership. It is the first step toward focusing your priorities.

- ◆ **Learn to think in terms of both *and* and:** Chapter 2 explains both–and thinking as it relates to the concept of polarities and how each of the leadership lenses in this book illustrates a basic interdependency between two seemingly competing poles.

- ◆ **Develop your understanding of emotional intelligence:** Chapter 3 explains the top-five truths about critical soft skills and then helps you to discover which of these are most important to you as they relate to the Twelve Lenses of Leadership.

- ◆ **Understand the leadership lenses that are most critical to you:** Chapters 4–15 each explain a specific leadership lens. Depending on the school you're leading, your goals for the short term *and* long term, and your focus for leadership development, you will use specific chapters to build your understanding of the leadership lenses and develop your leadership abilities.

◆ **Try the full Priority Focus™ process:** Chapter 16 outlines a process, including reflection activities, for setting your focus on a goal that will guide your leadership development. What happens as a result?

◆ **Partner with another leader:** This final step occurs after you've put this book's content to work for you. Meet with another leader to discuss ideas and to hold each other accountable in making progress toward your respective goals. In fact, use the reflection questions on page 209 (A Goal That Guides Development) together, offering the gift of listening carefully to each other to help clarify what is working.

Further, know that this book isn't a one-time read. Instead, it's a reference guide full of tools you can use for each new goal, position, team, initiative, responsibility, and more.

The goal is to become the best leader you can be by focusing your strengths, ensuring your blind spots don't get in the way, and building your capacity to reach the goals you've set to make your learning community a visionary place for students and adults. Great leaders never stop developing; may these pages help you meet the ongoing challenges of guiding the schools upon which every student's future, and the future of all who will benefit from what they can contribute to society, depend.

CHAPTER 1

Developing Leadership for Whole-Child Schools

ASCD (n.d.) well-defines the whole-child approach to education: "A whole child approach, which ensures that each student is healthy, safe, engaged, supported, and challenged, sets the standard for comprehensive, sustainable school improvement and provides for long-term student success." Before we delve into the importance of this critical statement, let's start where it all starts—at the top.

Here's the repeating story of my work with school leaders. I'm called in to work on a specific initiative: creating collective efficacy through building trust and collaborative skills; launching effective, sustainable collaborative learning communities; differentiating instruction; improving instructional coaching; or resolving conflict are a few examples. Over the weeks or months that I'm involved, the leader gains a heightened awareness of his or her leadership style, its impact on a diverse staff, and strategies for avoiding overuse of strengths and related blind spots.

The leader moves to a new position, or a new building, or perhaps launches a major new initiative. "I'm set for the time being, what with all I've learned about leadership," he or she tells me. "I'll start with getting a good read on my new colleagues and team, listening to their ideas and working on strategies. Then I might call you in again. Thanks."

And? Often within a month, I get a call, "I need you now. This staff is *so* different. We need to understand one another better." Or, "I focused on A, lost track of B, and I can feel resistance on the rise. Help!"

These are effective, intentional leaders. They quickly grasp the situational nature of school leadership and have internalized the following.

♦ Each learning community is unique, with different histories, personnel, resources, assets, and challenges.

- Staff chemistry, habits, beliefs, values, and fears vary widely.

- To truly lead for academic success and success for the whole child involves more roles and responsibilities than any one person can shoulder.

- The most important leadership roles and responsibilities vary from situation to situation.

- Prioritize everything, and nothing will get done.

Further, they have learned that leadership roles are often in tension with one another. For example, it isn't easy to communicate high expectations *and* create an atmosphere where teachers feel safe sharing dilemmas and mistakes. Nor is it easy for schools to ensure they are meeting each student's academic needs *and* physical, social, and emotional needs.

That's what this book is about: providing tools so that you can lead from who you are and focus on the right priorities for the students, teachers, staff, parents, local businesses, and other stakeholders that comprise your specific learning community.

To accomplish this, you'll use a process aligned with the conditions necessary for true leadership development. Through stories of leaders who have successfully navigated competing priorities and stopped the pendulum swings so rampant in education reform efforts, you'll learn about balancing twelve pairs of core leadership responsibilities that are essential for leading whole-child schools. These are the Twelve Lenses of Leadership I introduced at the start of this book.

You'll come to know each of these lenses well, but to start off, the key concept to understand is that these lenses represent ongoing interdependencies between two *equally important* sets of values. A simple example of one of these ongoing inter-dependencies is also a major theme of this book: focusing on academics while also focusing on the whole child. They're interdependent, aren't they? After all, we know that physical, social, and mental well-being affect academic performance—and academic performance can affect the physical, social, and mental well-being of students (Jensen, 2005; Mullainathan & Shafir, 2013). You'll read more about how these lenses work in chapter 2 (page 23). Here, you'll first tackle your own leadership mindset by gauging how your natural priorities align with these twelve lenses and how your skills with eight core competencies of emotional intelligence support or thwart your efforts.

Leadership lenses? Interdependencies? Mindsets? Priorities? Emotional intelligence? There are so many components because developing as a leader—not just mastering management skills but engaging everyone in effectively working toward a meaningful shared purpose—is *very* difficult. In fact, most leadership development programs have little or no impact on actual leadership practices. However, if you use this book's process, you will become a more thoughtful, balanced leader who is capable of adjusting to an ever-changing educational landscape. You'll be using all of these components to maximize your strengths while avoiding your blind spots. As theologian Richard Rohr (2013) puts it, "*We do not see things as they are; we see things as we are*" (p. 82).

Your journey begins in this chapter with exploring five elements crucial for effective leadership development along with learning a holistic leadership development process for establishing your focus on whole-teacher instruction and whole-child learning.

Five Essential Components for Effective Leadership Development

McKinsey & Company is a consulting firm heavily involved in understanding and implementing what works best in leadership and change initiatives. Its deep analysis of what it takes to develop leaders identifies four key components (Gurdjian, Halbeisen, & Lane, 2014). The fifth essential component that you'll find in the following list is something I believe is a crucial addition to the mix.

1. **The skills and dispositions you need depend on your context:** What works in one learning community may not fit with the needs, values, or chemistry of another. You'll be using the tools in this book to choose the right focus for your context.

2. **Skill development happens not in isolation, but while working and reflecting on real responsibilities and issues:** Case studies and retreats may have their place, but combining leadership development with important workplace projects and initiatives fosters real growth. As you will soon see, it's ultimately about setting a specific goal to focus on, and that will derive from your real work. (See Choosing Your Development Focus, page 14.)

3. **Leaders need to unearth and address mindsets:** We all have unconscious beliefs, biases, assumptions, and other mindsets that keep us from changing, keep us from hearing other viewpoints, and keep us from being free to see new solutions. Perhaps you've heard of some of the sources of biases, those blind spots that influence our thinking and actions. Jonathan Haidt (2012) summarizes some of the most important ones that keep us from seeing other points of view and courses of action.

- Our moral judgments come before our rational decisions, without cautious processing. We then reason to justify what we've already concluded. Paradoxically, the more education we have, the better we are at building one-sided arguments.

- Our genetic makeups, cultural backgrounds, and life experiences influence our instant reactions to people, things, ideas, and more.

- We're all guilty of outcome bias, a tendency to judge a decision by the outcome rather than by *how* the decision was made.

- We all have confirmation bias, a tendency to seek out and interpret new evidence in ways that confirm what we already think. Haidt (2012) summarizes research showing that it takes only one piece of evidence for us to say, "See? I'm right!" But it takes ten or more for us to consider changing our minds.

- Only through dialogue with people who think differently do we examine our beliefs and evidence that contradicts them—and through tools that point out when we can't see the other side.

The tools in this book are designed to help us see what we don't see. You'll know you're unearthing them if some of the exercises cause you to squirm as you realize, *I was wrong. . . . I misinterpreted their motivations . . . . There is another way . . . . I need the wisdom of that person who kind of drives me crazy!*

4. **Leaders need to measure whether they're developing:** You're investing time and effort in becoming a better leader—and the McKinsey research (Gurdjian et al., 2014) indicates that people don't really take it seriously unless they're gathering evidence as to whether that investment is paying off.

Perhaps you're relying on the SMART acronym for setting effective goals—goals that are strategic and specific, measurable, attainable, results oriented, and time bound (Conzemius & O'Neill, 2014). Supposedly, such goals are motivating and lead to higher performance. Many schools use the SMART goal framework to set goals and action steps based on student assessment data. However, these criteria will not help you measure whether you are improving your skills with empathy, nor whether you are mobilizing your staff around a common purpose, or if you are successfully reframing the questions and contributions of teachers whose backgrounds and strengths are very different from yours. Each chapter in this book has examples of more immediate ways you can constantly check whether you are continuing to focus on the right priorities to reach your goals.

If this sounds time-consuming, keep in mind that you'll be following this process while focusing on your real work—both leadership development *and* your core responsibilities. However, from my experience in coaching leaders, this concern unearths one more component (number 5 in this list) that isn't on the McKinsey list (Gurdjian et al., 2014).

5. **Set aside time for reflection:** We don't actually learn by doing. We learn by taking action and then reflecting on whether the action had the impact we desired, by examining how others were affected, whether we might have done something differently, what we've learned for the next time, and so on. In the busy life of a school leader, it's easy to overlook the necessity of reflection. Write it into your calendar like any other responsibility, or as if you were taking a class. If you can work with a leadership coach, do so; leaders in the business world have long recognized the worth of an objective, skilled outsider who can facilitate reflection. Or, find an accountability partner and schedule regular check-ins—someone with whom you could talk about your progress, frustrations, and next steps.

Before you dive into the journey of effectively leading for the whole child, let's understand the leadership development process this book uses.

The Whole-Child Leadership Development Process

The leadership development process in this book is one you can use again and again, for different *development* goals (short-term and long-term) that let you gain the skills, wisdom, dispositions, and understandings you need to lead a school that truly meets the needs of the whole child. Be intentional about using it. *Before* you run into difficulties with new people or new responsibilities, use the process to identify the potential focuses you will need (the right goals), and then coach yourself to a plan for action. The six-step process works like this. (You will find more detailed supporting material for these steps in the sections that follow.)

1. Choose an appropriate development focus or goal as I describe in the next section (page 14).

2. Sort your leadership priorities using the list in Choosing Your Priorities (page 16).

3. Locate those priorities in Aligning Priorities and Lenses (page 18), and work with the reflection questions on page 20 that follow the figure. These are all designed to help you consider your mindset. Think of this as a way to

discern where you may or may not be overusing your strengths or to perhaps discover where you are falling into the trap of one of your blind spots.

4. Use the steps in Aligning Priorities and Lenses (page 18) to narrow down your priorities to just three. Why? Because it's hard to focus on more than three priorities at once. In fact, until the 19th century, the word *priority* had no plural (McKeown, 2014). Think about it. You could only have one.

5. Check out the chapters that relate to your top three priorities (chapters 4–15 each cover a specific lens). Which leadership lenses are involved? What other roles or tasks require you to successfully navigate those lenses? How might the suggestions at the end of this chapter help you better balance the demands of that lens?

6. Create a plan for action—a priority focus. Chapter 16 (page 209) provides the process for turning your priorities into a guide that includes answers to the questions *Why is this important?* and *How will I know I'm making progress?* This process gives you a real-time tool for development.

That's it, a process you can use again and again to ensure you're focused on the right priorities and actions for your current situation. In the next three sections, we'll detail how you choose your development focus, how you choose your priorities, and how you can align those priorities with the Twelve Lenses of Leadership in this book.

ASK YOURSELF

What is a goal you already have for which you might use this process? Before reading further, take a moment to identify this goal, and then apply the criteria in the next section.

Choosing Your Development Focus

Each time, the development process begins with choosing a specific goal. *Becoming a better leader* is too general, but a wide variety of other goals works. You'll find that different goals may call for completely different priorities, making this process very different from other systems for determining values that you may have used in the past.

Although it is by no means an exhaustive list, here are some ideas of how you might identify your initial focus.

- **Lead a specific initiative or work toward a specific learning community goal:** Your focus might flow straight from the strategic plan and could be as large as successfully launching a district- or schoolwide PLC or smaller in scope such as increasing expert use of student-centered discussions in your building.

- **Improve a specific skill:** For the time being, set aside technical skills such as using data to inform instruction. Think about the soft skills that are actually the hardest to develop (Cherniss, Extein, Goleman, & Weissberg, 2006). For example, you might read through the eight components of emotional intelligence described in chapter 3 (page 33) and choose one that will improve your ability to positively influence and motivate others.

- **Focus on a new position:** If you are about to step into a new role, your focus could be on what you perceive as your most important goal for the first four to six weeks on the job. Maybe you need to listen to understand the culture or maybe you need a deeper understanding of what will be expected of you. Maybe you need to establish a clear purpose and vision or need to review, revise, or implement a specific plan.

- **Change your one key thing:** Do you have a mentor, supervisor, or colleague whom you trust and who really understands school leadership? Ask this person, "What one thing should I work on getting better at so that I can be a more effective leader?" It's amazing how often the answer people receive is surprising, a bit unnerving, and spot on. This may be the toughest starting place for a first foray into true leadership development, but the payoff can be huge.

Now, let's check whether your natural priorities truly support achieving your purpose.

Use these margins to make notes of related goals you might set; and if you don't like to write in books, attach a sticky note with your thoughts beside each one.

Choosing Your Priorities

Figure 1.1 lists forty priorities—priorities that leaders with very different strengths, mindsets, and styles view as naturally key to good leadership. None are bad or wrong; you are choosing between good and better priorities. In fact, some that seem unattractive to you for this goal may be key for a different goal. With your chosen focus in mind, select the top ten priorities that you think will be most important for reaching your goal. Another way to phrase it is, *Is this priority crucial to my making progress on this goal?*

From the following forty priorities, choose your top ten.

1. **Influencing:** I want to see my ideas, tools, or plans being used by others to create improvements, efficiencies, or significant change.
2. **Shepherding:** I work to ensure that everyone is clearly aware of our values and vision and that they are making decisions and choices that align with those values and our vision.
3. **Empowering:** I strive to enable others to learn to lead themselves and take the initiative in their work.
4. **Connecting:** I listen to understand the viewpoints, feelings, and aspirations of those I lead; doing so increases my effectiveness.
5. **Networking:** I am committed to making connections, sharing resources, and establishing relationships to enhance my team's effectiveness.
6. **Innovating:** I explore resources, research-based innovations, ideas, theories, and learning opportunities on multiple fronts to stay abreast of best practices.
7. **Legacy:** I want to be involved in new ideas, paradigm shifts, or solutions to problems that others thought were difficult or even unsolvable.
8. **Mastery:** I value seeing initiatives implemented in depth so that teachers and students develop needed skills and knowledge.
9. **Relationships:** I invest time in building bonds with others for mutual support that can go beyond what the task at hand might require.
10. **Collaboration:** I want to foster meaningful teamwork where people enjoy working together and keep everyone's best interests in mind.
11. **Individuality:** I value opportunities for solo efforts, making the most of each person's unique gifts, creativity, and inspirations.
12. **Personal development:** I am committed to continuous improvement of the skills and knowledge I and others need to reach our full potentials.
13. **Realism:** I value representing things as they really are and having the pulse of my team's capacity, engagement, and sense of efficacy.
14. **Balance:** I want to model limits on work so that I, and those with whom I work, make time for family, health, leisure pursuits, nature, and relationships.
15. **Visioning:** I believe in co-creating images of the future that motivate people and then leading them to work toward those common purposes.

16. **Optimism:** I want to inspire confidence in those I lead, so that our efforts will bring success.

17. **Experience:** I thrive when using our knowledge and past work, which are key to improving performance or to planning and implementing new but related work.

18. **Creativity with the known:** I value using sound judgment, proven routines, and known information for continuous improvement in practical matters.

19. **Challenge:** I am motivated by exciting problems or difficult and risk-filled tasks that enhance skills and prove competency.

20. **Creativity with the new:** I value using my imagination and inspirations to devise original ideas, theories, tools, methods, or plans that bring about change.

21. **Efficiency:** I want to organize our work environments, processes, tasks, and such, so that goals are met with little waste of time, talent, or materials.

22. **Adaptability:** I model being able to adjust to ever-changing circumstances, responding to the needs of the moment.

23. **Fair-mindedness:** I believe in calmness and objectivity, using consistent standards so that my decisions and actions are fair, just, and effective.

24. **Empathy:** I believe in stepping into the shoes of others and understanding their experiences, values, and points of view.

25. **Results:** I put meeting or exceeding our stated goals at the top of my priority list.

26. **Measurability:** I want to ensure we are using helpful data, soft and hard, to assess progress toward goals.

27. **Trust:** I am committed to creating an environment where people can rely on me and others, on our integrity, reliability, vulnerability, compassion, strength, and support.

28. **Appreciation:** I want to create an atmosphere where people demonstrate respect for each other, regardless of expertise.

29. **Expertise:** I model respect of competency—thinking highly of demonstrated skills, knowledge, work, and results.

30. **Openness:** I seek and ponder contrary data, new perspectives, and other points of view before reaching conclusions.

31. **Organization:** I emphasize thinking through project or systems processes, needs, and expectations to create workable plans and practices.

32. **Accountability:** I establish realistic expectations and responsibility for outcomes, striving for clarity regarding what is and isn't under our control.

33. **Originality:** I value tapping our imaginations, connecting ideas in unusual ways, and using artistic skills or other tools to find unique pathways.

34. **Autonomy:** I foster teams where each member can be effective when thinking and acting independently.

35. **Dependability:** I want to be known as trustworthy and reliable, carrying out the charges I have been given.

Figure 1.1: The forty leadership priorities.

continued →

36. **Complexity:** I recognize when linear solutions are inadequate and plan for uncertainty, paradoxes, multiple scenarios, and volatility.

37. **Achievement:** I believe in setting worthy goals, planning for how to reach them, and then doing so.

38. **Perseverance:** I want to model and encourage others in sustaining momentum and having fortitude while marking tangible progress.

39. **Enjoyment:** I want to create a work environment that is inspiring, congenial, and playful, where people can find a touch of fun and humor.

40. **Fulfillment:** I want to concentrate my efforts on the dreams and endeavors that bring meaning and purpose to me and to those I lead.

Visit **go.SolutionTree.com/leadership** *for a free reproducible version of this figure.*

Here's a tip for doing the sort: use small sticky note flags. Or, print a copy of figure 1.1 and cut apart the forty priorities so you can sort the strips of paper. *Do not simply circle your top ten.* Why? Because your brain reacts differently to setting aside a priority than to simply not circling one. Using the flags or paper strips expands your working memory to include the work surface in front of you—your brain holds on to the important focus of considering your goal while the surface allows you to move ideas around, group them in different ways, and reconsider discarded priorities.

Once you have your top ten priorities, let's see how they align with the Twelve Lenses of Leadership as a first step toward examining any mindsets that could get in the way of your goal.

Aligning Priorities and Lenses

In figure 1.2, you'll find the forty priorities distributed among the Twelve Lenses of Leadership. They're in the same order as the list in figure 1.1. For example, the first priority, *influencing*, is under lens 1 and the last (fortieth) priority, *fulfillment*, is under lens 12 (the last lens). Notice how each lens lists two, core polarities (poles), a topic we explore in detail in chapter 2 (page 23).

FURTHER DEVELOPMENT

The priorities and lenses are designed based on the leadership strengths and priorities of leaders with different Jungian personality-type preferences, a framework popularized through the Myers–Briggs Type Indicator, but

Lens 1	Leadership	Listening
	Providing leadership while helping everyone learn to lead themselves	
Priorities	Influencing, Shepherding	Empowering, Connecting
Lens 2	Breadth	Depth
	Implementing needed initiatives and ensuring mastery of initiatives	
Priorities	Networking, Innovating	Legacy, Mastery
Lens 3	Community	Individual
	Building a collaborative culture while meeting individual needs	
Priorities	Relationships, Collaboration	Individuality, Personal development
Lens 4	Reality	Vision
	Accounting for very real barriers of time, resources, and so on, while leading toward a purposeful vision	
Priorities	Realism, Balance	Visioning, Optimism
Lens 5	Continuity	Change
	Building on current success while changing to meet the future	
Priorities	Experience, Creativity with the known	Challenge, Creativity with the new
Lens 6	Short Term	Long Term
	Addressing current needs while working toward systemic change	
Priorities	Efficiency	Adaptability
Lens 7	Logic	Values
	Determining universal principles and rules and accounting for individual needs and perspectives	
Priorities	Fair-mindedness	Empathy
Lens 8	Outcomes	People
	Moving toward organizational success and creating a culture of collective efficacy	
Priorities	Results, Measurability	Trust, Appreciation
Lens 9	Power To	Power With
	Effectively using positional power while effectively sharing power	
Priorities	Expertise	Openness
Lens 10	Clarity	Flexibility
	Clarifying expectations and remaining open to new processes and ideas	
Priorities	Organization, Accountability	Originality, Autonomy
Lens 11	Predictability	Possibility
	Setting goals and making plans while preparing for ever-changing environments and an uncertain future	
Priorities	Dependability	Complexity
Lens 12	Goal orientation	Engagement
	Making whole-child achievement progress while ensuring that adults and students have purpose	
Priorities	Achievement, Perseverance	Enjoyment, Fulfillment

Figure 1.2: The Twelve Lenses of Leadership and related priorities.

*Visit **go.SolutionTree.com/leadership** for a free reproducible version of this figure.*

you can use them without knowing your personality type. The appendix (page 217) contains a version of figure 1.2 (page 19) with the related type preferences. If you would like to use the framework with this book but do not know your type, contact me through www.janekise.com/contact-me for a decision-maker code to access TypeCoach (the system I use with educators), to verify your preferences and receive a six-page report on how your type operates in the world of education.

Make a copy of figure 1.2 (page 19) and circle the top ten priorities you chose from figure 1.1 (pages 16–18). At this point, you have settled on your priorities, so it's OK to circle them. Then, use the following five steps to take a slow, reflective look at whether your priorities reveal any mindsets or blind spots that might hinder achieving your overall purpose.

1. Read the definitions of the lenses that are connected with the priorities you chose. Do they seem to match the intent of your overall goal?

2. Read the definitions of the lenses under which you circled no priorities. Do the themes for these lenses seem connected to your goal? Remember, the lenses define ongoing interdependencies in leadership roles and responsibilities. Reflect on which of the twelve are most likely to be problematic, given your development focus and your situation.

    •   Do your priorities point to the most relevant lenses, or are you overlooking some key priorities? Identify the two or three most relevant lenses.

    •   If the priorities you selected for one of the lenses appear on both sides, that often means that you're already aware of the ongoing interdependency the lens presents. Or, as one leader said, whose priority sort for an ongoing initiative revealed this pattern, "No wonder we haven't made much progress!"

3. For your chosen lenses, are you naturally drawn more to one pole or the other as being of higher priority? The chapter for each lens begins with a chart that provides a little more information that might help you identify such biases. Remember, each lens is made up of two equally valuable sets of priorities, but it's easy to over-focus on one side and create an unbalanced situation that will not bring long-term success.

4. The priorities on the left-hand side of each lens and those on the right-hand side of each lens correlate with the natural priorities of leaders with different sets of strengths. In other words, for each lens, some leaders more naturally choose priorities on the left and others choose those on the right. With this in mind, consider the following.

- Read the definitions of the priorities opposite the ones you chose. Do you find any distasteful or not very valuable? For example, one leader whose goal involved deepening community connections did not choose networking. When I asked about this, she said, "Networking is just selling snake oil." Of course, it was a key priority to her goal, but her past experiences had created a blind spot around its importance. Ponder what you *didn't* choose to flag any such hidden mindsets.

- Of the priorities you chose, are any so much a part of your leadership style that you will focus on them no matter what? If this is the case, consider substituting for something that is less automatic to your leadership style.

5. Think about which of the ten priorities are probably your top three. Eventually, these will form the structure for your development work.

Remember, this is a repeatable process. Your priorities will change with each goal—that's what makes this different from a values clarification. This process is not about deciding what your values are. Here, you are thinking contextually about forty different focuses you might use as a leader, depending on what you are trying to accomplish.

Once you've narrowed from forty to ten to three, you're ready to delve into the meat of this book. However, if you like to begin with the end in mind, turn to chapter 16 (page 209) for a preview of how you'll turn those three priorities into a useful tool for personalized leadership development.

Reflection and Next Steps

Chapter 2 (page 23) provides a deeper explanation of *polarity thinking*, a method for working with the ongoing interdependencies in the Twelve Lenses of Leadership. Chapter 3 (page 33) will help you understand the importance of these varied, hard-to-measure, core leadership competencies (the lenses) and how the ongoing interdependencies between them often result in either their underuse or overuse, both of which impede effective leadership. You'll learn how they fit with the Twelve Lenses of Leadership and identify which ones may require more focus from you. Then, you'll have what you need to use chapters 4–15 as a reference guide for your personal development around your current focus. Although you can read these chapters in order, you can also begin with the three to four lenses that are most relevant to your goal. In each chapter, you'll find the following.

- Information on the interdependencies inherent in the lens and examples of how they affect school leadership

- Stories showing leaders working with the lens—their experiences, struggles, successes, and wisdom

- Which emotional intelligence competencies support effective use of the lens

- Tips for developing your ability to employ both–and thinking with the lens that you can adopt or modify for your own development

Finally, chapter 16 guides you through forming a development plan and provides the reflection tools to ensure that you can continue to reflect to find what is working, adjust your focus, and truly continue the leadership development journey.

CHAPTER 2

Thinking in Terms of Both *and* And: A Core Leadership Competency

"We've seen this before."

"If we wait it out, the pendulum will swing back to what we're doing now."

"These reforms aren't actually reforms."

You've heard these comments about new initiatives, right?

For example, the longer you've been in education, the more labels you'll recognize for frameworks designed to create collaborative teams. Teachers spend too much time working in isolation, right? So, we need to bring them together. But then, something goes wrong, and things swing back to isolated practice again, until the pendulum swings yet again with another reincarnation of teamwork.

What's missing? Collaboration isn't actually a solution, but an interdependent set of values that coexists with values associated with working as individuals. Individual *and* team. We can't spend all our time with others, or we'd neglect the particular needs of our own students or fail to make the most of our own strengths. Yet if we spend all our planning time alone, we miss the wisdom and experiences of others, the chance to learn from dialogue, opportunities to share workloads, and the pursuit of shared goals. You'll read more about this ongoing interdependency between individuals and their communities in chapter 6 (page 75).

In fact, each of the interdependencies we explore within the Twelve Lenses of Leadership consists of paradigms that require looking two ways at once to work with two equally important sets of values. Another way of saying this is that the lenses consist of *polarities*—systems of interdependent sets of values and priorities that, over time, need each other.

In this chapter, we explore the concept of polarities and how those in this book connect to a core leadership competency—thinking in terms of both *and* and. You'll learn how to identify polarities instead of trying to solve unsolvable problems and see how they connect with leadership priorities and emotional intelligence. We'll wrap up with a reflection of what you've learned about polarities.

Polarities

Here's a quick illustration of a polarity: Take a deep breath, and inhale slowly. Now exhale, and ask yourself, "Which is better, inhaling or exhaling?"

It's a silly question, isn't it? Our bodies require both. The energy system that is reality for the breathing cycle is best illustrated with an infinity loop, as shown in figure 2.1.

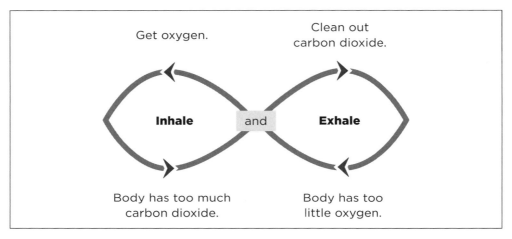

Figure 2.1: A simple polarity.

Inhaling brings needed oxygen, but breathing in for too long causes a problem: too much carbon dioxide. Exhaling releases that carbon dioxide, but eventually a new problem will arise: too little oxygen. We can't choose either inhaling or exhaling. Each accurately describes something we need, yet neither is complete without the other. They're interdependent. In fact, you can't exhale unless you've inhaled, nor inhale unless you've exhaled.

Polarities are thus part of our lives literally from our first breath. Unlike breathing, however, learning to handle real-life polarities well can take some time. Barry Johnson (2012) coined the term *polarity* as he developed organizational tools for working with these systems:

> Polarities are interdependent pairs that can support each other in
> pursuit of a common purpose. They can also undermine each other
> if seen as an either/or problem to solve. Polarities at their essence

are unavoidable, unsolvable, unstoppable, and indestructible. Most importantly, they can be leveraged for a greater good. (p. 4)

In each of chapters 4–15 (the lens-focused chapters), you'll see a diagram similar to figure 2.1 that captures the main interdependencies for each lens. These diagrams illustrate how each side or pole of the Twelve Lenses of Leadership holds only a partial solution for leaders. In fact, if you want to *guarantee* that you'll fail to reach a leadership goal, build it solidly on the positive results one pole has to offer while excluding the values of the other. This balance is what makes the lenses very different from a list of school principal responsibilities. The lenses acknowledge that over-focus on a crucial role can lead to ignoring something equally crucial. It isn't one or the other; it's both!

In the next two sections, we look at some polarities for both–and thinking, and the fact that some dilemmas can't be solved once and for all. No, this isn't a fixed mindset, but an acknowledgement that when working with systems, ignoring some elements results in predictable patterns. For example, what happens if you hold your breath and never exhale? How will that work in the long term? Inhaling and exhaling are interdependent. Over time, both are required. Ignore either and problems ensue. Similarly, for these dilemmas that involve interdependent pairs of values, we need to *leverage* both sides, just as we learn to leverage the value of inhaling and exhaling when we are exercising, singing, meditating, or otherwise paying attention to how we breathe to maximize a bigger goal or purpose.

Polarities for Both–And Thinking

We all know that either–or thinking can lead to problems—we need *and* thinking as well. Consider the tensions that arise when we need to honor traditions *and* implement necessary changes, or use standardized assessments *and* customize how we check for understanding, or think short-term *and* long-term. In each case, both sides are right. A more appropriate phrasing might be that both sides are accurate, but each is also incomplete. Using the concepts and tools of polarity thinking can help leaders discern when we are dealing with perpetual dilemmas rather than problems that are solvable once and for all.

I've written extensively on techniques for seeing, mapping, and leveraging polarities. In this book, the polarities in each lens serve as tools for recognizing and addressing common tensions school leaders face. Using them allows you to recognize when either–or thinking simply isn't appropriate. You'll be better able to see systems and address their complexities instead of falling into the trap of looking for a single solution to unsolvable, ongoing interdependencies that need constant rebalancing.

FURTHER DEVELOPMENT

You can start seeing and working with polarities immediately, and you can take a two-year master class to develop the expertise necessary to use the tools for systems thinking. Barry Johnson (2012), founder of Polarity Partnerships (www.polaritypartnerships.com), and his colleagues have generously shared their research and tools with me for use in education. *Unleashing the Positive Power of Differences: Polarity Thinking in Our Schools* (Kise, 2014) analyzes key polarities in education, has step-by-step information on seeing, mapping, assessing, and leveraging them, and provides tools for using polarity thinking with leaders, staff, and students.

An Example of Problem–Solution Thinking When Both– And Is Necessary

Let's look at a well-known solution often advocated in education circles: encouraging a growth mindset. Lauren Resnick (1999) draws attention to how a fixed mindset regarding intelligence—you either are or aren't smart—limits student learning. Carol Dweck (2006) extends the research base and popularizes the idea of a growth mindset. Jonathon Saphier (2005) paints a clear picture of the difference the two mindsets make in a classroom (table 2.1).

Table 2.1: Comparing Atmospheres of Fixed and Growth Mindset Classrooms

Ability-Based Atmosphere	Effort-Creates-Ability Atmosphere
Mistakes are a sign of weakness.	Mistakes help one learn.
Speed counts. Faster is smarter.	Care, perseverance, and craftsmanship count.
Good students do it by themselves.	Good students need help and a lot of feedback.
Inborn intelligence is the main determinant of success.	Effort and effective strategies are the main determinants of success.
Only the bright few can achieve at a high level.	Everyone is capable of high achievement.

Source: Saphier, 2005; Saphier & D'Auria, 1993.

Soon, schools were solving the problem of fixed mindsets with strategies for promoting a growth mindset. The result? By 2015, Dweck (2015) was publishing articles clarifying that there was more to it than praising students for effort:

> Recently, someone asked what keeps me up at night. It's the fear that the mindset concepts, which grew up to counter the failed self-esteem movement, will be used to perpetuate that movement. In other words, if you want to make students feel good, even if they're not learning, just praise their effort! Want to hide learning gaps from them? Just tell them, "Everyone is smart!" The growth mindset was intended to help close achievement gaps, not hide them. It is about telling the truth about a student's current achievement and then, together, doing something about it, helping him or her become smarter.

In effect, when educators see a fixed mindset, they treat it as a problem for which the solution is a growth mindset that they can create by teaching students that effort creates ability. They praise their effort rather than saying, "You're so smart."

However, while having a fixed mindset is a real problem, a growth mindset is only one of two interdependent sets of values. *Readiness* to learn specific content and processes is absolutely key, or effort will get you nowhere. Ask yourself, for example, "Am I *ready* right now to develop calculations to identify the gravitational pull of a black hole? Or might I need some prior knowledge and skills before I put in the *effort* required?"

Figure 2.2 (page 28) summarizes the interdependencies and dilemmas present in working with growth mindset strategies, using the infinity loop diagram we'll be using throughout the book to examine twelve big, ongoing dilemmas—the leadership lenses—that require both–and thinking.

Can you see how applying this kind of both–and thinking while planning an initiative, such as fostering growth mindsets, can ensure that students are ready for the tasks on which you'll be asking them to persevere, bringing the upside of both sets of values? That's the sort of systems thinking we'll be using to examine the ongoing dilemmas present in leading a thriving, whole-child school.

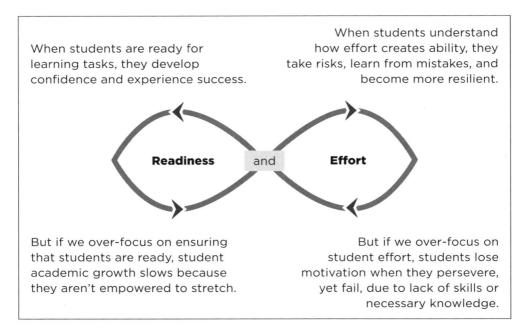

When students are ready for learning tasks, they develop confidence and experience success.

When students understand how effort creates ability, they take risks, learn from mistakes, and become more resilient.

Readiness   and   **Effort**

But if we over-focus on ensuring that students are ready, student academic growth slows because they aren't empowered to stretch.

But if we over-focus on student effort, students lose motivation when they persevere, yet fail, due to lack of skills or necessary knowledge.

Figure 2.2: The readiness *and* effort loop.

Polarity Identification Instead of Unsolvable Problems

Another example of an ongoing polarity that leaders often treat as a problem to solve is accountability. Teacher accountability encompasses just one set of values that is interdependent with the values of supporting teachers for growth and development even as we hold them accountable. No one is actually born with all the complex skills the profession requires. Too often, schools lack the resources or mechanisms to truly support new teachers in developing in multiple areas such as pedagogy, classroom management, building relationships, and more. The inevitable problems that arise when you treat a system as a linear problem to solve show up in teacher strikes, decreased job satisfaction, and stretched resources for evaluation at the expense of other forms of professional development. For accountability measures to actually improve teacher quality, we also need action steps for supporting teachers' growth.

How do you know when you have a polarity instead of a problem to solve? Here are four key factors.

1. **Is it ongoing?** Look back to the opening example of the waves of reform that often lead to a pendulum swinging back and forth between collaborative and individual work. This is indicative of a polarity.

2. **Are the alternatives interdependent?** Think of breathing, or how short-term goals add up to long-term goals.

3. **Over time, are both poles or solutions necessary?** Consider how school districts swing between centralizing and decentralizing how they make policies and other decisions—decentralization leads to schools with different practices, so certain things are pulled back to the district office, only to be farmed out again.

4. **What happens with only a singular focus?** Examine what happens, and might happen, if we focus only on one upside, and ask whether we might undermine our original goals, as Dweck (2006) articulates with mindset.

In grappling with these questions, consider the goal you've already identified that you'll be thinking about throughout these pages. In chapters 4–14, each lens establishes an underlying interdependency, providing plenty of thought for how the lenses most connected with your leadership development goals might require both–and thinking. (The interdependencies for chapter 15 work a bit differently.) The goal isn't balance between these sets of values, but instead placing the right amount of emphasis to get to the upside of each, avoid their downsides (look back at figure 2.2), and move ahead toward your purpose.

Note that the primary description of each lens comes through stories of leaders who have learned to work well with it. When people are locked into dualistic, either–or thinking, arguing your point of view often simply causes them to become even more entrenched in their own position. Telling stories that help them truly see the dilemma is often a crucial step into helping them see the bigger picture of both–and thinking (Rohr, 2013).

Polarities, Priorities, and Emotional Intelligence

Interwoven in the lens-focused chapters is the core idea that a thriving whole-child school requires an atmosphere of trust, safety, equity, and skilled collaboration. Creating that kind of atmosphere takes an entirely different set of leadership skills than a full-on accountability effort typically emphasizes. When leading holistically, the soft skills of emotional intelligence, which are often the hardest to learn, become vital. Leading a school for both whole-child success and academic success requires leaders who are physically, mentally, emotionally, and spiritually healthy. In the next chapter, we'll look at the far-ranging domain of emotional intelligence and how it fits into your developmental needs, given your goals and situation. As you ponder the dilemmas of both–and thinking, note that being able to work with seemingly contradictory ideas is a marker of both wisdom and adult development, especially as you lead in a VUCA world.

Three Ways to Improve Your Use of Both–And Thinking

Consider the following three action items for reflection.

1. Revisit figure 1.2 (page 19), listing the Twelve Lenses of Leadership. Read the description for each lens, which read as *and* statements. All of these are polarities. Where have you seen each interdependency in education policies, practices, initiatives, or dilemmas? Which are relevant to your current situation?

2. Review the following list of common polarities. Reflect or engage with another leader in conversation about when you have seen these in play in education. For example, you could examine the pushback against the Common Core State Standards in terms of the polarity standardization *and* customization.

    a. Top-down *and* bottom-up

    b. Centralized *and* decentralized

    c. Individual responsibility *and* organizational responsibility

    d. Competition *and* collaboration

    e. Content *and* process

    f. Individual freedom *and* community safety

3. For one of the interdependencies you identified in question 1 regarding figure 1.2, try to create a loop as it appears in figure 2.1 (page 24). What is the upside of each pole? Given the nature of a system, what might be an unintended consequence if you over-focus on one side or the other? Use the blank loop in figure 2.3 to capture your thoughts.

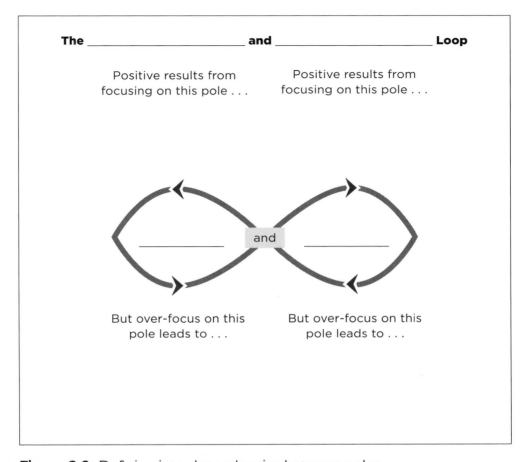

Figure 2.3: Defining interdependencies between poles.

*Visit **go.SolutionTree.com/leadership** for a free reproducible version of this figure.*

CHAPTER 3

Understanding Emotional Intelligence and Leading for the Whole Child

Consider the following scenarios.

A superintendent who prides herself on emotional self-control and objectivity unexpectedly loses her temper in a board meeting. No amount of effort or apology works to patch her relationship with two board members.

An elementary school principal underestimates the impact of reassigning teachers to different grade levels without their input. Grade-level team meetings erupt in shouting matches and a palpable resistance to the school's initiatives.

The director of instructional coaching who sees her efforts to embed coaching as ongoing professional development rather than remediation is shocked when her spouse insists on marriage counseling. "You have nothing left for us at the end of the day," he tells her.

I could make an endless list of examples of leaders who are focused on the strategic and technical aspects of leadership while underestimating the roles of emotional intelligence. I think this quote from Human Capital Institute (2013) best sums up the importance of high emotional intelligence:

> We argue that Emotional Intelligence is more than an amorphous concept related to "playing well with others." It is made up of a specific set of observable and measurable emotional and social skills that impact the way people perceive and express themselves, develop and maintain social relationships, cope with challenges, and use emotional information in an effective and meaningful way. (p. 1)

33

Since the start of the 21st century, the world of business has brought widespread recognition that these soft skills are not only vital but far harder to master and deploy day in and day out than the hard skills such as strategic planning, supervision, and financial management (Cherniss et al., 2006). In this chapter, you'll understand the case for developing your emotional intelligence quotient, or *EQ*, you'll be introduced to an accessible yet robust model for EQ development that we'll refer to throughout the book, and you'll determine those EQ skills most relevant to your goals.

The Top Five Truths About EQ

Dismissed at first by powerful executives as that touchy-feely stuff that might decrease organizational drive for results, a growing body of research and empirical evidence supports the key role of EQ in effective leadership. Here's what you need to know.

1. **EQ is the foundation for effective leadership:** Leaders in education are, by and large, a smart group, and the vast majority of promotions is the result of proven results with managerial and technical skills. However, the shift from effective manager to effective leader requires EQ. Bill George (2012), retired head of Medtronic, made this observation: "I have never seen leaders fail for lack of raw intelligence, but have observed . . . more than a hundred who failed for lack of . . . Emotional Intelligence" (as cited in Human Capital Institute, 2013, p. 15).

2. **EQ in education is often oversimplified:** EQ is far more than empathy, grit, resilience, and some other repeating themes. Although literature on school leadership often cites EQ, are you seeing investment in assessments and ongoing development and a broad definition that includes components as diverse as reality testing, independence, and stress tolerance? When coaching university and business leaders, I often use the Emotional Quotient-Inventory 2.0 (EQ-i$^{2.0}$) from MHS Assessments (https://bit.ly/2K4KXRZ), which I believe has the best norms, reliability, and validity of any of the self-reporting tools on the market. Without exception, the educators I work with find that they are overusing or underusing one or more of the fifteen subscales in the model; they need a plan for development. Later in this chapter, you'll learn more about the four core areas found in robust EQ models (see page 37).

3. **Teacher efficacy requires EQ:** Without EQ, it is nearly impossible for a leader to create the conditions necessary for collective teacher efficacy, an

atmosphere where teachers believe that they have the capacity to reach the goals set out for them and that their hard work will have the desired results (Sun & Leithwood, 2015).

Meta-analyses of over 150 instructional strategies and other influences on student learning show that collective teacher efficacy has the biggest effect size, 1.57 (DeWitt, 2017). However, building collective teacher efficacy requires leadership expertise in several skills involving EQ, including the following.

FURTHER DEVELOPMENT

Effect size studies quantitatively answer the question, "So how big an effect did this really have?" It is a numerical representation of an effort's impact on learning, and it derives from measuring the impact of implementing a change versus not doing so using an experiment group and a control group. John Hattie (2012) estimates that an effect size of 0.4 was the equivalent of providing a year's worth of academic growth.

- *Inspiring group purpose*—People who feel connected to an organization's purpose and values are more effective than those who are competent but lack connection to that purpose (Coyle, 2018).

- *Providing teachers with individual support*—Holding teachers account-able is only one side of the outcomes *and* people lens, the subject of chapter 11 (page 143). Think, for example, of the different levels of support teachers need to implement the same new strategy, depending on their experience levels, individual strengths, and content-area expertise. Collective teacher efficacy flows from all teachers experiencing the level and forms of support they need to learn. That takes empathy, listening skills, and coaching skills in school leaders.

- *Creating an atmosphere of safety and trust*—The number-one predictor of effective teams is an atmosphere of safety and belonging (Coyle, 2018). Team members consistently describe the experience of being in such atmospheres as being part of a family. Will Felps, Terence Mitchell, and Eliza Byington (2006) report three key leadership cues that create this safe space: (1) Their *energy* is invested in the immediate exchange. Group members feel safe sharing problems and mistakes because the leader listens intently and ensures that no critique or judgment comes from others. (2) This individualized attention makes each person *feel unique and valued* instead of like a problem to be solved or a nameless face in the crowd. (3) The leader makes it clear that the relationship and safe space are ongoing. When we know we are safe, we can tell the friend-or-foe filter in our brains (developed back in caveman days) to take a break and get on with collective efficacy.

- *Modeling self-care and care for others*—Teachers report increased job satisfaction, loyalty, and effectiveness when their leaders not only care for those around them, but for themselves as well. A leader without work–life balance, the focus of chapter 15 (page 195), the goal orientation *and* engagement lens, discourages others from striving for it in their own lives (Skakon, Nielsen, Borg, & Guzman, 2010).

4. **People crave leaders with high EQ:** *The Athena Doctrine* (Gerzema & D'Antonio, 2013) documents a worldwide study of the skills people seek in leaders. These include connectedness, humility, candor, patience, empathy, trustworthiness, openness, flexibility, vulnerability, and balance. That is basically a list of EQ competencies.

5. **EQ requires willpower:** Willpower is a finite (but replenishable) resource, and your job whittles away at your limited supply. Have you noticed that you have less patience at home after a tough day at school? Or, how tempting your favorite dessert is after you finish writing a difficult report or facilitating a conflict situation?

All of these things rely on willpower, and you only have so much. Roy Baumeister and John Tierney (2011) point out that our brain's large frontal lobes developed to facilitate being part of large social groups—in other words, for emotional intelligence. Successful participation requires self-control. Self-control involves willpower. Research into willpower reveals the following two key lessons that we cannot ignore in our quests for higher EQ:

1. You have a finite amount of willpower that becomes depleted as you use it.

2. You use the same stock of willpower for all manner of tasks. You might think you have one reservoir of self-control for work, another for dieting, another for exercise, and

> another for being nice to your family. But . . . there are hidden connections among the wildly different things you do all day. You use the same supply of willpower to deal with frustrating traffic, tempting food, annoying colleagues, demanding bosses, pouting children (Baumeister & Tierney, 2011, p. 35).

They specifically cite control of emotional intelligence as a willpower depleter. Developing EQ competencies can increase the willpower reservoir in many ways, as you'll see in the second half of this chapter. Think back to the opening vignettes in this chapter, though, and ponder how these otherwise competent leaders undervalued the importance of ensuring they had willpower available for EQ.

Fortunately, you can develop and increase EQ throughout your lifetime through deliberate practice while monitoring the impact on your effectiveness. Let's turn to using a working model for accomplishing this.

Your EQ Focus

Although we'll be exploring eight EQ skills (organized into four realms), a core principle of coaching—executive, group, or self-coaching—is to focus on no more than three goals or priorities at a time. In fact, one may be enough, considering how quickly that limited reservoir of willpower and self-control can drain away. You'll have a chance to reflect on all eight, ponder which are most closely tied to the goal you identified in chapter 1 (page 9), and see which of the Twelve Lenses of Leadership most likely require that specific skill. You'll find specific suggestions for EQ development in each of the lens-focused chapters (chapters 4–15).

In figure 3.1 (page 38), note the flow among the four realms and the eight specific skills. The model is neither static nor hierarchical. Further, most people find that their acumen with a skill ebbs and flows, depending on their environment, stress level, and even the EQ of those around them. They may get very different feedback at home and at the office.

Let's explore each of these four realms and the skills inherent in them. Each of these sections asks you to self-assess your current level of EQ with a specific skill. At the end of this chapter, you'll find a tool for making the best use of this information.

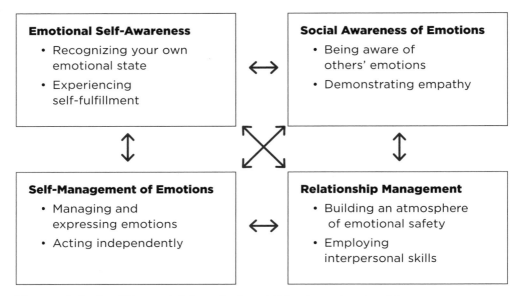

Figure 3.1: An EQ model for whole-child school leadership.

Emotional Self-Awareness

"Check your emotions at the door." "Don't smile until midterm." "Stay objective." These and other persistent workplace norms downplay the role of emotions as valuable information for taking action, making decisions, understanding how others see you, and many other things. Consider these two separate skills.

1. **Recognizing your own emotional state:** You can't regulate your emotions if you aren't aware of them. Do you sense when you are enthusiastic, frustrated, fearful, joyful, angry, and so on before others do? Do you note whether your emotions are healthy or unhealthy or productive or nonproductive for your current situation? Can you identify a remedy before it is too late?

2. **Experiencing self-fulfillment:** Imagine someone leading you who isn't sure that he or she has accomplished anything meaningful. This EQ skill involves having meaningful goals tied to your values, and the confidence to plan and take steps to reach those goals. You also need a healthy balance between confidence in your own talents and abilities and the humility inherent in knowing you'll need the talent and efforts of others to reach those goals.

Figure 3.2 highlights some markers you can use to assess your ability with these EQ skills.

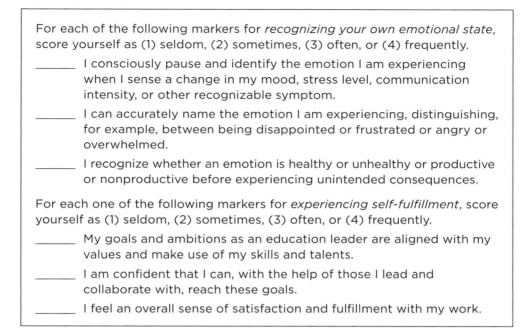

For each of the following markers for *recognizing your own emotional state*, score yourself as (1) seldom, (2) sometimes, (3) often, or (4) frequently.

_____ I consciously pause and identify the emotion I am experiencing when I sense a change in my mood, stress level, communication intensity, or other recognizable symptom.

_____ I can accurately name the emotion I am experiencing, distinguishing, for example, between being disappointed or frustrated or angry or overwhelmed.

_____ I recognize whether an emotion is healthy or unhealthy or productive or nonproductive before experiencing unintended consequences.

For each one of the following markers for *experiencing self-fulfillment*, score yourself as (1) seldom, (2) sometimes, (3) often, or (4) frequently.

_____ My goals and ambitions as an education leader are aligned with my values and make use of my skills and talents.

_____ I am confident that I can, with the help of those I lead and collaborate with, reach these goals.

_____ I feel an overall sense of satisfaction and fulfillment with my work.

Figure 3.2: Assess your emotional self-awareness.

*Visit **go.SolutionTree.com/leadership** for a free reproducible version of this figure.*

Self-Management of Emotions

Recognizing emotions is only the first step; managing them is essential to real effectiveness. Also note that exhibiting too much or too little control of emotions can be equally dangerous. For example, coaching clients often ask, "What could be bad about my ability to handle lots of stress?" The answer? You might have a tendency to assume, "If I can handle it, so can everyone else."

Again, let's look at two separate skills.

1. **Managing and expressing emotions:** The more accurately and specifically you can appraise your emotional state, the easier it is to identify and apply a remedy. For example, knowing you are overwhelmed rather than simply frustrated might spark an idea for delegating, seeking support, or saying no to the next request. Or, you might note rising impatience as a teacher describes a classroom incident and prompt yourself to employ active listening skills to ensure you exhibit the empathy the teacher deserves.

   As a leader, your goal is expressing emotions appropriately and effectively in ways that build relationships and the vital atmosphere of trust. Emotional neutrality may actually decrease trust people have in leaders; people report that trust falters when they don't think they can accurately read a leader's mood (Pearman, Lombardo, & Eichinger, 2005).

Controlling your impulses falls into this skill as well. If you are a planner who seldom gives into impulses, remember that interrupting others, pushing for quick decisions, slips in emotional expression, and poor follow-through can all come from lack of impulse control.

2. **Acting independently:** One way to assess your ability with this skill is to ask yourself, "Can I make a tough call, even if it means facing disapproval or lack of harmony or worse?" A leader who can act independently works toward consensus. John Glaser (2005) cites the Quaker definition of consensus as "a process used to find the highest level of agreement *without* dividing the participants into factions" (p. 148). Effective leaders can make the tough call *and* employ other EQ skills as necessary to maintain trust and safety.

Figure 3.3 highlights some markers you can use to assess your ability with these EQ skills.

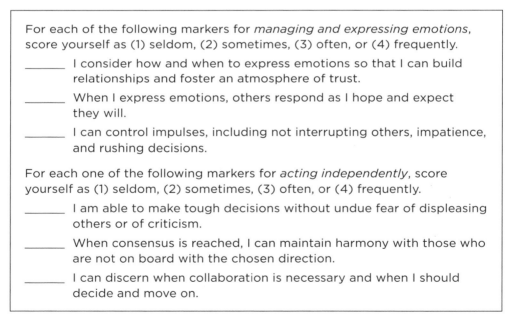

For each of the following markers for *managing and expressing emotions*, score yourself as (1) seldom, (2) sometimes, (3) often, or (4) frequently.

_____ I consider how and when to express emotions so that I can build relationships and foster an atmosphere of trust.

_____ When I express emotions, others respond as I hope and expect they will.

_____ I can control impulses, including not interrupting others, impatience, and rushing decisions.

For each one of the following markers for *acting independently*, score yourself as (1) seldom, (2) sometimes, (3) often, or (4) frequently.

_____ I am able to make tough decisions without undue fear of displeasing others or of criticism.

_____ When consensus is reached, I can maintain harmony with those who are not on board with the chosen direction.

_____ I can discern when collaboration is necessary and when I should decide and move on.

Figure 3.3: Assess your self-management of emotions.

*Visit **go.SolutionTree.com/leadership** for a free reproducible version of this figure.*

Social Awareness of Emotions

Emotions—your own and others—are soft data as valuable as any hard data about test scores, classroom observations, or other common tools for data-informed decisions. Back to the opening scenarios in this chapter, the school principal who moved teachers among grade levels was unaware of the potential emotional impact of her decisions and therefore created conflict, unintentionally sabotaging the level of trust in the building. The following two skills are necessary when making decisions that have an impact on others.

1. **Being aware of others' emotions:** Views such as, "If it's best for students, then the adults need to deal with it" negate the way our brains work. Adults can't simply turn off their emotions, so leaders need to be aware of undercurrents. We are wired to connect with other humans; after all, we survived saber-toothed tiger attacks by working together. In the modern workplace, researchers find that when people pause from focusing on specific tasks, their attention defaults to social cognition. We think about ourselves and our relationships (Lieberman, 2013). Think how the example of grade-level moves violated core needs such as perceiving fair treatment, being valued as individuals, and feeling safe. Social awareness lets you not just recognize emotions in others but gain insights into their root causes and potential ramifications.

2. **Demonstrating empathy:** There is no doubt that people want leaders who are empathetic and that it is a core skill. However, the truly empathetic leader goes beyond feeling another's pain to being able to grasp the root causes and impact of those emotions.

   Overusing empathy can cause problems just as big as underuse. In coaching and in leading, too much empathy may encourage someone to indulge too long in self-pity rather than employing skills that lead to resilience. Too much empathy can also get in the way of a leader's independence.

   Empathy has one other downside: there is a fine line between using empathy for good and using it in ways that may eventually be interpreted as manipulative. After all, if you can empathize, you know exactly how to create maximum pain. As an extreme example, psychopaths are actually capable of demonstrating high levels of this skill (Meffert, Gazzola, den Boer, Bartels, & Keysers, 2013).

Figure 3.4 (page 42) highlights some markers you can use to assess your ability with these EQ skills.

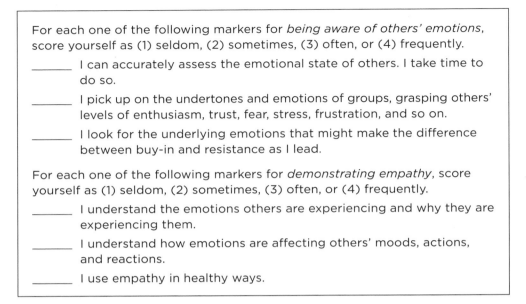

For each one of the following markers for *being aware of others' emotions*,
score yourself as (1) seldom, (2) sometimes, (3) often, or (4) frequently.

_____ I can accurately assess the emotional state of others. I take time to
do so.

_____ I pick up on the undertones and emotions of groups, grasping others'
levels of enthusiasm, trust, fear, stress, frustration, and so on.

_____ I look for the underlying emotions that might make the difference
between buy-in and resistance as I lead.

For each one of the following markers for *demonstrating empathy*, score
yourself as (1) seldom, (2) sometimes, (3) often, or (4) frequently.

_____ I understand the emotions others are experiencing and why they are
experiencing them.

_____ I understand how emotions are affecting others' moods, actions,
and reactions.

_____ I use empathy in healthy ways.

Figure 3.4: Assess your social awareness of emotions.

*Visit **go.SolutionTree.com/leadership** for a free reproducible version of this figure.*

Relationship Management

The first three areas of EQ skills are foundational to a leader's biggest task—
creating an environment where people are effectively engaged in working collaboratively toward a meaningful vision or purpose that inspires them personally. Effective
leaders take what they know about the organization and the goals and use both
strategic thinking and EQ to guide and motivate. Further, school leaders need to
manage external relationships as well—with parents, the community, school district
personnel, and so on.

If that sounds like a huge, nebulous responsibility, perhaps this lends weight to the
premise that developing EQ is far more difficult than mastering the technical skills
of leadership. Concentrating on the following two skills is an ongoing journey.

1. **Building an atmosphere of emotional safety:** You've already seen how this
   is key to collective teacher efficacy. People need to know they are accepted
   for who they are. They don't have to change their essence to fit in and gain
   acceptance. Safe in an atmosphere of unconditional acceptance, they can
   freely seek help in meeting high expectations. Again, the leader cues this
   acceptance through energetic attention to conversations, ensuring that each
   person feels valued as an individual and establishing that this safe space for
   relationships is ongoing and permanent. Further, if you are the top leader

in your building, department, or school district, then everyone who reports to you needs to have this same EQ competency so that people at every level experience being accepted.

2. **Employing interpersonal skills:** You could probably generate a long, long list of interpersonal skills to include here, but those that are most critical to the other EQ skills are active listening, working collaboratively, giving feedback, and modeling balance.

    Active listening means hearing what another person is saying to understand their position, needs, circumstances, and so on. If you paraphrase what they've said, their reaction is, "Yes! That's exactly what I was thinking!" This skill takes practice, since most of us listen with one ear while judging, readying a response, or critiquing with the other ear.

    Collaborative skills involve being open to other points of view and different paths for reaching the same goals as you share responsibility and learn from collective reflection.

    People on your teams might see providing effective feedback as being a friendly mirror. The person you are coaching grasps what he or she needs to see, and your relationship strengthens in the process.

    As for modeling balance, in chapter 15 (page 195), you'll explore more deeply how your personal approach to work–life balance, the workplace norms you can influence, and the policies and expectations you set affect not only everyone's well-being but their ability to be energized, effective, efficient, and engaged.

Figure 3.5 highlights some markers you can use to assess your ability with these EQ skills.

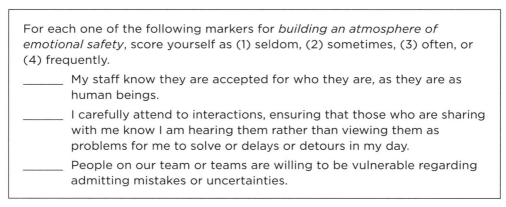

For each one of the following markers for *building an atmosphere of emotional safety*, score yourself as (1) seldom, (2) sometimes, (3) often, or (4) frequently.

_____ My staff know they are accepted for who they are, as they are as human beings.

_____ I carefully attend to interactions, ensuring that those who are sharing with me know I am hearing them rather than viewing them as problems for me to solve or delays or detours in my day.

_____ People on our team or teams are willing to be vulnerable regarding admitting mistakes or uncertainties.

Figure 3.5: Assess your relationship management.   continued →

For each one of the following markers for *employing interpersonal skills*, score yourself as (1) seldom, (2) sometimes, (3) often, or (4) frequently.

_____ I receive feedback that people feel I truly listen to them.

_____ My staff see me as a team player who welcomes opportunities to collaborate or share leadership.

_____ My staff seek coaching and feedback from me.

_____ I demonstrate good health habits, boundaries between my work and personal life, and effective use of social media and mobile devices.

Visit **go.SolutionTree.com/leadership** *for a free reproducible version of this figure.*

The EQ Skills Most Relevant to You

Figure 3.6 shows which of the eight EQ skills are most relevant to the Twelve Lenses of Leadership. Note that in any situation, *any* of these eight key EQ skills may be where you need to place your priorities.

Lens 1	**Leadership** **Listening** Providing leadership while helping everyone learn to lead themselves	
Priorities	Influencing, Shepherding	Empowering, Connecting
EQ Areas	Demonstrating empathy, Being aware of others' emotions, Interpersonal skill: active listening	
Lens 2	**Breadth** **Depth** Implementing needed initiatives and ensuring mastery of initiatives	
Priorities	Networking, Innovating	Legacy, Mastery
EQ Areas	Managing and expressing emotions, Interpersonal skill: working collaboratively	
Lens 3	**Community** **Individual** Building a collaborative culture while meeting individual needs	
Priorities	Relationships, Collaboration	Individuality, Personal development
EQ Areas	Being aware of others' emotions, Acting independently	
Lens 4	**Reality** **Vision** Accounting for very real barriers of time, resources, and so on, while leading toward a purposeful vision	
Priorities	Realism, Balance	Visioning, Optimism
EQ Areas	Building an atmosphere of emotional safety, Acting independently	

Lens 5	*Continuity*	*Change*
	Building on current success while changing to meet the future	
Priorities	Experience, Creativity with the known	Challenge, Creativity with the new
EQ Areas	Acting independently, Building an atmosphere of emotional safety	
Lens 6	*Short Term*	*Long Term*
	Addressing current needs while working toward systemic change	
Priorities	Efficiency	Adaptability
EQ Areas	Acting independently, Interpersonal skill: active listening	
Lens 7	*Logic*	*Values*
	Determining universal principles and rules and accounting for individual needs and perspectives	
Priorities	Fair-mindedness	Empathy
EQ Areas	Demonstrating empathy, Building an atmosphere of emotional safety	
Lens 8	*Outcomes*	*People*
	Moving toward organizational success and creating a culture of collective efficacy	
Priorities	Results, Measurability	Trust, Appreciation
EQ Areas	Experiencing self-fulfillment, Building an atmosphere of emotional safety (through effective feedback)	
Lens 9	*Power To*	*Power With*
	Effectively using positional power while effectively sharing power	
Priorities	Expertise	Openness
EQ Areas	Experiencing self-fulfillment, Interpersonal skill: giving feedback	
Lens 10	*Clarity*	*Flexibility*
	Clarifying expectations and remaining open to new processes and ideas	
Priorities	Organization, Accountability	Originality, Autonomy
EQ Areas	Building an atmosphere of emotional safety	
Lens 11	*Predictability*	*Possibility*
	Setting goals and making plans while preparing for ever-changing environments and an uncertain future	
Priorities	Dependability	Complexity
EQ Areas	Recognizing your own emotional state, Being aware of others' emotions	
Lens 12	*Goal orientation*	*Engagement*
	Making whole-child achievement progress while ensuring that adults and students have purpose	
Priorities	Achievement, Perseverance	Enjoyment, Fulfillment
EQ Areas	Demonstrating empathy	

Figure 3.6: The Twelve Lenses of Leadership and related EQ skills.

Three Ways to Improve Your Emotional Intelligence

Consider the following three action items for reflection.

1. Look back over how you scored yourself; how others score isn't as important as how you score each scale in relationship to the others. How would you rank your abilities with the eight areas? Use figure 3.7 by placing a 1 in front of the area you have the most skill with, and so on. Use this as a reference to establish how much focus on the EQ skill you might need if your current focus involves lenses that are related to the EQ competencies you ranked lower.

Assess your level of EQ with each associated skill. Rank the highest skill with a 1, your second highest skill with a 2, and so on.

_____ Recognizing your own emotional state

_____ Experiencing self-fulfillment

_____ Being aware of others' emotions

_____ Demonstrating empathy

_____ Managing and expressing emotions

_____ Acting independently

_____ Building an atmosphere of emotional safety

_____ Employing interpersonal skills

Figure 3.7: Rank your EQ skills.

*Visit **go.SolutionTree.com/leadership** for a free reproducible version of this figure.*

2. When it comes to emotional intelligence, what may seem like common sense when setting goals and plans is often anything but. Daniel Goleman, Richard Boyatzis, and Annie McKee (2002) report on characteristics of strong goals and plans:

    > Goals should build on one's strengths, not on one's weaknesses. Goals must be a person's own——not goals that someone else has imposed.
    >
    > Plans should flexibly allow people to prepare for the future in different ways——a single planning method imposed by an organization will often prove counterproductive.
    >
    > Plans must be feasible, with manageable steps: Plans that don't fit smoothly into a person's life and work will likely be dropped within a few weeks or months.
    >
    > Plans that don't suit a person's learning style will prove demotivating and quickly lose his attention. (p. 144)

Consider using these points to build your own goal.

- How can you use an EQ strength—say, empathy, to work on another area, such as giving feedback?

- Talk with someone you trust about the eight competencies and where they see you using them well and where you are struggling to use them well, but set your own goal for moving forward.

- Consider trying the planning method in chapter 16 (page 209) once, but then change it for your own style.

- Ask yourself, "Can I do this, or should I adjust the plan?"

- Ask yourself, "Is this my style or someone else's? What do I need to change?"

3. Reflect on the following emotional intelligence attributes needed for collective teacher efficacy. Which ones can you honestly say you have mastered? Where might you focus your leadership development efforts?

- Inspiring group purpose

- Providing teachers with individual support

- Creating an atmosphere of safety and trust

- Modeling self-care and care for others

CHAPTER 4

Leading Toward a Common Vision *and* Guiding Others in Leading Themselves

As a leader, you are responsible for establishing a vision for your team. At the same time, the people you lead come to you with widely diverse backgrounds and experiences, and they have valuable wisdom to offer you. This chapter's lens is about leveraging the priorities in table 4.1 to ensure that you find the right mix of setting direction (leadership) *and* gathering the wisdom of those you lead (listening).

Table 4.1: The Leadership *and* Listening Lens Domain

Lens 1	Leadership *and* Listening	
Priorities	Influencing Shepherding	Empowering Connecting
Common initiatives, issues, or leadership responsibilities that involve this lens	Setting school direction Influencing beliefs Sharing leadership Building relationships Leading for collective teacher efficacy	
EQ component	Demonstrating empathy Being aware of others' emotions Employing interpersonal skills: active listening	

In this chapter, we explore the interdependency of leading *and* listening by learning from a school principal who understands how to best leverage the priorities inherent in this lens. We follow this by explaining how you strike a balance between the leadership and listening poles, establishing an emotional intelligence connection for this lens, and explaining how you can best leverage the priorities inherent in this lens.

An Example of Leading While Listening

When Timothy Brown first became an elementary school principal, he announced that he was devoting his first months at the school to listening, observing, and working to understand all of its staff (what was working well, the challenges they faced), and helping them get to know him. The broad reaction was roughly, "Yeah, right. When are you going to start changing things?"

The staff reaction isn't surprising, is it? Most new leaders bring tools that have worked elsewhere, mandates from the district office, and other elements of overall direction for the year. Often, the district hires them on the basis of changes they promise to bring about.

Tim acknowledges that being born into a more introverted culture (he is an enrolled member of the White Earth Band of Ojibwe), and being introverted himself, perhaps make it easier to prioritize the listening pole of this lens. However, his experiences fostered his belief that the listening pole is an imperative for school leaders:

> I think leaders know this, but think they don't have time in their day. . . . Kids and adults don't just walk into a building and become students and teachers. They have Venn diagrams of things going on, complex and competing and conflicting diagrams. The more you try to steamroll, simplify, flatten that landscape, the more you potentially disenfranchise and alienate people. I don't know how to slow down and unpack that more other than to listen to people to understand them as individuals. If they feel listened to and respected, they can bring their better selves to work that day. (T. Brown, personal communication, August 8, 2017)

Listening for those first months on the job let Tim confirm that he'd been given the right advice by a mentor regarding his new position: "Don't mess it up." The staff already worked collaboratively and held each other to high standards. Listening helped Tim understand the culture he was joining, what motivated his staff, their shared values and purpose, and how he could become part of an existing safe and trusting environment.

Listening also allowed him to unearth some unproductive norms, such as the staff believing "if I'm in the principal's office, I'm in trouble." They were trying *too* hard to solve their own problems, whereas running interference for staff, seeking additional resources, facilitating difficult conversations, and so on, are part of a principal's job.

Tim took concrete steps to counteract this norm. First, he communicated the value of time for one-to-one conversations by talking about how ineffective walking meetings were for true listening, what with inevitable interruptions from happenings in the hallway or questions from others along the way. Instead he told his teachers, "Make an appointment. Let's really dedicate time without texting or watching students or anything else."

Then, when the meetings happened, he explicitly talked about his desire to both support and protect teachers. Teaching is stressful! He conveyed that whether it's a particularly difficult parent situation or a personal crisis or other frustration, he wanted staff members to involve school leaders before they were fighting back tears or otherwise being overwhelmed by stress. It was common for him to say things like, "You don't get points for beating yourself up. It's a long school year. If something is exhausting you, or you sense verbal, physical, or mental abuse, it is not okay. Come and talk to me sooner, not later."

Then, he took time to thank them for coming and urged them to come sooner. The word spread, and the one-to-ones slowly became a new norm. Why slowly? Because while Tim ranks listening as a top leadership responsibility, it took time for teachers to grasp that the one-to-ones were as valuable to him as his other responsibilities.

Tim wanted one more new norm—*percolating*. For him, silence is natural as he digests new information or thinks through a decision, but he knows that most people are uncomfortable with silence. Normalizing it and helping others embrace it were important to his style. His staff got used to his longer-than-expected silences and learned to ponder their own ideas. They frequently bantered about "He's percolating on that" or "Let's give this time to percolate" and other like phrases in a good way, because they knew they were placing more value on establishing time to think. Tim also prioritized the leadership pole, knowing that the ultimate responsibility for student learning rested with himself as the school's top leader. In his first months, he used the listening pole to find the pockets of excellence regarding the school's existing initiatives and then shifted to the leadership pole to spread best practices. For example, some teams were more adept at using data to inform instruction. Tim invited them to capture their strategies in formats they could pass on to other teams—presentations, videos, protocols, and so on. He then worked with the other teams to ensure they had the time, support, and other resources to master the skills they needed.

Leadership *and* listening can work together on the most practical of issues. For example, as a newcomer, Tim noticed that how the school used its physical space was less than optimal. He provided a clear purpose by asking the staff to rethink the building as a blank map and consider what would work best for students. He asked questions like, "Can we get rid of hallway bottlenecks?" "If we move where our specialists are located, might we do less dashing about for interventions?" "Does our space create any problems among older and younger students?" and "What else might we change?"

As a result, several teachers volunteered to draw maps—and the ways in which their maps overlapped became the new building space plan. Their collective plan fostered buy-in for the immense task of packing up and moving classrooms during the last days of the school year. The staff figured out not just the *what* of the new map, but the *how* and *when* of the move.

Leadership Priorities, Listening Priorities

Not every school has a culture like the one Tim entered. If, unlike Tim, you take the lead in a building or on a team where the common vision has dimmed, the leadership pole may take priority; focusing on the listening pole for months might be disastrous if people need immediate inspiration. But imagine the disruption of change, change, and more change in a school like Tim's, where collective teacher efficacy already exists. Will it continue if a new leader comes in on day one with a bold vision but fails to listen and understand how the existing culture already works?

Figure 4.1 illustrates the competing priorities inherent in the leadership and listening poles.

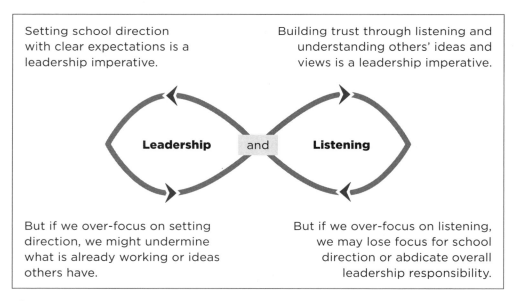

Setting school direction with clear expectations is a leadership imperative.

Building trust through listening and understanding others' ideas and views is a leadership imperative.

Leadership and **Listening**

But if we over-focus on setting direction, we might undermine what is already working or ideas others have.

But if we over-focus on listening, we may lose focus for school direction or abdicate overall leadership responsibility.

Figure 4.1: The leadership *and* listening loop.

It's the principal's job above all, and a key priority for every school leader, to ensure that all students are learning—a clear responsibility for the leadership side of this lens. The leadership pole—setting direction, advocating, influencing beliefs—thrives on extraversion. Leadership means setting direction and ensuring that expectations are clear.

FURTHER DEVELOPMENT

These points refer to the Jungian definitions of extraversion and introversion as a source of energy. See the appendix (page 217).

Listening can feel a bit countercultural in many countries because of cultural bias toward being extraverted (Kirby & Kendall, 2008). Traditionally, schools reward adults and students for speaking up quickly and participating in discussions. We expect leaders to be visible and involved, not tucked away in their offices. We worry about shy children. More and more, we expect teachers to collaborate. The fast pace of the school day, with multiple changes in activities and groups, also favors those who get their energy through action and interaction, but balance is possible.

Tim sums up his aha moment as realizing, "Leadership *is* listening!"

Consider two key interdependencies between the equally valuable leadership roles of leadership *and* listening: (1) leading the why and listening for the what and how and (2) leading for new norms and listening for obsolete norms. How might these affect your goals and initiatives?

Leading the Why and Listening for the What and How

Answering the question, "Why are we doing this?" is an ongoing leadership responsibility. It applies to the big picture (overall) vision of the school and to each task that members of the learning community are asked to engage in. How much of the vision comes from the top and how much a full staff can co-create may depend on the current level of collective efficacy. The right mix of top-down and shared leadership may change quickly, depending on the issue, how quickly trust is built, and a myriad of other factors.

Remember, though, that a common thread in literature on change in organizations is that it takes three to five years for a significant change to take hold and become part of the culture (Hall & Hord, 2010). As a leader, with all of the outside pressures on schools, it is tempting to jettison initiatives sooner than that, especially if they began under another leader. This is where both–and thinking is of great value. Yes, you (or those above you) may decide to shift strategic focus for very good reasons. However, using the listening pole will help you determine when to switch focus and when to work with what already exists. Consider listening to uncover the following.

- **Consistencies and inconsistencies:** Look for examples of effective practices not being maintained across all stakeholders. For example, a new leader might notice that although students receive consistent messages on behavior from adults in the hallways and cafeteria, classroom teachers are inconsistent on positive behavior interventions.

- **Pockets of excellence:** Look for specific areas of your school where there is excellence in practice. In the example about Tim Brown that started this chapter, he unearthed not just who was having the most success with using data to inform instruction but how and why they were having success. This allowed him to expand that pocket of excellence.

Listening provides these insights. Leadership turns the insights into action.

ASK YOURSELF

What are the patterns or ideas that everyone might benefit from, and who needs support? Are you more hands-on or hands-off? When are you comfortable setting the vision and letting others decide the what and the how?

Leading for New Norms and Listening for Obsolete Norms

Leaders who expect everyone to accept, adjust to, or work around their styles are usually abrasive, arrogant, or uncaring. However, each of us has strengths and tools or habits that support our own effectiveness, and it's important to maintain those to be effective. As Tim did with percolating, helping those you lead understand and become comfortable with some of your tools can, if done right, increase both trust and effectiveness. To accomplish this requires naming, modeling, and encouraging the practice in others.

The flip side, though, is adapting to the productive norms in your new environment, and carefully working to change any unproductive ones, whether that involves something as simple as ensuring everyone takes a true lunch break or as complex as normalizing one-to-one time with the principal.

ASK YOURSELF

What is your natural approach to a new role? More leadership? More listening? How does this tendency fit with your current environment?

The EQ Connection

The key EQ areas for this lens are demonstrating empathy, being aware of others' emotions, and employing the interpersonal skill of active listening. The following are a few key points about being aware of others' emotions that pertain to this chapter.

- This kind of awareness takes time. It may mean pausing in meetings. Tim would remind staff "there is no awkward silence—just silence." It may mean taking time before a meeting to consider how others may act and why, and then reflecting afterward on the accuracy of your predictions.

- Remember that emotions are data that may clarify patterns in resistance—the levels of support necessary in change, overall stress, the presence of initiative fatigue, and more. These data can be more crucial to reaching goals than any objective data.

The following are a few key points on demonstrating empathy that pertain to this chapter.

- Remember that empathy involves not just understanding others' emotions but grasping the root causes and using the information in a beneficial way.

- Overusing empathy can cause a leader to try to please everyone or to solve all their problems in ways that sabotage resilience and empowerment.

- Using empathy may nudge a leader to change a course of action or adjust how he or she communicates information. It doesn't have to be wishy-washy.

The following are a few key points on active listening that pertain to this chapter.

- Through brain-imaging studies, Dario Nardi (2011) finds that only 7–10 percent of people naturally listen well. The rest of us think ahead to what we are going to say or get caught up in silently critiquing what we are hearing. Don't assume you're in the 10 percent who are good listeners!

♦   The visible presence of a smartphone or other digital device during a conversation decreases the level of connection people feel with one another and the perceived level of empathy. People conversing with casual acquaintances, with no smartphone present, felt a deeper connection than those who had a deeper relationship but had their phones on the table (Misra, Cheng, Genevie, & Yuan, 2014). Focused attention is crucial.

Priorities Inherent in the Leadership and Listening Lens

Table 4.2 highlights the equally valuable competing priorities and common initiatives that involve the leadership *and* listening lens.

Table 4.2: Priorities Connected to Leadership *and* Listening

Leadership Priorities	Listening Priorities
Influencing	**Empowering**
I want to see others use my ideas, tools, or plans to create improvements, efficiencies, or significant change.	I strive to enable others to learn to lead themselves and take the initiative in their work.
Shepherding	**Connecting**
I work to ensure that everyone is clearly aware of our values and vision and that they are making decisions and choices that align with those values and our vision.	I listen to understand the viewpoints, feelings, and aspirations of those I lead. This increases my effectiveness.

In the next two sections, we'll look at strategies to increase your use of both the leadership pole and your use of the listening pole. Remember that it may take at least six tries using a strategy before you feel comfortable or see results.

Five Ways to Increase Your Use of the Leadership Pole

To strengthen your use of the leadership pole, use the following five strategies.

1. **Be intentional about the why:** Many leaders think they've communicated why they made a decision and what needs to happen but people on their staff would disagree. Have a leadership team in place and run your vision past them or past someone who thinks differently than you. Can that group

or person paraphrase the overall purpose? Do they understand what action to take?

2. **Gauge buy-in for the why:** Jim Kouzes and Barry Posner (2010) find that, when it comes to organizational purpose, it didn't matter as much what the person at the top had to say as much as what the leadership at subsequent levels conveyed to their teams. If you are the principal, do your teacher leaders, coaches, and other leaders convey a clear message? How might your full leadership team help reinforce the school's vision and ensure that everyone feels connected to it in a meaningful way?

3. **Know yourself:** Viewing your competencies and areas for development through lists developed for school leaders may not provide the kind of information you need on your strengths or practices that bring out your best leadership. Think of Tim making percolating a school norm.

4. **Create an advocacy checklist:** Sometimes, the day-to-day demands of the job are so crazy that we forget to think strategically or beyond the regular scope of responsibilities. At least once a month, work through the following checklist.

   When have you:

   ❑ Sought opportunities for visibility for your students, teachers, or other colleagues?

   ❑ Made sure that others know of successes in your building? Educators sometimes shy away from tooting their own horns, not understanding that proven success can generate more support and sometimes even more resources.

   ❑ Advocated for needed professional development or other forms of support?

5. **Practice reading emotions:** If paying attention to others' emotions isn't a natural skill, practice with someone who does it well. A low-risk method is watching movies together, targeting scenes that involve decisions—*The Martian*, *The Big Short*, *Norma Rae*, and so on. The possibilities are endless. Compare notes on your conclusions from facial expressions, body language, and tone of voice. A higher-risk method is comparing notes with someone after meetings. Remember that emotions are data. How might what you are noticing inform your decisions?

Five Ways to Increase Your Use of the Listening Pole

To strengthen your use of the listening pole, use the following five strategies.

1. **Develop active listening skills:** Do this as a key strategy for showing more empathy. Practice paraphrasing what someone says to you, to check for understanding, before you share an opinion or suggest a solution. Check the Wikipedia entry for active listening skills ("Active listening", n.d.) for great descriptions of other techniques and links to online resources.

2. **Make time:** Never underestimate the value of ensuring that you and your staff or team have casual time for connections. Having coffee ready before staff meetings, arranging lunch gatherings, ensuring that professional development time allows for connecting, and hosting small gatherings to simply check in on school climate are all good uses of time because they add to team trust. One group I worked with instituted a sacred donut hour. While they also had healthy food available, the leaders set a clear expectation that everyone would gather for this weekly time to simply talk with each other.

3. **Provide the what and why without the how:** Be clear about the goals and the results you expect, but let those you lead determine the how for themselves; this is a sure path to empowerment. Let them come up with the timeline as well as how they will inform you of progress. If you are hands-on by default, watch for your own impatience. Stay hands-off unless they fail to update you as they promised.

4. **Read for empathy:** Read a book with literary merit or watch a character-driven movie—this is an effective, research-based strategy for improving empathy in leaders. Name the characters' motivations and why they do what they do. Check your understanding of the characters with someone else—with a friend, members of a book club, or through discussion groups at an online site such as Goodreads (www.goodreads.com). Empathy means understanding another's viewpoint even if you disagree with its merit.

5. **Check your technology use:** Hiding your phone when listening is a priority—at work and everywhere else. If you find you've become quite addicted to your phone, check out the experiments and advice in the book *Bored and Brilliant: How Spacing Out Can Unlock Your Most Productive and Creative Self* (Zomorodi, 2017).

ASK YOURSELF

This lens is about providing direction while gathering wisdom. How well are you doing on balancing leadership *and* listening?

CHAPTER 5

Implementing Initiatives *and* Making Them Meaningful

A core part of school leadership involves choosing and putting into place initiatives that improve learning outcomes, but effective implementation has two major components: (1) ensuring that its scope adequately covers the issues it is meant to address and (2) that it is both effective and sustainable for the long term. Often, leaders fall short on one component or the other and the initiative fades away. This lens is about using the priorities in table 5.1 to ensure that you identify the goals, strategies, or initiatives necessary to move your learning community forward *and* plan for sustainability and effectiveness.

Table 5.1: The Breadth *and* Depth Lens Domain

Lens 2	Breadth *and* Depth		
Priorities	Networking Innovating	Legacy Mastery	
Common initiatives, issues, or leadership responsibilities that involve this lens	Instructional leadership Equity Professional development		
EQ component	Managing and expressing emotions: impulse control Employing interpersonal skills: working collaboratively		

In this chapter, we explore the interdependency of breadth *and* depth by building understanding that initiative fatigue is one of the most difficult barriers to overcome, and we explore how to invest teachers in new ideas while setting up a new initiative for success. From there, we explain the balance between the breadth and depth poles, establish an emotional intelligence connection for this lens, and explain how you can best leverage the priorities inherent in this lens.

Initiative Fatigue and How to Overcome It

As an education consultant, I've become quite sensitive about emphasizing teacher readiness as I begin working with a new school client. Oh, how I prefer hearing, "We're assuming that today will be filled with useful information, strategies, and collaborative time" to "Is this going to be another professional development flavor of the month? As if we don't have enough on our plates!"

To lessen the feel of one more thing (and to be honest, to protect myself from that sort of critique before I even begin!), I always ask leaders what initiatives are underway besides the one I'll be part of. I've asked for textbooks to be dropped at my hotel so I can peruse them for examples to use in hands-on activities. To make connections between the ideas I'm bringing and the other frameworks they're using, I've gone to workshops on behavior management models, student motivation, high-level thinking strategies, and more. I do these things because not everyone naturally pinpoints the synergy among seemingly diverse topics, nor do teachers necessarily have reflective time to do so.

However, with the increasing complexity of education, it's easy to see how so many schools have initiatives underway for the following.

- Equity
- Technology
- Instruction
- Assessment and data-driven decisions

- Collaborative teaming
- Social-emotional learning
- School climate and safety
- Behavior management
- Instructional coaching

Even reading the list is tiring, isn't it? No wonder teachers are stressed and experiencing initiative fatigue (Freedman, 1992), that sinking feeling you get when you're handed yet another strategy or program when you know you don't have time or resources to do what's already on your plate. Check out these causes of initiative fatigue (Kise, 2014).

- **Abbreviating:** An initiative is on the list, but leaders don't allocate enough time for professional development, collaborative conversations, instructional time, or other requirements for success.

- ◆ **Assuming:** This commonly occurs after extensive professional development has taken place, but leaders assume it is enough and don't assess whether further support is needed—or if anything is even being implemented.

- ◆ **Animosity:** Anger toward initiators results in side conversations, sapping the energy necessary to move forward.

- ◆ **Abandonment:** Many initiatives, such as PLCs, are a long process, taking three to five years to fully implement. When a school takes on initiatives but moves on without investing the necessary time for them to work, it makes buying into future initiatives that much harder.

- ◆ **Apathy:** Teachers comply without deep engagement. This is common when a school has a history of abbreviating or abandonment as teachers assume that, just like initiatives in the past, this one too will not get the resources necessary for success and will go away.

So how do you move forward on multiple fronts *and* move well on every front? Let's look at my long-term partnership with school principal Beth Russell and our breadth *and* depth journey together.

The Ongoing Dilemma of Ideal Initiatives and Immense Investment

From 1998 until her retirement in 2016, I partnered with Beth at three very different middle schools in three very different school districts. As an assistant principal, she first hired me to facilitate a career day for eighth graders. I brought in four other consultants who had experience working with teens. The day went really well—for half of the students. The other half? As Beth put it, "We didn't give enough information to the teachers who were chaperoning them from activity to activity. Some teachers participated with the students, but others used the time for grading, and so on. Next time we start with the teachers, not the students!" (B. Russell, personal communication, May 27, 2018).

Yes, we'd erred too far on the side of breadth. We thought, *Let's have a career day! This will be great, and the teachers can just learn along with the students.* However, the teachers saw the day as just one more thing that wasn't relevant to teaching. When Beth and I ran into each other at a store a few days later, she said, "I've just accepted a school principalship for next fall, and I'm going to bring you in. We've got ninety minutes a week for professional development, and we're going to go steep and deep, all year long."

That year, September to February, we used the framework of personality type (see the appendix, page 217) for team building and as a lens for instruction. I worked directly with students the school considered at risk academically or socially, and the teachers then introduced the framework to all students. About two-thirds of the teachers volunteered to attend extra after-school sessions to become certified type practitioners.

Success? Yes! The student who had been responsible for the most disciplinary problems wasn't back in Beth's office the entire remainder of the school year. Teachers came with stories of engaged classes. Students expressed that they felt understood. So, when Beth moved to a different school a few years later, we thought we knew what we were doing. However, we met with a few surprises.

Two big differences between the schools forced us back to the drawing board. With far more free and reduced lunch students, and far more diversity, Beth knew there was more to do on the instructional side. Beth remembers:

> I knew we simply didn't have time or resources to roll out thorough type training as we had before—not in the midst of major budget cuts and some district-wide initiatives that were valuable and required. I pitched to Jane, "What if we ask for volunteers? A grade-level team that has seen enough of the type framework in our teambuilding sessions that they want to try it with students? I'm going to assume it'll work in the classrooms here as well as it did in my former school, the word will spread, and more teachers will sign up next year." (B. Russell, personal communication, May 27, 2018)

I really liked this idea—it allowed for depth with those who were involved without adding to the breadth of everything the entire staff was working on. A sixth-grade team volunteered. By February, the other sixth-grade team joined in. Both seventh-grade teams signed on for the following year because they were inheriting students who had been through the process and they wanted to be ahead of the game. The eighth-grade teams soon followed suit for the same reason.

Great, right? Now we could deepen learning about type during all-staff professional development time, team time, and instructional coaching. But meanwhile, Beth had identified other core school-improvement needs and potential programs, including:

- The Institute for Learning (IFL) Principles of Learning, to address organizing for effort, setting clear expectations, and academic rigor

- Schoolwide implementation of the International Baccalaureate (IB) Middle Years Programme, instead of just for some classes

- National Urban Alliance (instructional strategies)
- Advancement Via Individual Determination (AVID)

We continued with collaborative teams, using type as a framework for differentiating instruction, and more. At this point, you can see how quickly breadth can grow. It looks like *a lot*, and it is, but Beth was keenly aware of the need to avoid initiative fatigue. She knew the staff needed to see all of these vital efforts holistically. She recalls:

> Using the big whiteboards in an empty classroom, I made a huge matrix, with the nine Principles of Learning across the top as my organizing umbrella. Then I slotted in the other strategies we were using under each. To me, this synthesis made for a tight, doable bundling of expectations for my great teaching staff. Everything we were doing supported everything else. For example, the IB curriculum fulfilled the IFL principle of rigor, differentiation through personality type helps plan rigor for all, and NUA strategies support rigor. We were really just doing a few things. The matrix made clear how we were accomplishing those few things. It took up the two front whiteboards.
>
> I asked my professional development committee to join me for a meeting in that classroom. They looked at the boards and said, "Um . . . don't show this to anyone else. We understand this but you're going to terrify the rest of the staff." I took their advice. (B. Russell, personal communication, May 27, 2018)

As a result, she tailored all communication about professional development to one of the IFL Principles of Learning, thus emphasizing depth while benefiting from the added breadth of the other initiatives.

The Need to Test Depth Before Breadth

Beth, her team, and I planned professional development for one IFL Principle at a time—perfect for nine months of the school year, right? Because of its excellence as an equity strategy, we started with student-centered conversations, often called high-level discourse or Accountable Talk (University of Pittsburgh, n.d.).

Teachers received the professional development well, so we were ready to move on to the next principle, right? Well, not quite. I did a set of classroom walkthroughs and saw exactly zero Accountable Talk going on. I discussed my findings with Beth. The following is an approximation of our dialogue.

Jane: What do you think? Do they need more information? Do they think it's too risky? Or are we up against the "I didn't think it would work, so I didn't try it, and it didn't work" syndrome?

Beth: We set up the professional development calendar as we did for a reason. We've got eight strategies yet to go.

Jane: I know, but isn't this one of the highest-impact? You were so enthused after seeing videos of actual classroom discussions and the evidence of the resulting learning.

Beth: I know, but I can't make the teachers try it. Their hearts won't be in it if I force them, and you know that means it may not go well.

Jane: But think of the resources we've already invested, with no yield. What if they don't try the next principle either?

Beth: I'm still hoping some will try when they see a perfect application in one of their unit plans, and then spread the word about how well it works. Type spreads so well that way.

Jane: Or, they may forget all about discourse as we move on. How about this—we give them some choices, to preserve the autonomy they need, but ask them to all bring student data to the next professional development session. That gives them time and choice.

Beth: Hmmm, better yet, let's let them work in their collaborative teams. Let's scratch out a planning sheet—the list of discussion techniques we've covered, a slot for the team to discuss which one they will all use, and the data they'll bring to the next meeting.

Can you see how Beth was right—so much to cover, so little time? And how I was right—why move on if we haven't seen any impact from the first strategy? Striking the balance between breadth *and* depth is a dilemma you never solve once and for all.

Often, Beth used me or other members of her professional development committee as interpreters. For example, I attended a workshop on equity strategies with several teachers. My role was to unobtrusively make the connections between whatever strategies were introduced and the school plan—an onsite buffer to help avoid triggering apathy, animosity, abandonment, abbreviating, and assumptions. That hard-working group of amazing teachers stayed with her even though they joked about Beth's penchant to come home from a conference with a dozen new ideas to try!

The Breadth You Need With the Necessary Depth

Figure 5.1 illustrates the interdependency between the breadth and depth poles.

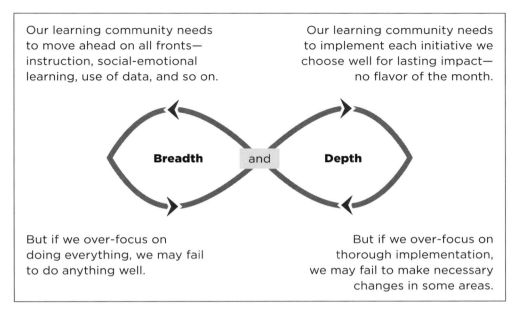

Our learning community needs to move ahead on all fronts—instruction, social-emotional learning, use of data, and so on.

Our learning community needs to implement each initiative we choose well for lasting impact—no flavor of the month.

Breadth and **Depth**

But if we over-focus on doing everything, we may fail to do anything well.

But if we over-focus on thorough implementation, we may fail to make necessary changes in some areas.

Figure 5.1: The breadth *and* depth loop.

There is no magical number of right initiatives—I'm still in awe of how Beth and so many other school leaders I've worked with manage to keep multiple plates spinning, and spinning smoothly. However, Beth credits her professional development team with keeping the staff on her side by, for example, advising her to not share the initiatives matrix.

As you look at this balance between doing enough and doing each part well enough, here are two key interdependencies to keep in mind: (1) generalist and specialist and (2) preparation and implementation.

Generalist and Specialist

Are you more of a generalist? For example, are you comfortable knowing just enough about a lot of instructional leadership topics and allowing others to dive deeper into them? Or are you more of a specialist? Are you someone who is comfortable when you have in-depth knowledge of the initiatives in your building? Being aware of your own preference can help you better understand those who prefer the opposite.

Beth, for example, is more of a generalist. She knows a very adequate amount about personality type, AVID, the IFL Principles of Learning, and so on. As a school principal, she thrived with lots going on in her buildings, and she collaborated with teacher leaders to coordinate deep implementation. Note that the higher you are in leadership, the more the role calls for generalist knowledge.

I'm more of a specialist, with deep knowledge of how to apply personality type in several ways that apply to education—instruction, leadership, classroom management, conflict resolution, and so on. Note that as a leader, being a specialist always brings the danger of seeing your area of expertise as *the* solution when others might be more applicable. Beth points out:

> There are times and positions that require you to be a generalist, and realistically there is no possible way to be a specialist in those positions. Recognizing when that knowledge is needed is key, however. I sought expertise from Jane and others. I didn't have to be an expert, but I had to have a general idea in order to move the work ahead.
>
> For leaders, being an expert can be dangerous if it becomes the only lens through which you look at things, unless you acknowledge that and make sure you surround yourself with other perspectives. (B. Russell, personal communication, May 27, 2018)

Some teachers are comfortable trying strategies or buying into new ideas with a bit of knowledge, and love drawing on all kinds of ideas and frameworks. Others love becoming experts in a few domains and dislike being asked to try things before they understand them. Remember that even as you are balancing time and resources for needed breadth *and* depth, you are also working with staff who have different needs as far as knowledge depth.

ASK YOURSELF

How is your balance between generalist and specialist, given your current position? When do you seek the expertise of others, and when do you seek to broaden your own ideas?

Preparation and Implementation

How much do teachers need to know about a topic (for example, Accountable Talk) before they start trying it out in their classroom? If we concentrate too much on the depth pole, we may never get around to actually using what we are learning! It takes conscious thought, as well as planning with flexibility in mind, to leverage the interdependency between learning and putting ideas into action.

For example, Beth was rolling out the ideas behind having a growth mindset (Dweck, 2006) before books had been published on the subject. We accessed the original research articles (establishing depth) and synthesized them into a four-page article for staff to read (establishing breadth). Because reading the article was preparation for the real work, the staff discussed it in their collaborative teams along with a protocol they could use with students. Thus, they were ready to do the actual work in the classrooms.

It's also possible to make doing the work in classrooms part of the preparation process. Beth's idea for collaborative team discussions around the data each teacher collected during student discussions is an example of this. Think of it as a double-leverage professional development move when teachers are practicing what they will do with students while simultaneously gaining background knowledge.

ASK YOURSELF

Are you more likely to spend too much time preparing your team or to have them jump in before they're really ready?

The EQ Connection

The key EQ areas for this lens are managing and expressing emotions through impulse control and employing interpersonal skills—working collaboratively. The following are a few key points regarding managing and expressing emotions that apply to this chapter.

◆ Both breadth and depth require controlling impulses, an important component of managing and expressing emotions. Getting the right, complementary set of initiatives takes careful selection and implementation planning and the willpower to resist adding one more thing. Once you select an initiative, understanding the depth of knowledge it requires and then implementing a plan to get everyone there take willpower. However, a leader also needs to recognize when flexibility is crucial—as when we rethought the plan and spent more time on Accountable Talk (University of Pittsburgh, n.d.) at Beth's school.

◆ Be aware of your own reactions to potential new initiatives and strategies for school change. Are you easily enthused or cautious? Have you missed opportunities because you didn't want to chase the next new thing, or have you missed opportunities because you chased too many good things? What might you learn from how you've worked with breadth *and* depth in the past to leverage it better in the future? For example, at the third school where Beth and I partnered, she decided to just have me work with mathematics teachers. The dynamics and demands on teacher time were different than at the other schools. Segmenting what was going on in the content areas while still pursuing all-school initiatives allowed for movement on more fronts with the depth required.

The following are a few key points and thought-provoking questions on working collaboratively that apply to this chapter.

- ◆ Remember that collaboration is not an innate human skill. Part of preparing to do the work is ensuring that you and your team, and every team in the building, believe that collaborating will be valuable. Ensuring that all members of each team have the skills to collaborate is also part of that preparation. Note, for example, the key roles that Beth's professional development team played in delivering the right messages, planning the calendar, and prioritizing learning. This was only possible because they trusted that Beth was open to their feedback and valued what they created together.

- ◆ How competitive are you? For example, as a leader at some level, do you hope to build a legacy through improvements in your team or school? How might that affect your collaboration efforts?

- ◆ Do you see collaboration as more work? As in, do you tend to tackle things alone because it's faster? When have you needed other voices?

- ◆ Are you afraid of losing control, and of collaborative efforts leading to conflict? Of being seen as not having enough instructional or organizational knowledge? How can you reframe these fears in light of the immenseness of school leadership responsibilities, making collaborative leadership a necessity? Note that chapter 12 (page 155) also addresses a facet of collaboration, the lens of power to—positional power—*and* power with—collaborative power—another very important and ongoing interdependency.

Priorities Inherent in the Breadth and Depth Lens

Table 5.2 highlights the priorities connected with this lens. Which of these resonate more with you? Which may be more key to your current leadership goals?

Table 5.2: Priorities Connected to Breadth *and* Depth

Breadth Priorities	Depth Priorities
Networking	**Legacy**
I am committed to making connections, sharing resources, and establishing relationships to enhance my team's effectiveness.	I want to be involved in new ideas, paradigm shifts, or solutions to problems that others thought were difficult or even unsolvable.
Innovating	**Mastery**
I explore resources, research-based innovations, ideas, theories, and learning opportunities on multiple fronts to stay abreast of best practices.	I value seeing initiatives implemented in depth so that teachers or students develop necessary, lasting skills and knowledge.

In the next two sections, we'll look at strategies to increase your use of both the breadth pole and your use of the depth pole. Remember that it may take at least six tries using a strategy before you feel comfortable or see results.

Five Ways to Increase Your Use of the Breadth Pole

To strengthen your use of the breadth pole, use the following five strategies.

1. **Read, watch, and attend with variety:** Avoid the rut of attending only one conference, reading only journals connected to education, or limiting yourself to a narrow range of nonfiction topics. Instead, read from other fields. What insights or connections might you make? Try out the immense variety of speakers at TED Talks (www.ted.com), featuring experts in nearly every field. What might you learn from chef Jamie Oliver or anthropologist Jane Goodall? What about from leading authors, such as Daniel Pink? What about biologists or entrepreneurs? What do you need to know about trends in the fields your students might aspire to, or about how other professionals are adapting to a rapidly changing world?

2. **Join a network:** *Bowling Alone* (Putnam, 2000) chronicles the loss of community in America—because of busyness, long commutes, devotion to youth sports, and many other factors, fewer and fewer people join professional, service, or recreational organizations. If this includes you, make room for regularly attending a local professional organization meeting. Find out what others are doing, and how they're tackling difficulties similar to your own and staying abreast of changes. Check out the local affiliates of such organizations

as Learning Forward (www.learningforward.org), the Association for Supervision and Curriculum Development (ASCD; www.ascd.org), as well as business groups.

If nothing appealing is nearby, then invite other leaders to meet for breakfast or for an informal book club. If you choose books tied to something generally available, like a TED Talk, people can at least access the video in their spare time. Remember that your goal is to expand your sources of new ideas, tools, and other resources.

3. **Find the enthusiasts:** Leading for breadth means sharing leadership. If you *know* something needs to be done on your team or in your building, and you know you don't have time to become the expert or to shepherd the implementation, pitch it to your staff with clear connections to the dilemmas it will solve or the way it will enrich your school. Once you find an enthusiast, work together to determine what your team needs. Is there a creative way to give them more planning time? Perhaps there is a grant available to cover training?

   What if no enthusiast comes forward? Maybe everyone's plate is full, but consider the three key factors in motivation: (1) autonomy, (2) mastery, and (3) purpose (Pink, 2009). Which factor might be missing in what you are proposing?

4. **Look for synergy:** If you prefer depth, then bolster your belief in the value of adding to your school's agenda by finding the connections among different programs, initiatives, strategies, and more. In fact, make that a decision criterion when choosing among alternatives. What is a seamless addition to what you are already doing? Or, how can you form connections? For example, when conducting workshops, I try to incorporate texts teachers are already using.

5. **Ask:** Design a staff meeting to find out what your teachers, specialists, and administrators are enthusiastic about. What have they learned from other buildings? What have they read about? What have they recognized through working with their own children? What would they like to bring to your school? What are they so enthused about that they'd like to participate in seeing it well-implemented?

   Open Space Technology (Owen, 2008) is a great tool for such conversations because it facilitates organizing and running a meeting, conference event, or professional development session. The protocols are actually technology-free. Instead, they facilitate creating the casual yet rich conversations that often happen over coffee or after meetings, using a process that quickly self-organizes participants into groups to discuss topics of mutual interest.

Five Ways to Increase Your Use of the Depth Pole

To strengthen your use of the depth pole, use the following five strategies.

1. **Study depth:** Find schools that make for good role models because they have made great strides on student achievement through in-depth implementation of a key strategy or program. How much time did they spend on professional development before teachers were proficient? What outside support did they require? How did they build internal expertise? How many days, months, or years passed before they began seeing results? What is similar and different to your situation and your goals? Too often, when we view initiatives from the outside, they seem to happen seamlessly when, in fact, a few years of consistent, persistent effort led to the systemic changes.

2. **Survey your staff:** Where are staff members seeing results? What would they like to do more of, and what do they need to do to achieve these goals? What isn't working, from their perspective? Why aren't those things working? Do they have the necessary time, knowledge, and resources? Or, can they articulate why it doesn't seem to fit their working groups or community? In other words, uncover where your staff would like to develop mastery.

3. **Key in on a dream:** Brainstorm the answer to: *If our school could do one thing so well that we could be a lighthouse to other schools, what would it be?* Once you have an idea—from how your school is teaching mathematics to how teachers team up to do problem-based learning to community partnerships—map out where you are and where you need to go. What would students and staff be doing if your learning community were the exemplary? How could you start down that path?

4. **Define mastery:** Before launching something new, take the time to define what mastery looks like. Robert Marzano (2011) suggests defining stages of developing expertise, such as Not Using, Beginning, Developing, Applying, and Innovating. Set up what each level looks like so that teachers feel safe indicating where they are and what they need to do to get to the next level. Set expectations as to when staff should be at each stage and the resources available to support their growth. Note that in the example of implementing

Accountable Talk (page 65), Beth and I did this halfway through the process rather than at the start. This was not at all as efficient as having clear expectations up front.

5. **Count the cost:** Think back through your education career and list the professional development initiatives, new approaches to teaching, and so on, that you've been part of. Which were you most enthusiastic about? Of those, which were implemented at a deep enough level that you saw lasting results? If you were successful, what percentage of those around you also saw success? Choose a few and think about them in terms of the breadth *and* depth lens. Which received the necessary investments, and which were nearly worthless because they needed more time, training, resources, or longevity? What do you want to make sure you remember as you launch new ideas?

ASK YOURSELF

This lens is about moving your learning community forward while implementing plans at a deep enough level for effectiveness and sustainability. How well are you leveraging breadth *and* depth?

C H A P T E R 6

Building a Collaborative Learning Community *and* Ensuring That Individuals Have Autonomy

For some purposes, systems work best when people work together as a collective. For other purposes, the best outcomes derive from individual effort, allowing people to be their best, unique selves. This concept isn't limited to one individual and a team. One can quickly generate a list of examples of this part–whole interdependency in action in a variety of education systems, such as: the needs of the kindergarten teachers and the needs of the whole staff; the needs of the middle school and the needs of all the schools in the system; and the needs of school principals and the needs of all the leaders in the district. In every case, community needs and individual needs both require careful consideration and balance.

This lens is about using the priorities in table 6.1 to ensure that you are building a collaborative culture *and* meeting individual needs.

Table 6.1: The Community *and* Individual Lens Domain

Lens 3	Community *and* Individual	
Priorities	Relationships Collaboration	Individuality Personal development
Common initiatives, issues, or leadership responsibilities that involve this lens	Learning communities Teambuilding for effective collaboration Supporting teacher growth Differentiation	
EQ component	Being aware of others' emotions Acting independently	

In this chapter, we explore the interdependency of community *and* individual by examining the factors that play into an organization's need for honoring community and honoring the individual. From there, we explain the balance between the community and individual poles, establish an emotional intelligence connection for this lens, and explain how you can best leverage the priorities inherent in this lens.

The Dilemma of Community and Individual

I could tell from their almost-late arrival time and restlessness that the secondary science teachers weren't all that excited about spending a day with me on collaborative lesson planning. They were polite as I asked for their expectations for our time together, indicating that they would welcome more of the differentiation strategies such as those I'd introduced in an all-staff session a few months before. "We don't get handed many days for actual lesson planning, though," one of the team leaders said, "and we're wondering about individual planning time today. After all, I teach chemistry, Eli teaches biology, Kayla teaches physics, and the middle school teachers all have different content, too."

Their politeness turned to rather heavy skepticism when I suggested that the collaborative planning time would help them individually. To their credit, they dug into using a student-friendly discussion protocol to build a shared understanding of information on developing growth mindset classrooms. They seemed to have fun with an activity where they each had different science facts on paper strips and had to compare and contrast to discover the main topic, and they engaged deeply in rating the rigor of tasks and how to implement them at a high level.

Then I posted one of the state standards on chemical bonding, gave each of them a big strip of paper, and said, "Use a marker and write down the big idea that students need to remember from this unit long after the exam. When you've finished, bring them over to this empty table."

The biology teachers shrugged. The chemistry teachers started writing immediately and were the first to place their strips on the table. It wasn't hard to guess that they were thinking: *This is our stuff. Why would the others have more of a handle on it than we do?* But as they perused the strips other teachers added to the table, their attitudes changed. The chemistry teachers began sliding them around, grouping by commonalities. The whole group discussed which words would resonate most with students, which best conveyed the essence of chemical bonding, and how to wrap up the key ideas contained on the strips into a single, sentence-length summary.

One of the chemistry teachers remarked on how her content knowledge actually got in the way of conveying to students why some of the material was important, noting that the final core idea was far better than her initial sentence. Heads around the table nodded.

Together, they worked to flesh out the learning progression for the unit. We then took what remained of the day for each of them to identify a standard for their content area and get the same help from the group in crafting a useful, student-friendly gem describing the essence of the content.

This is a visible example of the community and the individual working together for the benefit of all, but the dilemma of how much and when individuals should work as a group comes up in other areas in a school. Consider questions, such as the following.

- For each grade-level or content-area-focused team, what does everyone need to teach? What can be optional? The same goes for instructional strategies and classroom procedures.

- For student discipline, where is it essential to strive for consistency?

- What professional development topics benefit all staff or contribute to community building? What do individual teachers need?

- In what ways should learning team meetings be consistent in content and processes? How might they be different? What about school specialists?

- In working to build a classroom community, when are the needs of the group more important than those of the individual students and vice versa?

Again, collective teacher efficacy has one of the highest positive effects on student academic growth (DeWitt, 2017). Worthwhile collaboration fosters this efficacy when the other conditions are present (see page 34, The Top Five Truths About EQ). Think for a moment about your own work habits and preferences. How natural is collaborating for you? It isn't actually a natural skill for anyone—we all grow in listening, give and take, trusting others enough to be vulnerable, sharing ideas, and more. Yet some of us naturally thrive on working with others, and others of us need to experience the benefits before we really embrace collaboration.

Compare your reactions to the pairs of statements in figure 6.1 (page 78). Which is more attractive to you? For example, I truly value working with coauthors (six over the course of my writing career), who have enriched my ideas and pointed out my blind spots. However, my best ideas, and the form of each sentence, happen when I work alone. I know the value of collaboration but, like Tim Brown in chapter 4 (page 50), I need time for ideas to percolate before working with others.

Think about your natural preferences, and place yourself on each of the following continuums by circling a marker or placing a dot.

Collaborative		Individual
I get my best ideas when I'm talking with colleagues.	⊢─┼─┼─┼─┤	I get my best ideas when working alone.
Collaborative		**Individual**
In my experience, I receive more than I give when I'm part of collaborative teams.	⊢─┼─┼─┼─┤	In my experience, I end up doing more than my share of the work when I'm part of collaborative teams.
Collaborative		**Individual**
I'd prefer to spend more of my planning time collaborating with others than working alone.	⊢─┼─┼─┼─┤	I'd prefer to spend more of my planning time working alone than collaborating with others.
Collaborative		**Individual**
I'd rather brainstorm a lesson plan with my team and then tweak it on my own so it works for me.	⊢─┼─┼─┼─┤	I'd rather develop a lesson plan alone and then ask colleagues for suggestions.
Collaborative		**Individual**
Often, when I'm working alone, I find myself wishing I could talk through ideas with someone.	⊢─┼─┼─┼─┤	Often, during collaboration time, I find myself wishing I could work on my own.

Figure 6.1: Comparing preferences for collaborative and individual contributions.

*Visit **go.SolutionTree.com/leadership** for a free reproducible version of this figure.*

Note that the beliefs and therefore the actions of leaders, and thus the practices of those they lead, often reflect how they place themselves on these continuums. I once facilitated a workshop for a group of instructional coaches whose leadership had charged them with supporting learning teams. When asked, they struggled to list what was valuable about teachers working independently. Conversely, I once worked with a school principal who only brought his staff together for a few hours during the professional development days before school started—he didn't want to waste their time with collaborative sessions when they could be in their own classrooms, planning.

Your Personal Collaboration Meter

Figure 6.2 maps the interdependency between the community and individual poles.

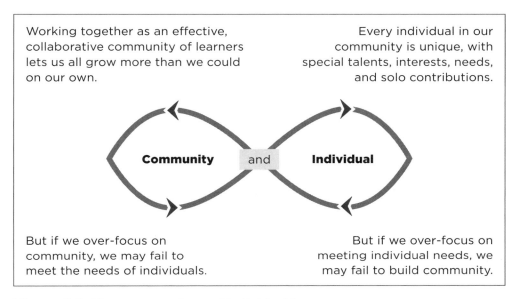

Working together as an effective, collaborative community of learners lets us all grow more than we could on our own.

Every individual in our community is unique, with special talents, interests, needs, and solo contributions.

Community and **Individual**

But if we over-focus on community, we may fail to meet the needs of individuals.

But if we over-focus on meeting individual needs, we may fail to build community.

Figure 6.2: The community *and* individual loop.

As a leader, understanding which side you favor—and which downside you're more afraid of—can help you balance the interdependency between these equally valuable considerations. Often, if leaders are *too* enthusiastic about collaborative time, teachers begin to feel that it comes at a cost—they lose the individual prep time they need for grading, or they end up focusing on needs the school identified rather than their own biggest concerns about their students. On the other side, if leaders are *too* enthusiastic about allowing teacher autonomy, wisdom and success remain in individual classrooms rather than being shared across the community. Knowing whether or not you struggle to enthusiastically embrace both sides of this lens can help you avoid the traps of your preferred style.

Again, this lens describes multiple part–whole relationships, not just a teacher and a team: the needs of the kindergarten teachers and the needs of the whole staff, the needs of the middle school and the needs of all the schools in the system, and the needs of school principals and the needs of all the leaders in the district. In every case, community needs and individual needs both require careful consideration and balance.

One way to move forward is to focus on the overall target of this lens: building community while meeting individual needs. Consider the following two interdependencies as you work out how to get the right mix for this lens: (1) standardization and customization and (2) the classroom and the student.

Standardization and Customization

In *Differentiated Coaching* (Kise, 2017), I point out that when we differentiate professional development for teachers, we are modeling what we expect them to do for students. There are a few differences, though. First, although teachers may have different levels of skill and expertise, different interests, and different content to teach, school leadership is still viewing professional growth for each teacher through the lens of the school's vision and values. A shared understanding of the vision and values can't happen without collaborative conversations and decision making about how to stay aligned with those values. Yes, teachers might choose from a menu of professional development options, but some things need full learning-community participation even as you meet teacher needs.

One-size-fits-all professional development has the same problems as one-size-fits-all reading instruction. Just as students have different levels of reading interest and proficiency, so too do teachers have different levels of interest and proficiency with new classroom strategies—and neither all students nor all adults have the same informational needs. However, the inverse of the one-size-fits-all approach is also true. Completely customized professional development—everything delivered via individual coaching or online modules—has the same disadvantages in terms of cost, loss of social learning, and other factors, as completely customized student learning, whether through tutoring or online instruction. We can standardize the goal and even offer several standardized strategies. But then, we can meet the needs of the individual teachers by customizing based on the following.

- Teacher experience level
- Self-reported or observed classroom-management struggles
- Teaching style and current strengths for building rapport with students
- Teacher expertise with the proposed strategies; consider allowing them to self-assess with questions that make apparent that they aren't expected to be experts yet: Have they heard of the strategies before? Have they tried them but hope for more support? Do they use them regularly? Have they changed them so they work even better? Are they ready to coach others in their use?

When teachers trust that disclosing their expertise will result in support, not evaluation or judgment, limited resources can target the biggest needs.

The Classroom and the Student

Ensuring that the adults in the building experience the benefits of collaboration and the benefits of individual development and contribution can reinforce how to ensure that students gain the same benefits. Frequently, teachers favor one over the other, and it shows in their classrooms. Perhaps students are always seated in groups and there are few opportunities for pursuing independent ideas—in fact, one of the schools I worked with had moved to *all* learning as cooperative learning. In other cases, schools emphasize individual work—another school had moved to all computerized mathematics instruction and students were complaining, "Can't we solve some problems together?"

This is not merely about meeting the needs of extraverted and introverted students or teachers. All of us need to learn how to work with others, respect their viewpoints, and benefit from different ideas. Likewise, all of us need to learn how to work alone, think for ourselves, and trust our own wisdom.

Further, students benefit from being part of a classroom community, just as adults do, even while each needs to be recognized as a unique individual with talents to share.

The EQ Connection

The key EQ areas for this lens are being aware of others' emotions and acting independently. The following lists a few key points regarding being aware of others' emotions that apply to this chapter.

◆ Remember that collaboration isn't a natural human skill. Leaders need to have the pulse of each team under their purview—their attitudes toward collaboration and toward one another.

◆ Within learning teams, appropriate protocols can be of great use in helping each team member build awareness of one another's level of trust and emotions. However, many protocols do the opposite—using them allows for sharing at a shallow level, or calls for such positive platitudes that no real collaboration can take place. Work with people who don't think like you to find ones that allow for what I term deep, Level III collaboration (Kise, 2017):

> Level III collaboration is as follows:
>
> - Based on robust knowledge regarding teaching and learning. Otherwise, teachers may simply reinforce each other's incorrect assumptions or bad habits.
> - Nitty-gritty deliberation regarding present practice and future direction. Teachers feel free to question each other about why a practice works, what kinds of students it reaches, who might be left out, and changes that might improve it or adapt it.
> - An interdependency that reduces planning time, spreads effective teaching practices, develops a culture of shared meaning, concentrates resources where they are most needed, and makes the best use of the strengths of each member of the team. Synergy, synthesis, reinforcement, and sharing are the result. (p. 75)

The following are a few key points on acting independently that apply to this chapter.

◆ Because collaboration comes with a built-in bandwagon effect ("Wow, this is great—let's all do this!"), developing independence in leaders and in everyone else is critical to ensuring that people feel free to advocate for their own ideas and needs.

◆ One way to encourage independence in everyone is to formalize each person considering what excites them and concerns them about a strategy, teaching method, new content, and so on. Have them rate their experience level, list the support they need—or the support they can provide to others— and if appropriate, where it ranks in their own agenda for professional development. Then have teams compare answers and negotiate how to move forward together.

Priorities Inherent in the Community and *Individual Lens*

Table 6.2 highlights the values connected with this lens. Which of these resonate more with you? Which may be more key to your current leadership goals?

Table 6.2: Priorities Connected to Community *and* Individual

Community Priorities	Individual Priorities
Relationships	**Individuality**
I invest time in building bonds with others for mutual support that can go beyond what the task at hand might require.	I value opportunities for solo efforts, making the most of each person's unique gifts, creativity, and inspirations.
Collaboration	**Personal Development**
I want to foster meaningful teamwork where people enjoy working together and keep everyone's best interests in mind.	I am committed to continuous improvement of the skills and knowledge that I and others need to reach our full potentials.

In the next two sections, we'll look at strategies to increase your use of both the community pole and your use of the individual pole. Remember that it may take at least six tries using a strategy before you feel comfortable or see results.

Five Ways to Increase Your Use of the Community Pole

To strengthen your use of the community pole, use the following five strategies.

1. **Reward teaming:** Make sure that collaborative time is viewed positively by ensuring that teachers also have enough individual planning time. Get creative. You might give each collaborative team a day for collaboration once a semester if creative schedule shifts allow for their classrooms to be covered. How might you fund substitutes? What staff meetings can you do away with to allow for collaboration?

2. **Care for outliers:** Identify whose responsibilities are truly different from anyone else's in the building or team. Do you have collaborative buy-in from teachers for subjects such as art, physical education, or music? Or, are these teachers frustrated by not getting the same level of value from collaborative time as do teachers in naturally homogenous groups, such as third-grade teachers? Share group leadership with them—get their input on what is and isn't working and consider whether virtual meetings with specialists at other

schools might be beneficial. Decide whether your teachers might benefit from some collaboration such as the example of the science teachers at the start of this chapter who were working on collaborative lesson planning. Identify other ideas individuals might have for being part of a collaborative effort while still getting their individual needs met. If you've already solved this, great! In too many places, it's left to chance.

3. **Get help:** Teambuilding requires special expertise, and research indicates that partnering with outside expertise often shortens the time required to establish effective, sustainable collaborative groups (Hord, 2004). Further, although leaders can indeed lead teams through many skill-building endeavors, it is nearly impossible to participate yourself and also observe the interactions among individuals. If trust is already shaky, the investment is doubly worthwhile.

4. **Get a framework:** Too often, leaders think, *We need something new to hone our skills,* so they move from one instrument or theory for group dynamics to the next, never taking time to live with any deeply and perhaps evolve it. I favor Jungian personality type, as described in the appendix (page 217), because after twenty-five years, I'm still developing and learning about new applications for it. Do you have a framework that provides a common language for discussing and making connections among initiatives for equity, classroom management, differentiation, collaboration, stress management, cultural competence, assessment, and more?

5. **Invest time:** Relationships need tending. Time spent on adult-collaboration skills or time for deepening the quality of relationships on your team might seem to detract from the focus on students, but it actually deepens the quality of Level III collaboration (Kise, 2017).

ASK YOURSELF

Is being aware of others' emotions one of your blind spots? Consider an anonymous poll of your staff to get a better read on trust levels, listening, and collaboration skills.

Five Ways to Increase Your Use of the Individual Pole

To strengthen your use of the individual pole, use the following five strategies.

1. **Examine collaborative efforts:** Collaboration can move a school forward, but individual brainstorming can be more effective than group efforts, many creative tasks are best done individually, and most people need solo, deliberate practice to gain expertise. List some of your recent collaborative projects. Might any have benefited from more solo effort? When was team effort helpful? Did it ever get in the way? Teachers won't always have their leader or team around to help them, and they sometimes need to be able to get as far as they can as individuals before seeking advice.

2. **Avoid micromanaging:** Although people differ in the amount of instruction and feedback they desire, few take kindly to micromanagement. My very first supervisor checked every morning to ensure we were all at our desks by 8 a.m. (I was there at 7:42 thanks to bus schedules, but that wasn't worthy of his notice.) Think through how you might be micromanaging and thus taking away individual development and autonomy. Do you do any of the following?

   - Lay out exactly how something should be done
   - Set the timelines
   - Frequently ask people whether they are on track
   - Insist on frequent, regular meetings so people can report progress
   - Expect to see drafts, correspondence, meeting notes, and so on?

   If you say, "Isn't all this part of leadership? Ensuring people are tracking with the vision?" consider how it might be if you instead practiced the following.

   - Ask the team to plan how it will be done.
   - Ask them to provide a realistic schedule.
   - Tell them you'll assume they're on track unless they tell you otherwise.
   - Discuss and agree together as to when in the process a check-in would be wise.
   - Ask where they might need your input to ensure that they understood your expectations for them to complete the work in alignment with your requirements.

3. **Plan for divergence:** Whenever possible, set the overall goal and allow people to reach it in their own way. Or, be clear—hopefully after receiving collaborative input—as to what everyone should do uniformly and when people can diverge. For example, one school was working toward a more uniform curriculum. Previously, teachers had taught content as they wished, so the first-grade teachers never were sure what students had done the year before. As I worked with the kindergarten team on planning a specific unit, they quickly agreed on four activities they would all do, and on two learning goals where the students would benefit from each teacher doing things differently. Collaboration and autonomy, with clear expectations, kept everyone motivated. You'll find more on this in chapter 13 (page 167).

4. **Prime your ideas:** If you prefer to work through things with your team, do some preparation in advance of a meeting. Where do your strengths align with the work you'll be doing together? Ideally, how would you like to see it done and why? How might research, practical considerations, or the needs of your particular students back up your ideas? Identify where you really want to take a stand to ensure that you are able to proceed with your own idea and where you are most open to group consensus. Remember that teams benefit both from an atmosphere of agreeableness and from healthy sharing and testing of ideas.

5. **Choose depth:** In a learning community, everyone, from the top leader to the students, should be seeking to learn every day. If you're more of a generalist, pick something to explore more deeply than you usually do—something tied to your own professional development goals. You might read books, find research via the online search engines at your local or university library, network with other educators to understand how they are addressing a need or developing a program, or attend a workshop. Then, add to your learning. Take time to reflect on questions you still have, and then go and find the answers. Learn less about something else to make time for going deeper.

ASK YOURSELF

This lens is about building the collaborative team that will move forward student learning while ensuring that everyone's needs are met. How well are you balancing and honoring community *and* individual?

CHAPTER 7

Taking Reality Into Account *and* Pursuing a Vision

The best ideas for any initiative start with a vision of the future, one that is generally ambitious and bold. This is a *good* thing. But leaders need to balance this with reality and what can be done with the available resources. This lens is about leveraging the priorities in table 7.1 to ensure that you find the right mix of leading toward a powerful vision *and* accounting for the very real hurdles of limited time, resources, energy, and passion.

Table 7.1: The Reality *and* Vision Lens Domain

Lens 4	Reality *and* Vision	
Priorities	Realism Balance	Visioning Optimism
Common initiatives, issues, or leadership responsibilities that involve this lens	Maintaining school focus Evaluating implementation strategy Setting clear expectations and providing feedback Setting school direction Influencing beliefs	
EQ component	Building an atmosphere of emotional safety Acting independently	

In this chapter, we explore the interdependency of reality *and* vision by looking at a scenario where an established vision needed adjusting as reality changed. From there, we explain the balance between the reality and vision poles, establish an emotional intelligence connection for this lens, and explain how you can best leverage the priorities inherent in this lens.

When Vision Meets Reality

Patrick Duffy describes the work of making a vision become reality as, "Building support without priming resistance." Patrick's passion around building systems for equity has its roots in his experiences growing up in a small Minnesota town as the son of a Lebanese mother and Irish father. In his roles in different school districts as a teacher, assistant principal, district leadership development coordinator, and director of secondary schools, Patrick's personal vision or purpose has remained the same. "I develop people and develop systems for equity. I'm passionate about helping people articulate and live up to their values" (P. Duffy, personal communication, September 21, 2018).

However, Patrick's approach to the work is anything but static. He'd be the first to say that what works in one place may not work in another, and he's learned the importance of paying attention to the realities of each new situation before taking the first steps toward a vision.

Patrick's initial conversations about race began when he noticed that several of his students were reading and discussing *Why Are All the Black Kids Sitting Together in the Cafeteria?* (Tatum, 2017). At about the same time, interns from a nonprofit organization trained a dozen or so students in facilitating antiracist conversations. Realizing that something more systemic was necessary, Patrick asked the students who had formed their own study group if they would be interested in developing a student-leadership program.

These students met with him for several months, culminating in a Dare 2 Be Real program that sixty-seven students attended. They went on retreat, met weekly for eight months, and learned to facilitate conversations about race that included staff members. Then a colleague introduced him to Anthony Galloway, an African American deeply involved in the same kind of work. Together, they deepened the curriculum, taught workshops, and collaborated to increase the impact they were having on students.

Patrick soon moved to an administrative position in another district. Anthony worked with different organizations throughout the region, keeping Patrick connected with people involved in equity work. With just a small percentage of minority students in his new district, there was little urgency around equity work. However, Patrick was able to find interested students, and a few staff, willing to attend a Courageous Conversation retreat, which he and Anthony led (https://courageousconversation.com). This small group worked over the next year to master protocols and develop their personal racial narratives. Patrick had the students share their narratives with staff, at conferences, and via video, greatly increasing the credibility of the initiative.

Eventually, Anthony was able to guide discussions about racially predictable achievement not only at Patrick's school but throughout the region.

Patrick was then recruited to be a school principal. His new staff had done some equity work but seemed to be avoiding some hard conversations. He repeatedly heard negative language around using data. The teachers did not trust standardized test scores and believed they should resist data-driven instruction. To avoid priming resistance, Patrick started the school year with a data walk, redefining data for them by including emails from parents, student work examples, quotes from student forums, *and* the test scores. He explains how:

> I asked them, "What story do you see as the strength of our school? What needs to happen? What needs to be attended to? What pieces of the story aren't told?" I summarized their responses in themes and brought them back to groups of teachers and parents and students, asking, "Are these aspirations for the school what we stand for?" The values were to guide everything forward, allowing us to ask whether decisions moved us toward or away from who we said we were. (P. Duffy, personal communication, September 21, 2018)

The process helped the entire school community re-examine reality and use it as input for a relevant, useful vision.

Eventually, Patrick took on a district leadership development role. The vision called for a progressive, but by no means radical, plan for equity. Patrick would first work with leaders, developing their capacity to do the work. They would then develop their teams' capacities.

However, that vision ran into reality. Personal transformation around race frequently precedes any hope of systemic change, but people are generally in different places as to the need and the urgency. Patrick's own doctoral research focused on white paralysis—the stages of guilt, blame, pity, and fear that often paralyze white people's ability to move forward. He points out:

> The personal work of equity is messy, and you need to be okay with making some mistakes. Our systems aren't set up to allow for that. Public confidence is connected to the idea of perfection. That perpetuates a culture of fear of saying the wrong thing or standing up in support of someone who may be appearing too radical in their approach. (P. Duffy, personal communication, September 21, 2018)

This fear-driven resistance drove home yet another key reality: the power of the status quo. He was asking people to move out of their comfort zones, comfort zones that provided some stability in the fishbowl of public scrutiny they were experiencing.

The equity work would eventually ask them to give up some power as students' voices began to inform best practices. He had to slow down and spend more time working with the leaders; and some of them truly struggled, not ready to have the difficult conversations with their teams regarding bringing about equity for students.

Patrick knows that the clearer his own vision, his sense of his values and strengths and limitations, the easier it has been to move forward the big vision of schools that work for all students. He summarizes, "How do we help our teams recognize that by sharing power with our students, with our historically marginalized community, we aren't losing but gaining something of our own? I believe we gain something in our own humanity" (P. Duffy, personal communication, September 21, 2018).

The Need to Bring Vision to Reality

Some leaders look at the reality of their organization and become paralyzed by the lack of time, employee complacency, limited professional development resources, or priorities imposed from the outside. Others push and push and push for progress, only coming to terms with a failed effort when the reality of inadequate resources or game-changing resistance is too disastrous to ignore.

Figure 7.1 depicts the interdependency loop between the reality and vision poles.

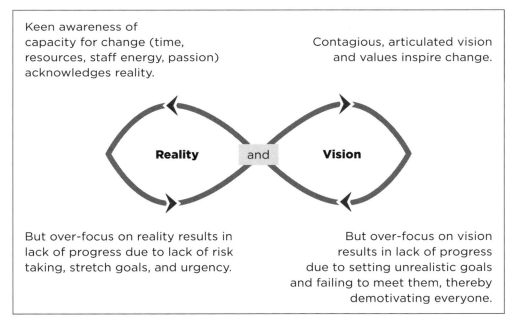

Figure 7.1: The reality *and* vision loop.

Uniting people around a shared vision is one of the top five practices of effective leaders (Kouzes & Posner, 2010). It isn't enough to simply articulate a vision, though. It has to *mean* something; and it shouldn't sound like everyone else's, because your school, your students, your community, and your needs are all unique. However, googling *school vision* brings up a string of statements that are likely to include phrases, such as *student academic excellence, college and career pathways, caring citizens,* and *success in an ever-changing world.*

None of these phrases are bad in and of themselves. In fact, it's hard to argue against any of them; but the true test of a school's vision is what it does, not what it says. Fortunately, researchers have teased out what it takes for a vision statement to be worth the time it takes to craft it.

First, the vision needs to contain the organization's ultimate purpose. It may not reflect current reality, but to be meaningful and motivating, the vision needs to resonate with employees. Further, employees need to be able to connect it to their own, personal values. Think of it as giving them a compelling purpose to get out of bed in the morning. In fact, research shows that the feeling of purpose is even more important to ultimate organizational success than how passionate they are or even if they are the most skilled employees you could have (Coyle, 2018).

Second, leaders need to communicate that shared vision frequently and concretely. Communicate the vision through concrete images. For example, instead of saying, "We will achieve gender equity," say, "No adults will be surprised when a girl takes the top mathematics award" (Carton, Murphy, & Clark, 2014).

How often must you express this? John Kotter (1996) finds that because of the barrage of other communications people receive, employees need to hear the vision about ten times more often than they do. In *Originals*, Adam Grant (2016) reports on Kotter's research:

> In one three-month period, employees might be exposed to 2.3 million words and numbers. On average during that period, the vision for change was expressed in only 13,400 words and numbers: a 30-minute speech, an hour-long meeting, a briefing, and a memo. Since more than 99 percent of the communication that employees encounter during those three months does not concern the vision, how can they be expected to understand it, let alone internalize it? The change agents don't realize this, because they're up to their ears in information about their vision. (pp. 76–77)

Third, make the vision into an actionable shared purpose through three to four values statements. The strongest cultures have a short list that sets clear expectations for day-to-day actions. We're tempted to list more than three or four values to sell our visions by including all kinds of phrases that parents, communities, and other stakeholders might be seeking. That's how catch phrases, like *global* and *college and career*, make their way into so many schools' web pages. However, with more than four values, shared purpose starts to fade (Carton et al., 2014). This happens for two reasons.

1. Three or four priorities are all an organization can maintain focus around. More than that, and people pick and choose the priorities of most interest to them.

2. The ways in which people interpret the values diverge more and more as leadership attention becomes divided among the values competing for focus.

Effective organizations narrow down values lists by asking whether they'd still retain their unique organizational identity if it isn't included.

Fourth (and finally), ask, "Is this vision realistic?" Motivation throughout an organization comes from believing that the vision is attainable. It can be audacious, but your staff need to believe it can happen (Pink, 2009).

With the complexity and ever-changing vista of any implementation effort, it's easy to forget the exact strategies that resulted in progress and apply them in new situations. Among the many lessons Patrick has learned is the importance of two key interdependencies in making visions a reality: (1) incrementalism and urgency and (2) the students, the staff, and the leaders. How might these affect your goals and initiatives?

Incrementalism and Urgency

How fast you can move is a key factor in balancing the reality *and* vision lens. Whatever initiative you're leading, there's a tension between getting immediate results and ensuring effectiveness and sustainability via long-term planning and strategies.

Think about this fundamental difference in beliefs: Do those around you think that your current system just needs a few tweaks? Or, are people articulating that your system isn't meeting the needs of all students and that the system needs big changes before this can happen? Are they looking for incremental change or big change?

Perhaps you've seen mathematics initiatives fail because an incremental change, such as a new curriculum, didn't address the big need of increasing teacher mathematical knowledge. Or, perhaps plans for extra tutoring time for students fell apart because they would have required huge changes to the school day. Odds are, you can easily name your own failed effort that enacted an incremental change when big change was vital.

In equity work, like the work you read about in When Vision Meets Reality (page 88), the trap can be jumping into workshops and protocols for discussing race and improving the system before people are ready to acknowledge that they have some personal work to do around their concepts of race and racial identity.

Consider how you might use these key indicators of the reality pole to inform the pace at which to proceed. The following are some useful indicators.

- **Listen for the language in use:** As you listen, what can you learn? The following example shows some of what Patrick learned by listening when he worked with another school on its vision:

  > In one setting, talk of race just fostered anger. So, I began by suggesting intercultural programs for students. Slowly, I peppered in the concept of race. In meetings, people would whisper, "the black students . . ." as if they were saying something wrong rather than acknowledging that we were talking about reality. Those conversations allowed me to introduce race in productive ways.
  >
  > Then I moved to another district where I was charged with beginning equity work. I assumed they were ready for race, so I started with antiracism. They definitely shared their feelings about that—and I pulled back! My work is about equity for all students, and through that principle, I can gradually move toward race. (P. Duffy, personal communication, September 21, 2018)

- **Note that language is a *reality*:** Patrick helps change language to ready people for more change.

- **Understand the social and political power of the status quo:** Change, even change we choose to undertake, involves discomfort. Patrick points out, "There's an urgency to do things for kids, something substantive for the students we have in front of us right now. And a fear that we've got to move slow so we don't create waves." Gauging that fear correctly, and understanding the level of power, are crucial.

- **Assess the scope of change needed:** How do you check for root causes—the needed big changes—before implementing what might turn out to be an unneeded incremental change?

The Students, the Staff, and the Leaders

What is the best starting place for your effort? Often, limits on time and resources dictate an incremental approach. Patrick has seen change happen whether the work starts with leadership, teachers, or students, but he also found that if adults interact with students at least weekly, it increases their willingness to do the work. Part of this happens through increasing student voice, a popular trend in education. Patrick cautions:

> It's in vogue to have student voice, but to what end? Is it helping us create a system to serve all kids or to feel good about what we're already doing? Are we rallying around students who say how their needs aren't being met and getting them what they need?
>
> Before kids speak truth to power, we need to set the staff up to hear things from a place of openness to growth. It's huge if their attitude is, "How can I learn from what the students are saying?"
>
> And, flipping the question, are the students ready to have voice? In one school, I had focus groups of white students and students of color talk about their experiences in front of the staff. The white students left saying, "That was a great experience." But the students of color told me they felt they'd sold out. One said, "I couldn't bring myself to say in front of everyone what a teacher did to me."
>
> I've had it backfire the other way, too, where a student of color blasted a teacher in front of peers in ways that didn't respect the teacher's humanity. Protocols, or sharing audio clips, or sharing with a small group of trusted adults who then spread the themes and patterns with the rest of the staff, are all great ways to include student voice. (P. Duffy, personal communication, September 21, 2018)

Visualize what might happen if students have knowledge before teachers. How might that inform or catalyze your efforts? What if teachers receive their training first? What about a train-the-trainer model? How might the starting place alter the path, and where do you begin? With leaders? Students? Staff? Parents?

The EQ Connection

The key EQ areas for this lens are building an atmosphere of emotional safety and acting independently. The following are a few key points on emotional safety that apply to this chapter.

◆ Remember that the number-one predictor of effective teams is an atmosphere of safety and belonging (Coyle, 2018). Revisit the three key leadership cues that create this safe space (see page 34, The Top Five Truths About EQ).

◆ Whether you are changing school schedules or changing the conversations about equity, part of assessing reality is expecting people to be in different places, with different fears and different needs. Proven protocols, such as the Courageous Conversation tools (see https://courageousconversation.com) that Patrick used, can be invaluable. Be aware that many Intuitive types (see the appendix, page 217) see protocols as straightjackets and either avoid them or fail to use them with the level of fidelity necessary for effectiveness. If this describes you, reframe protocols as benefiting from the wisdom and experience of others rather than as limits to your own creativity!

The following are a few key points on acting independently that apply to this chapter.

◆ By definition, visionaries have original ideas. Even if the vision you're bringing into reality came from somewhere else, it is still original in your setting. Make sure you are aware of why it is of value to you and how it aligns with your own purpose. Without that clarity, it is all too easy to trigger issues of trust or to miscommunicate the goals and hoped-for outcomes of what you are asking people to do.

◆ If you tend toward the logical thinking style of decision making (see the appendix), making tough calls based on your principles may be relatively comfortable. Acting independently may be natural, especially when implementing proven strategies or making data-backed decisions; however, remember that logic does not sway everyone! You may need to use other forms of argument or evidence after making a necessary tough call.

Priorities Inherent in the Reality **and** *Vision Lens*

Table 7.2 (page 96) highlights the priorities connected with this lens. Which of these resonate more with you? Which may be more key to your current leadership goals?

In the next two sections, we'll look at strategies to increase your use of both the reality pole and your use of the vision pole. Remember that it may take at least six tries using a strategy before you feel comfortable or see results.

Table 7.2: Priorities Connected to Reality *and* Vision

Reality Priorities	Vision Priorities
Realism	**Visioning**
I value representing things as they really are and having the pulse of my team's capacity, engagement, and sense of efficacy.	I believe in co-creating images of the future that motivate people and then lead them to work toward those common purposes.
Balance	**Optimism**
I want to model limits on work so that I, and those with whom I work, make time for family, health, leisure pursuits, nature, relationships, and so on.	I want to inspire confidence in those I lead that our efforts will bring success.

Five Ways to Increase Your Use of the Reality Pole

To strengthen your use of the reality pole, use the following five strategies.

1. **Think it through:** List three recent endeavors that fell short of your expectations. Use figure 7.2 to reflect on these. Do you see any patterns?

Endeavors	1. _____	2. _____	3. _____
Was I unrealistic about the time the project would take?			
What information did I discount because of past experiences or my own enthusiasm?			
Did others share my vision? My reality? How do I know?			
What did I know about the motivations of others working on the project?			
What should I have done differently to reach my original goals?			

Figure 7.2: Assess three recent endeavors.

*Visit **go.SolutionTree.com/leadership** for a free reproducible version of this figure.*

2. **Find a critic:** If you've received feedback that your plans are overly optimistic, consider who among your team members or peers might help you think through scenarios. This is a part of accountability, identifying and preparing for possible problems for which prevention is under your control. For example, Patrick learned to use current vocabulary to gauge where to start his equity work. Balancing optimism with a hard look at very possible pushback or roadblocks can increase trust and loyalty.

3. **Test your perceptions:** After announcing a plan, facilitating a meeting, or otherwise interacting with your team, take some time to reflect. How do you think each person reacted? Then, ask about their reactions. Frame your questions so that you're more likely to get honest feedback with information such as, "I'm not sure I heard everyone's questions or concerns" or "This project is very important—I need everyone's honest take on the opportunities and barriers we face." Do they feel sufficiently informed? Are they optimistic? Enthusiastic? Frustrated? Overwhelmed? Heard? If you aren't sure they'll speak frankly, consider using a quick and anonymous online survey through surveymonkey.com or a similar easy-to-use tool.

4. **Find a partner:** Who doesn't think like you? Who asks you the most questions? Who might even be somewhat annoying? Seek that person's input. One school principal invited the person who raised the most concerns in meetings to be on her professional development committee. The teacher said, "I thought I drive you crazy." "You do," replied the principal, "and it keeps me from assuming I have everything figured out. I need you."

5. **Rethink your expertise:** You may be experienced at leading change. You may have several years of experience in your current role. You may be a content expert on the change you're leading. However, if any one of these three isn't true, you may be missing a key area of expertise. Erik Dane, Kevin Rockmann, and Michael Pratt (2012) find that we should only trust our instincts in our areas of expertise. Otherwise we need to do a far more thorough analysis. Rely on your expertise in the right areas, and do your homework for the others.

Five Ways to Increase Your Use of the Vision Pole

To strengthen your use of the vision pole, use the following five strategies.

1. **Practice using images:** You, and those you lead, need a clear picture of where you're going, and the more concrete you can make it the better. For

example, instead of saying you want to develop lifelong readers, describe how student growth as readers can be seen when students beg to finish the page they're on, groan when independent reading time is over, or pull out a book as they wait for the next class to start.

Also consider when an analogy will get your message across better. For example, when I'm observing teachers, I suggest that I'm their second set of eyes at the back of the room while they're up there singing and tap dancing at the same time. Since they've had input into what I'll be looking for, this simple description works to help them feel the partnership between teacher and coach.

2. **Craft your personal vision:** Do you have a purpose, a cause, or something outside of your own needs or the specifics of your job that guides your decisions? In other words, are you clear on your own values and beliefs as a leader? If not, take the time to craft a statement. Identify what gets you out of bed in the morning, the values you want to see in reality, and the talents you bring to the table. Craft them into a short statement that captures your passion.

3. **Gauge your optimism:** Optimism is another piece of emotional intelligence, reflecting your daily approach to life. Too little optimism not only blocks us from taking appropriate risks, but can lead to depression if everything seems to be out of our control. Consider three simple actions: (1) Keep in regular contact with optimistic friends and coworkers. (2) Reflect on past times when you felt pessimistic. How often was it truly warranted? People often realize that they overestimate the frequency of negative events. (3) If your pessimism truly is warranted, consider meeting with a coach or counselor. What skill might you hone, or what other proactive strategy might warrant new optimism?

4. **Team for vision:** Whether it's a vision for a particular initiative or for your entire school, consider using Patrick's method of starting with the reality of data and finding the themes.

5. **Repeat your vision:** Remember that employees need to hear the vision about ten times more often than most leaders communicate it. Look for opportunities in meetings, correspondence, and the signage in the building. Be explicit about how different actions or decisions align with the vision. Ask others to share what they've seen that is evidence of the vision in action.

ASK YOURSELF

This lens is about accounting for very real barriers of time, resources, and readiness while leading toward a purposeful vision. How well are you balancing reality *and* vision?

CHAPTER 8

Building on Current Success *and* Changing to Meet the Future

Instructional practices and broader education policies exist on an always-evolving spectrum. Some solid strategies stand the test of time; for example, John Dewey (1990) describes practices similar to project-based learning in *The School and Society, and the Child and the Curriculum*. However, many initially ground-breaking initiatives to address critical deficiencies outlive their usefulness and require changes to remain relevant. Sometimes those changes may require abandoning the tried and true for entirely new initiatives. This lens is about using the priorities in table 8.1 to ensure that you find the right balance between maximizing the use of existing best practices *and* introducing new initiatives and ideas.

Table 8.1: The Continuity *and* Change Lens Domain

Lens 5	Continuity *and* Change	
Priorities	Experience Creativity with the known	Challenge Creativity with the new
Common initiatives, issues, or leadership responsibilities that involve this lens	Being situationally aware Maintaining school focus Managing administrative processes and standardizing procedures Acting as a change agent	
EQ component	Acting independently Building an atmosphere of emotional safety	

In this chapter, we explore the interdependency of continuity *and* change by examining change and how what looks like resistance from stakeholders often represents wise fear of mismanaged change that you have the power to diminish. From there, we explain the balance between the continuity and change poles, establish an emotional intelligence connection for this lens, and explain how you can best leverage the priorities inherent in this lens.

The Difference Between Resistance and Fear

Whole books have been written on working with resistant teachers, but whenever I'm working with instructional coaches, I ask them to accept as a norm for our time together that there are no resistant teachers, but rather only teachers whose needs during change haven't yet been met.

Often someone laughs and says, "You haven't been in our school." Actually, as an outside consultant, school leaders often ask me to work with teachers they consider the most resistant. However, early on, I learned an important lesson about classrooms and a healthy fear of change, which is very different from resistance.

I'd been working on differentiated instruction with a middle school teaching team for a couple of months when they asked me to facilitate a highly interactive exercise that I'd done with school staff for their 120 energetic, urban sixth graders. I said, "Yes," but I barely slept the night before. At 3 a.m., I was thinking through ways to head off problems: tape the floor in advance, leave more room for extraverts, and type out note cards for myself in case I got flustered. (I hadn't used notes in these kinds of sessions for years.) Could I make myself heard over 120 students? I'd spent time in the school cafeteria. I'd heard reports about assemblies. I had no trouble thinking of things that could go wrong.

But nothing did go wrong. The students enjoyed the exercise and small group conversations. The experience made me realize how intimidating it could be to try something new in a school. I'd done that exercise a hundred times, indoors and outside, in rooms where we couldn't move the furniture, with a group of school principals who were in deep conflict with each other—so why had I lost sleep over it? Because I didn't know how the students would respond.

Yet, I was asking the teachers to shed practices they knew would keep order in their classrooms for ones that I claimed had worked in other settings. After all, even with the *continuity* of using an exercise that I knew backward and forward, *changing* it for this group of students caused anxiety. The experience solidified for me the practical approach of having teachers begin differentiating lessons they were familiar with rather than brand-new curricula or lesson plans. Continuity *and* change.

Before we proceed further, let's look at two stories that demonstrate how changes happen even if you aren't changing anything.

When Continuity Isn't Named

A colleague and I were called in to work with the leaders of a school district who were in open conflict with each other. As a starting place, I talked with each leader individually so that they would hopefully feel free to share their points of view and provide us with some insights for planning the conflict-resolution session.

Almost every leader expressed frustrations with change. The district had seen a huge surge in student population and, as new building after new building opened, the leaders had moved from place to place, starting over with staff and programming. Superintendents had come and gone, the state had changed its proficiency tests and then changed them back, their town had gone from mostly rural to a bedroom community for the nearby city (with far more two-income families), and the percentage of English language learners had doubled—all within ten years. They also knew from the strategic plan that more changes were coming, albeit changes they knew were necessary.

We decided to make this huge flow of change visible. To open the group session, we made a timeline on the wall depicting the past ten years. Each person got a stack of sticky notes. We said, "Record the changes you've been involved with, one per sticky note, and then place them on the timeline."

When everyone had finished, the space was a sea of yellow paper squares. "No wonder we're stressed," was the overwhelming reaction in the room.

We then asked them to brainstorm what had remained constant. Slowly, they identified some significant things that hadn't changed. The elementary school principals had remained at the elementary level as they changed buildings, and sometimes assistant principals or lead teachers had moved with them. The mathematics curriculum had stayed the same. The parent-teacher organizations remained vibrant and helpful. We could feel the tension in the room diminish.

The school superintendent, who had been briefed on the agenda for the session, then articulated the specific items in the strategic plan that reflected continuity. While we had more work to do to restore harmony to the team, this exercise helped them stop focusing the blame for their difficulties on each other, recognize the role of circumstances beyond anyone's control, and start identifying the collaborative actions that would move them forward.

When Continuity Becomes a Tool

Another district asked me to work with a magnet program. The coordinators and the teachers were well aware of how funding cuts, changes in student population, the opening of similar programs nearby, and other factors had affected their classrooms. The head of the program noted the need for changes, but also the need for everyone to be on the same page before those changes began.

She asked me to run a *visioning day*. To her, the vision would be a constant, guiding staff through change. She warned me, though, that some staff members were already discouraged because a similar effort the year before had ended in a stalemate.

We started with experiences that involved some meaningful fun—exercises designed to highlight different approaches to planning and work that influence educator views on how to run their classrooms. This helped them grasp how each person's strengths influence their beliefs about teaching and learning, another constant factor in their work together.

They then each articulated and shared their answers to the following prompt: *What is the best outcome you could achieve together for your students that would be personally meaningful—and delightful—for you?* As they compared answers and looked for themes, their common values began to emerge. Before leaping to the vision, though, other exercises gave them more shared experiences in reflecting on values and fears, as well as their hopes for the program.

I then introduced the definitions I use in this work.

- **Mission:** Your reason for existing
- **Vision:** What you will look like if you achieve your goals
- **Values:** What you believe, and how you will behave; these guide decisions and establish a standard for assessing actions.

Note how both mission and values involve continuity—why the program exists would not change, and the values would be a constant tool as they worked toward the vision. Even if you're changing your vision, you are signaling, "In the years ahead, this is what you can count on. In fact, you can hold me accountable as your leader to be consistent with our mission and values."

The team quickly identified what it wanted to keep. Their program emphasized academic programming, even though similar programs focused on the arts or on service learning or on other perfectly acceptable choices. They would continue to concentrate on, and improve their skills for, meeting the unique social and emotional needs of the students in their program, and they wanted to foster creativity and intellectual risk-taking in their students. They broke into groups to reword the mission, vision, and values. Then they tested them with the decisions they were making about the program. Did the values provide guidance? If not, what was missing?

Although this process happened over three separate sessions totaling over a day and a half of intense work, the end product was rapid agreement on recommendations to the district leadership on the optimal restructuring of their magnet program. Remember, they started with a stalemate over what they wanted to be. They ended with knowing they were united on their core beliefs about their program and would stay true to those in whatever form the district revamped their program.

Deliberate Continuity, Constant Change

Both of the preceding stories reflect how changes happen even if you aren't changing anything. Both also involve deliberate changes. Ensuring that you keep and improve what is working, articulate what is constant even as external changes affect your learning community, and identify and act to bring about needed change, sums up a complex and crucial task of leadership. Even if a team, department, learning community, or school district needs to change from top to bottom, and from side to side, changing everything is not only a bad idea, it's almost guaranteed to be unworkable. We can only focus on so many goals at a time—we humans have limits. Based on both research and my experience and extensive conversations with other organizational consultants, three seems to be a doable number of robust goals (Carton et al., 2014).

Maintaining continuity is about continuous improvement with what is already working. You're giving your team the time they need to develop true mastery of a complex strategy. Or, you're letting them work with familiar materials even as they learn to use them differently. Continuity lets you keep things that are working, that are consistent with core values, and that tap hard-earned wisdom. Change, on the other hand, lets you stay current, provides room for creativity, and allows new wisdom to emerge. Figure 8.1 (page 106) maps the interdependency between the continuity and change poles.

Does one side of the loop feel more energizing than the other? Do you see more of one or the other in your learning community? Let's look at which pole might be your natural bent.

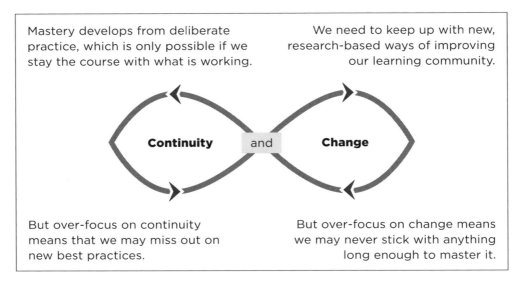

Mastery develops from deliberate practice, which is only possible if we stay the course with what is working.

We need to keep up with new, research-based ways of improving our learning community.

But over-focus on continuity means that we may miss out on new best practices.

But over-focus on change means we may never stick with anything long enough to master it.

Figure 8.1: The continuity *and* change loop.

Table 8.2 is a chart with a subset of twenty-six leadership roles tied to improved student achievement (Kise & Russell, 2008). Which set of school leadership roles best describes your preferred leadership style? Yes, you may be able to do all of them, but which do you *prefer*? What heads up your to-do list and gets done?

Table 8.2: Leadership Roles Tied to Student Achievement

Continuity	Change
• **Maintaining school focus and evaluating strategy implementation:** This role involves continuing to monitor resource allocation, progress, and results throughout the three to five years it takes for initiatives such as professional learning communities to bear fruit. • **Establishing standard operating procedures and routines:** This role involves ensuring that best practices that bring results are recorded and shared so that everyone benefits from successes. • **Managing school administrative processes:** This responsibility includes managing budgets, overseeing compliance requirements, filing reports, scheduling, and other detailed tasks.	• **Setting school direction:** This role involves communicating strong ideals and beliefs that lead to student achievement— and ensuring that all learning community members feel connected to the vision. • **Acting as change agent and optimizer:** This responsibility involves challenging the status quo and inspiring others, leading them in new innovations, and is often seen as a core leadership imperative. • **Influencing beliefs:** This role includes making the vision concrete, providing experiences that help change beliefs, and linking results with the school vision.

Source: Adapted from Kise & Russell, 2008.

Note how the three on the left are more closely tied with continuity, keeping what is working. Notice that I am *not* saying "Keeping everything the same." Also notice how the three on the right are mostly tied to change.

Sometimes, people term the list on the left as management while they refer to the right as leadership. This isn't a problem *unless* one is prioritized over the other by default when they are, in fact, interdependent. For example, launching a new school focus may be visible, game-changing, and crucial to success, but so is maintaining that focus and ensuring that everyone is supported in making progress toward goals. Similarly, school leaders need to be a source of inspiration—someone who can tell the right story, articulate the right value, or bring in the right training or resource to bring the vision to life—but have you seen that inspiration evaporate via not addressing key factors, such as unaccommodating school schedules or unclear disciplinary policies?

Obviously, only focusing on the left side can result in a school being nicely managed while stagnating, but only focusing on the right can end in stagnation because of lack of attention to sustainability. A leader's role is to ensure the right mix—whether you do it all yourself or share the roles with those with complementary skills—toward successful, sustainable change.

As you ponder your own strengths and struggles with this responsibility, consider the following two embedded interdependencies: (1) experience and creativity and (2) tradition and innovation.

Experience and Creativity

Experience and creativity are equally valuable contributors to whole-child schools. Do you appropriately value experience? This includes the experience teachers have with what has and hasn't worked and with what is required to make something work, the experience necessary to develop a certain skill or way of thinking about students, and the effort that has gone into perfecting current methods that have shown success or great promise.

Also, do you appropriately value creativity? This includes the ideas teachers have for doing things differently so that their teaching flows from their strengths and the creativity inherent in taking something and morphing it into a fresh approach.

ASK YOURSELF

Are you more comfortable when you have experience in an area, or is creativity second nature? How does this affect your expectations of those you lead?

Tradition and Innovation

Similarly, tradition and innovation are in tension with each other. Yes, some traditions need to change—maybe an all-school family event doesn't accommodate the schedules of working parents. Or maybe academic awards that parents revere are creating inequities. Sacred cows can include schedules, who is assigned to which classroom, whether recess is before or after lunch, dress codes, and a myriad of other traditions.

However, even as you innovate, is there a way to link to the past? Consider how one family changed up a Thanksgiving tradition. Although the jello salad had always had a place of honor next to the turkey and mashed potatoes, few members of the younger generation wanted to eat it. Then someone had the brilliant idea of having a jello sculpture contest. Cousins competed with waterfalls, castles, ships, and more, all made out of jello, all of which also made great side dishes. Similarly, a creative elementary teacher who agreed on the reasoning behind downplaying Halloween celebrations, but knew that children would miss assembling costumes and the festivities involved, designated October as *biography month*. Each child read a biography of someone they admired, dressed as that person on October 31, and prepared questions for being interviewed by the class so it could receive a history lesson in the midst of other fun but standards-based activities.

Recognizing the high value that some personalities naturally place on tradition or on innovation can help leaders pinpoint how they value each, determine how they might inadvertently over-focus on one or the other, and make visible the links between the old and the new.

ASK YOURSELF

What value do you place on traditions? Are you likely to maintain them, or are you quick to dismiss them and start new ones? How has this played out in past decisions you have made?

The EQ Connection

The key EQ areas for this lens are acting independently and building an atmosphere of emotional safety. The following are a few key points regarding acting independently that apply to this chapter.

◆ Think through current practices and the changes you are involved in. Which practices or changes, by *your* choice, have continuity—you deliberately decided to retain them because of your effectiveness with them? Which, by *your* choice, are changes? Have you ardently advocated for some of these choices, showing independence? If someone above you asked you to keep or change something you had decided to change or keep, what would you fight for? Because so many leaders at the top seem to seek change, change, and more change, pinpointing first how you are balancing continuity *and* change can be helpful in advocating for the right balance for those you lead. If you are at the top, consider when you jumped on the bandwagon of what other schools or districts were doing or thought through what might continue and what might change.

◆ Remember that autonomy makes just about everyone feel motivated (Pink, 2009). Identify and communicate where people can make their own choices and where your learning community needs uniformity.

The following are a few key points on building an atmosphere of emotional safety that apply to this chapter.

◆ If you're continuing a practice, strategy, or initiative for the long haul, remember that people will naturally master the requisite skills at different rates. If something is changing, it will no doubt be more natural or exciting to some people than others. Make it a norm to expect these differences so that people feel able to share both triumphs and struggles and are empowered to reach out for the support they need. To build skills in this sort of differentiation for adults, consider reading *Differentiated Coaching* (Kise, 2017).

◆ Elizabeth Gilbert (2015) points out:

> If your goal in life is to become fearless, then I believe you're already on the wrong path, because the only truly fearless people I've ever met were straight-up sociopaths and a few exceptionally reckless three-year-olds—and those aren't good role models for anyone.

> The truth is, you need your fear, for obvious reasons of basic survival. Evolution did well to install a fear reflex within you, because if you didn't have any fear, you would lead a short, crazy, stupid life. You would walk into traffic. You would drift off into the woods and be eaten by bears. You would jump into giant waves off the coast of Hawaii, despite being a poor swimmer. You would marry a guy who said on the first date, "I don't necessarily believe people were designed by nature to be monogamous." (pp. 22–23)

Thus, you aren't trying to create an atmosphere where no one feels fear when trying new practices or making changes in their classrooms. Instead, your job as a leader is ensuring that people feel safe expressing their fears so that they can hear what worked for their colleagues, ask for support, or otherwise move forward in spite of their concerns. What can you do with professional development— meetings, workshops, coaching, feedback—to ensure people feel safe expressing their fears?

Priorities Inherent in the Continuity and Change Lens

Table 8.3 highlights the values connected with this lens. Which of these resonate more with you? Which may be more key to your current leadership goals?

Table 8.3: Priorities Connected to Continuity *and* Change

Continuity Priorities	Change Priorities
Experience	**Challenge**
I thrive when using our knowledge and past work, which are key to improving performance or to planning and implementing new but related work.	I'm motivated by exciting problems or difficult, risk-filled tasks that enhance skills and prove competency.
Creativity With the Known	**Creativity With the New**
I value using sound judgment, proven routines, and known information for continuous improvement in practical matters.	I value using my imagination and inspirations to devise original ideas, theories, tools, methods, or plans that bring about change.

In the next two sections, we'll look at strategies to increase your use of both the continuity pole and your use of the change pole. Remember that it may take at least six tries using a strategy before you feel comfortable or see results.

Five Ways to Increase Your Use of the Continuity Pole

To strengthen your use of the continuity pole, use the following five strategies.

1. **Acknowledge the changes:** As you saw in the sticky-note timeline exercise, giving everyone a chance to articulate the changes they have experienced goes a long way toward building trust by acknowledging the inherent stress and uncertainty that change creates. In contrast, brushing away the changes

with statements about urgency or necessity fosters resentment. Barry Johnson (personal communication, December 11, 2012), creator of many of the tools of polarity thinking, points out, "Both sides hold part of the truth. Vicious cycles escalate when you can't see the other viewpoint, *or* when you tell those who *do* see it that it doesn't exist. That is a sure-fire way to generate resistance."

2. **Articulate the constants:** As you saw in the vision and values story, articulating the constants may not only lessen stress, but can bring about unity as you move forward. You may think some of the constants are obvious, but stress narrows our vision, and people may lose sight of positives in the wake of too many changes.

3. **Limit your list:** Take a look at your list of changes you hope to see in your community. Rank them in order of importance. Then, lop off all but the top five. Think about the work involved in taking each of those to successful sustainability. Is there room for anything else? Some of the people on your team naturally weigh change in this way. They *know* how long things take, the resources required, and the things they will have to stop doing to start the new. Instead of seeing their pleas to wait as resistance, benefit from their wisdom.

4. **Ask, "Why are we doing it this way?":** Work to see the value in routines others have created—what depth of expertise did they apply? Study how given classroom practices or procedures save time, help students with certain needs, or flow from teachers with strengths that differ from your own. If you are new to a building or team, ask how a strategy was chosen, and reconsider its fit with shared values. In other words, check out its foundation before assuming that change is the best strategy.

5. **Relate to the hedgehog:** In *Good to Great*, Jim Collins (2001) describes how foxes have many tricks, but hedgehogs have just one defense—rolling into a ball:

> [They] simplify a complex world into a single organizing idea, a basic principle or concept that unifies and guides everything. It doesn't matter how complex the world, hedgehog reduces all challenges and dilemmas to simple—indeed almost simplistic—hedgehog ideas. . . . Anything that does not somehow relate to the hedgehog idea holds no relevance. (p. 81)

If you identify your own hedgehog strategy as a leader, such as troubleshooting before problems arise or supporting strategies that involve some risk, you can help others see how the changes you are making relate to your core competencies and constant philosophy of leadership—you're walking the talk.

Five Ways to Increase Your Use of the Change Pole

To strengthen your use of the change pole, use the following five strategies.

1. **Change a process or routine:** Identify a few procedures or routines that you use, and analyze them by asking the following questions.

    -   What glitches have I experienced when using this?

    -   What changes to our work, my responsibilities, or our learning community have taken place since I started using this routine?

    -   When is this process most vulnerable to error? When is it vulnerable to outside pressures or changes? When is it vulnerable to other problems?

    Use your answers to guide you in changing at least one of these processes or routines.

2. **Embrace your creativity:** If you don't think of yourself as a creative person, consider reading Adam Grant's (2016) *Originals* or Gordon MacKenzie's (1998) *Orbiting the Giant Hairball*. MacKenzie points out that if you ask a class of first graders which of them are artists, nearly every hand goes in the air. Ask second graders, and about half will raise their hands. By sixth grade, ask the same question and the students all point to one student as *the artist*. In other words, when did you start feeling pressured to be normal, or when were you told you weren't creative?

    If you don't consider yourself creative, keep in mind that most innovations come from changes to existing products and processes. Think of the transistor radio and how it is an ancestor of many of the devices in common use today. What have you improved through your thorough knowledge of how things work best? Embrace that form of creativity even as you strive to see how the environment is changing and how new ideas may connect with what you already know.

3. **Understand the motivations for change:** In *Switch: How to Change Things When Change Is Hard*, Chip Heath and Dan Heath (2010) provide an excellent way of thinking about change. Define why change is necessary ("direct the rider"), engage your emotions as well as your mind ("motivate the elephant"), and make it easier to go in the right direction ("shape the path"). The book is filled with practical strategies.

    For example, if you decide that being more consistent about articulating the long-term vision is a change you need to personally make, you would state the why: Members of a learning community need to hear that vision far more often than leaders talk about it. You could motivate that elephant by identifying a few concrete ways you will talk about the vision in the next few weeks and by talking with key people about the impact your words are having. You might shape the path by designating places where you will post a Thought of the Week, with a date at the top, so that you have to keep coming up with new quotes or ideas to spread that vision.

4. **Meet with change agents:** Whom do you admire for chasing and carrying out big, hairy, audacious goals? Perhaps it's someone in your own learning community, an administrator in another building, or a teacher who constantly brings new ideas to his or her colleagues. Or, perhaps you would benefit from regularly attending a local gathering of educators. Besides formal affiliates of national and international organizations, who else gathers in your state? Network to find out, and then join up to find out what is going on and how people stay energized for the long haul to success and sustainability.

   Kouzes and Posner (2012) find that over half the innovations leaders oversee come from either those around them—those they lead—or from outside the boundaries of their experience. Are you out actually *seeing* what is going on in other schools? Exactly how are they having success? What might you bring back to your learning community after shadowing other school leaders?

5. **Listen to your dreams:** Gilbert (2015) puts a different spin on the question, "What would you do if you had no fear of failure?" To paraphrase her spin for leaders, What are you so keen on seeing happen that the words *failure* and *success* essentially become irrelevant? What do you envision for your team that you long to see become reality even more than you worry about your own ego? Identify that *one big thing*, and you have the motivation for the hard work of change.

ASK YOURSELF

This lens is about maintaining and improving your current best practices while also innovating for the future. How well are you balancing continuity *and* change?

CHAPTER 9

Moving Ahead Quickly *and* Moving Ahead for the Long Haul

Just as it's a balancing act to sustain and improve current practices while eyeing new ones to address future needs, it's equally important to strike a balance between supporting initiatives that serve immediate needs while also planning for sustainability. This lens is about using the priorities in table 9.1 to find the right mix of short-term results *and* moving toward long-term success.

Table 9.1: The Short-Term *and* Long-Term Lens Domain

Lens 6	Short Term *and* Long Term	
Priorities	Efficiency	Adaptability
Common initiatives, issues, or leadership responsibilities that involve this lens	Response to intervention Professional development School goals and strategic plans	
EQ component	Acting independently Employing interpersonal skills: active listening	

In this chapter, we explore the interdependency of short term *and* long term by establishing the full breadth of the challenges inherent in keeping short-term priorities in focus while also keeping an eye on longer-term priorities and outcomes. From there, we explain the balance between the short-term and long-term poles, establish an emotional intelligence connection for this lens, and explain how you can best leverage the priorities inherent in this lens.

A Focus on Tomorrow While Thinking Five Years Ahead

Think for a few moments about the following questions.

- What time horizon do you target when engaged in long-term planning?

- Do you look for differences between student short-term gains on standardized tests and whether they have retained that knowledge for the next school year?

- What is your balance between short-term and long-term goals? Do you tend to find yourself focused on one more than the other and suddenly realize you need to refocus?

- How do you decide whether a learning strategy that seems to be bearing fruit might have long-term consequences? Or, how do you decide when one might have too long of an implementation horizon for your current students' needs?

We live in a culture that seems to think short term most of the time. Think about it.

- Stock prices, not long-term strategies, often drive corporate decisions.

- Have you ever seen an advertisement for slow weight loss?

- Google research indicates that over 50 percent of website visits are abandoned if it takes more than three seconds for the site to load (Zomorodi, 2017). Three seconds!

- Instead of slowing down until students grasp the big ideas of mathematics, the United States has one of the highest percentages of students who are taught mathematics procedurally—memorization and practice (Boaler & Zoido, 2016). The United States also follows the pattern of lackluster performance on international measurements of learning compared with countries that teach students conceptually with self-monitoring and a focus on grasping the big ideas.

Let's focus on this last item for a moment. Does it matter for mathematics instruction? Doesn't repetition transfer learning into long-term memory? If students remember "Yours is not to reason why, just invert and multiply," aren't they set? Brain imaging is giving us some solid answers. Joonkoo Park and Elizabeth Brannon (2013) measure proficiency for subtraction problems and find clear differences between students who were more and less proficient in the brain areas they used while doing mathematics. It turns out that understanding and using symbols, arrays, estimation techniques, and other tools trains us to use more brain pathways, which results in more number sense—being able to understand, think about, and use numbers creatively.

Teaching students through the more conceptual, guided inquiry-based approach requires time. It also requires a higher level of mathematical expertise in teachers. It requires a long-term focus. Where do you see education flexing to somehow keep short-term efforts going while undertaking the deep professional development and dedicated instructional time necessary to truly improve mathematics instruction?

Let's look at a story of one school I worked with—details changed to protect the innocent, of course—to understand how difficult managing this lens is. Then we'll highlight some ways you can think about your own difficulties with balancing short-term and long-term needs.

When Short-Term Needs Take Over

A school principal had attended a workshop I taught on differentiating mathematics instruction for gifted students in the regular classroom and asked me to work with her staff. She told me that due to district mandates, she could only allocate an hour a month for this work even though she agreed that the problem-solving strategies I intended to show her staff, which required more than an hour a month, seemed useful and doable.

I finagled three hours of professional development time with all her teachers the week before school started. As they engaged in hands-on problems that they could use with their students, I quickly realized two things.

1. A high number of the teachers suffered from mathematics anxiety. This is common among primary grade teachers, as they often learned mathematics skills in a procedural way.

2. They were extremely worried about how their students would perform on accountability tests and on the district's common assessments for each unit.

During the last hour of our time together, I asked them to work in grade-level teams on a problem from their curriculum that they'd be teaching in the first couple of weeks of school. The first-grade team called me over to discuss a problem from the previous year. They noted how they'd changed everything about the problem and couldn't come up with a method that students understood.

The problem? *I have eleven balls. Some are soccer balls, some are baseballs, some are tennis balls. How many of each might I have?* I said, "Wow, this problem requires a lot of big math ideas."

Given this was the first common assessment they were to use with their students, my comment surprised them. So, I pressed further. "Well, students would have a lot of strategies if they understand one-to-one correspondence, combinations that make five and ten, conservation of quantity, and unitizing."

From the looks on their faces I realized that they didn't understand these underlying concepts that make up the building blocks of understanding mathematics. They'd been drilling the students on the whole problem rather than on concepts they'd be able to use again and again.

The school principal agreed with me that those big ideas should be our focus. For the next several months, in the one hour we had each month, we explored how to assess student understanding of them, activities that helped students master the concepts, and problems in which they were embedded. The teachers searched for examples in their upcoming units and planned for reinforcing them. The mathematics specialist quickly realized that the curriculum didn't build on the concepts sequentially, and so he helped the teachers see where the sequence of lessons assumed students had already mastered a concept they hadn't yet introduced. We discussed using mathematics tutorial time to reinforce these concepts rather than drilling for upcoming assessments. They worked together to develop preassessments to identify which students needed help with each one.

I must have said more than once, "Camp on these concepts—when students grasp them, their problem-solving ability can skyrocket." Right before the winter break, one of the special education teachers described how she'd worked with a second grader, session after session, on combinations of five and ten (for example, 2 + 3 and 4 + 6). "I kept hearing you say, 'Camp on these,' even as I worried that I wasn't accelerating him. But you were right. One day he caught on, his math confidence grew, and he's made loads of progress ever since."

The teachers reported that they were able to use what they were learning in their classrooms and that students seemed to be enjoying mathematics more. The teachers, too, were enjoying it more. Several times, as I walked toward the building as teachers were guiding their students to the buses, teachers commented, "Oh good, we're back with you today!"

Then, in early spring, the school district announced that every school needed to collect data on assessment problems the district assigned. Teachers were to spend professional development time analyzing the data to group and tutor students for the upcoming accountability tests. There were forms to submit and requirements to meet. We had to stop working on the long-term focuses of increasing teacher mathematics instructional knowledge and student understanding of the building blocks of big mathematics concepts, and instead turn to the short-term focus of test-taking strategies and memorization of certain terms and procedures.

I'm *not* saying that no short-term strategies exist to increase student learning. The teachers and I, in fact, worked with some heuristic techniques that students can apply in many situations. However, when strategies, such as timed tests to increase automaticity, are actually shown to increase mathematics anxiety (Lyons & Beilock, 2012), why are we still using them?

One of the big rationales I hear over and over is short-term expediency. "With all we have to cover, we can't spend that much time on any one thing." And of course, there are long-term consequences. Only a small percentage of educators in the United States, let alone the general population, see mathematics as a source of pleasure as they might art or reading; and T-shirts with sayings, such as "There. Another day where I didn't use algebra," are worn with pride.

Areas of Interdependency Between Short-Term and Long-Term Needs

Mathematics instruction isn't the only place where we fail to work well with this interdependency between short term and long term in education. For one thing, long-term planning is usually considered at least three to five years in scope, yet the tenure of urban school superintendents is only three to four years. That's not enough time to plan well and see the plan through. Consider the following.

- When new teachers are hired, what is the multiyear plan for their development?

- When do we assess students for the attitudes they are developing toward lifelong learning?

- How long-term are the staffing plans and leadership development plans in your building or district? Yes, student enrollment numbers drive decisions schools make, but how do you identify, train, and retain teacher leaders? How do you factor the long-term culture of a school's staff into hiring, reassignments, and so on?

Take the time to list some more areas you're aware of. There are long-term over-emphases too, so don't forget to think about these. For example, it's common for schools to overestimate the degree to which getting into college (too far in the future to seem real) or learning a life skill (that they won't need for years) motivate students until they're well into their teens.

The Long and Short of Planning in Schools

Figure 9.1 maps the interdependencies between the short-term and long-term poles.

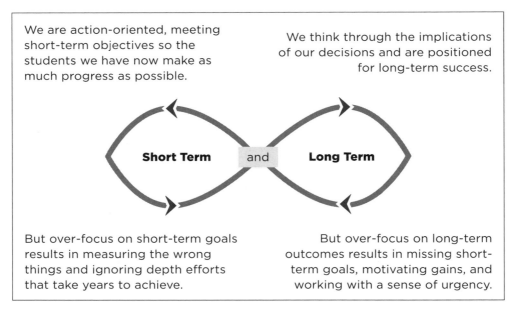

We are action-oriented, meeting short-term objectives so the students we have now make as much progress as possible.

We think through the implications of our decisions and are positioned for long-term success.

Short Term and **Long Term**

But over-focus on short-term goals results in measuring the wrong things and ignoring depth efforts that take years to achieve.

But over-focus on long-term outcomes results in missing short-term goals, motivating gains, and working with a sense of urgency.

Figure 9.1: The short-term *and* long-term loop.

Compounding the difficulty of this interdependency is the fact that each of us is naturally wired to think either six to twelve months out or three to five years out when someone says, "Long term" (Kise, 2017). Look back at the opening questions in A Focus on Tomorrow While Thinking Five Years Ahead (page 116). Which way do you lean? Again, leadership requires leveraging the upsides of both poles. As an easy example, the commutative property of multiplication is one of those big concepts schools often teach through worksheets or drills—short-term strategies. However, teaching addition strategies beyond the common algorithm is time-consuming even though it improves long-term results. But, it becomes worth remembering if we introduce the commutative property, and show students how useful it is for solving problems such as the one in figure 9.2.

Let's look at two key interdependencies that can help focus the bigger dilemma of making short-term progress while keeping our eyes on the long-term prizes: (1) now and later and (2) the urgent and the important.

> Solve the problem 14 x 25. Are you tempted to use the common algorithm? Instead, try halving the first number and doubling the second:
>
> 7 x 50 = 350
>
> Slick, eh? No calculator, paper, or pencil needed. It's called halving and doubling. But you have to know that 2 and 7 are factors of 14, and that the commutative property of multiplication allows you to change the order of the numbers involved without changing the value of the equation. Halving and doubling makes factoring and the commutative property of multiplication, the big ideas, useful and worth remembering.

Figure 9.2: Making the commutative property useful and memorable.

Now and Later

How do we ensure that students complete homework, engage in enough free reading, get the help they need, and so on *and* ensure that they have learned to take responsibility for their own homework, make time to read enjoyable books on their own, and recognize when they need help and know how to get it? How do we ensure our classrooms are a haven for emotional safety for all students *and* ensure that students develop skills to solve dilemmas around friendships or group dynamics on their own?

We can list dozens of questions like these regarding instruction, equity, resilience, physical fitness, nutrition, social dynamics, and more. The bigger question is, When we pick strategies to help students in these areas, are we thinking about both short-term and long-term benefits and priorities? Surely, you've been part of struggles on both sides?

For example, secondary teachers often say, "I'm tough because I'm preparing them for the real world" without teaching students the short-term strategies they need to learn to be responsible. They may also cringe when asked to allow students to retake tests because they've seen students use the first as a study session and dig in for the next one, creating more work for the teachers. The trick is to balance the pros and cons of strategies in the short term *and* long term. Ask yourself, "What can we do better now that will pay off in the long run?" (Think of showing students how factoring can make arithmetic problems easier.) The problems most often come when we only consider one time frame at the expense of the other.

The Urgent and the Important

Stephen Covey, A. Roger Merrill, and Rebecca Merrill (1994) point out how our time is allocated among four quadrants (figure 9.3).

Urgent Not Important	Urgent Important
Not Urgent Not Important	Not Urgent Important

Source: Covey et al., 1994.

Figure 9.3: The urgent and important quadrants.

Do you, and does your school, have the right mix of these quadrants? All are actually necessary—not urgent and not important might include some of the fun activities that simply make school more enjoyable and engaging for students and staff but don't influence their growth. But the urgent tend to grab our attention—including the urgent and not important items that arise from phone calls or circumstances that perhaps aren't really first on your agenda but creep in.

The big point is that these urgent tasks, which can include some very important ones, are so visible and loud that they can take our eyes off the important.

What steps are you taking to ensure that the not urgent, but important aspects of improving your learning community aren't crowded out? Are plans in place? Are you and your staff monitoring them to ensure their progress alongside the urgent demands of the school day, month, and year?

The EQ Connection

The key EQ areas for this lens are acting independently and employing the interpersonal skill of active listening. The following are a few key points regarding acting independently that apply to this chapter.

◆ If you recognize that a top-down directive is ignoring the short-term or the long-term needs of staff or students, independence is a crucial skill. Yes, it's risky because, too often, those higher up will simply look for someone else who will carry out their agendas. Using language such as "Can we modify this to avoid the unintended consequences of _____?" can help. Having research to back up your points, such as the research showing that timed mathematics tests increase mathematics anxiety (Lyons & Beilock, 2012), can also help.

◆ Being able to talk in terms of the core values of your teams can also be helpful. The whole idea of core values is to use them as guides for decisions; asking questions designed to help others see whether a policy is in alignment can sometimes allow you to hold up your point of view without being seen as too difficult to work with.

The following are a few key points on the interpersonal skill of active listening that apply to this chapter.

◆ When those you lead resist a new idea or strategy, listen for how they view it short term *and* long term. Although this isn't a consideration in every instance, they may be concerned about short-term time constraints, competing initiatives, or unidentified long-term consequences or additional work that will be necessary. What can you learn that will help for implementation or for improving the idea?

◆ It's very easy for any of us to lose track of the important in the tyranny of the urgent. Listen to others to get a feel for whether they think your school is addressing both urgent and important needs. After meetings or conversations, consider how you might categorize comments using the quadrants in figure 9.3 (page 122).

Priorities Inherent in the Short-Term and *Long-Term Lens*

Table 9.2 highlights the priorities connected with this lens. Which of these resonate more with you? Which may be more key to your current leadership goals?

Table 9.2: Priorities Connected to Short Term *and* Long Term

Short-Term Priorities	Long-Term Priorities
Efficiency	**Adaptability**
I want to organize our work environments, processes, tasks, and such, so that we meet goals with little waste of time, talent, or materials.	I model keeping the end goal in mind, even while responding in the moment and adjusting to ever-changing circumstances.

In the next three sections, we're going to approach the poles in this lens a bit differently. First, we'll look at strategies to increase your use of both poles; note that these double-leveraging strategies are easy to work with for this lens, and you may develop one for the lenses in other chapters that similarly contribute to the upside of both poles. Then, we'll look at strategies to increase your use of both the short-term pole and your use of the long-term pole. Remember that it may take at least six tries using a strategy before you feel comfortable or see results.

Two Ways to Increase Your Use of Both Poles

If you want to simultaneously strengthen your use of both the short-term pole and the long-term pole, use the following two strategies.

1. **Know your horizon:** Take the time to assess whether you tend to plan for the future or for the now. Few of us are truly balanced. One way to think about it is to ask yourself: What do you measure? What points to short-term goals? What tracks progress toward the long-term goals? What does both? Do you need more balance?

2. **Plan with your opposite:** Make sure your leadership team either uses protocols to think short term *and* long term (see the suggestions for both

poles) or recognizes and listens to those who naturally work more from one pole or the other. A simple protocol is to ask the following before finalizing plans.

- Have we thoroughly thought through any unintended consequences of what we are deciding? Have we done so with a focus on teachers? On student academics? On student social and emotional growth? On equity?

- Do we have measures in place that will indicate the things we truly want to measure?

Five Ways to Increase Your Use of the Short-Term Pole

To strengthen your use of the short-term pole, use the following five strategies.

1. **Listen for the truly urgent:** One long-range planning leader told me that he was often so far ahead of the troops that he was vulnerable to fire from the rear. Instead of just extolling the virtues and necessity of your plans, are you out and about and listening so that you understand what teachers think they should be doing instead? Who tells you straight up whether things are moving too fast or too slow? What do they need right now—another hour for planning, a glimpse of what is happening in other classrooms, a slight revision to make something more practical or manageable? What are you missing in the short term that would add to efficiency and effectiveness?

2. **Let someone else write your to-do list:** You don't need to follow every aspect of it, but perhaps you should. Ask someone who works closely with you to list exactly what he or she would realistically like to see you accomplish in the next few weeks, why those things are important as well as urgent, and how they tie to the school vision. What can you learn from their vision of what you should be doing? How can you integrate their viewpoint with your own priorities?

3. **Make a short-term plan:** Use the process in chapter 16 (page 209) to set a short-term, thirty-to-sixty-day leadership development goal for yourself. Then, measure your progress. Note when you fall short on your self-determined measurements. Did any long-term goals take your eyes off the urgent?

4. **Ask for the urgent and important:** Ask your team, "If we could make one thing happen in the next two, six, or twelve weeks, what realistic goal do

you think would have the biggest impact on student achievement, school climate, equity, or another important factor?" Tell them, "We can only have one or two such priorities, but I'd like your input on what they should be." Sort for patterns, choose one or two, and gather a team of those who see it as the one big thing to make it happen. Then, ask yourself what you learned by focusing on the short term.

5. **Dissect a goal:** Plan backward from one of your long-term goals. For example, if your aim is increased teacher mathematical knowledge, what will sustained work toward this goal look like at the end of three years? What topics do your staff need to cover? How much professional development time will that take? What other support will they need, and when will it need to be in place? With all of that information, what is your six-month plan that will move you toward your three-year goal? Can you really accomplish it in three years? If it isn't doable, it threatens teacher efficacy.

Five Ways to Increase Your Use of the Long-Term Pole

To strengthen your use of the long-term pole, use the following five strategies. Remember that it may take at least six tries using a strategy before you feel comfortable or see results.

1. **Use scenarios:** If you struggle with long-term planning because nothing about the future is knowable, use scenario planning. For example, what if your school stays the same? What if the teacher champion of an effort leaves? What is most important to do now—and later—if there is the possibility that an initiative might be replaced? What is most important if it might be permanent?

2. **Think possible instead of probable:** Yes, the future is unknowable, but many predictions are within the realm of very real probabilities. For example, although you may not know exactly how first graders will react to a different schedule, it is very predictable that they will have short attention spans and won't want to sit still for long periods. While you may not know your exact staffing needs until way too close to the start of the new school year, it is probable (and you already know this and plan for it) that you will have a few new teachers. Explore how separating probable things from those with infinite variables can help direct some decisions. You'll find more on this in chapter 14 (page 179).

3. **Make a long-term plan:** Use the process in chapter 16 (page 209) to set a long-term, three-to-five-year leadership development goal for yourself. Then,

measure your progress. Note when you fall short on your self-determined measurements. Did any short-term goals take your eyes off the important?

4. **Use your values:** Take a good look at your learning community's values. Are they all in play in the way you think they should be? If so, what needs to happen so that is still true five years from now? If not, create a plan to evaluate whether the values are still right and how you will move your organization toward alignment for the long haul.

5. **Think legacy:** When you leave your current position, what would you like to ensure continues after you're gone? Is there a particularly successful strategy or initiative? What about the camaraderie you helped foster? Or what about an equity practice that led to staff harmony around discipline? Think hard, and then do some succession planning. Who will become the new champion, and how will they develop expertise?

ASK YOURSELF

This lens is about ensuring that we help students and teachers as much as we can, right now, while staying aligned with their long-term needs, hopes, and dreams. How well are you balancing short-term *and* long-term priorities?

CHAPTER 10

Balancing Logical Objectivity *and* Valuable Subjectivity

Society often treats objectivity as a paragon virtue, and certainly logical objectivity has its place, especially in the realm of leadership. But we should not be too quick to dismiss the kind of subjective thinking that holds together the values that also make a school successful. This lens is about using the priorities in table 10.1 to determine universal principles and rules *and* still account for individual circumstances and perspectives.

Table 10.1: The Logic *and* Values Lens Domain

Lens 7	Logic *and* Values	
Priorities	Fair-mindedness	Empathy
Common initiatives, issues, or leadership responsibilities that involve this lens	Discipline Teacher accountability systems Effective use of data, assessments, and testing Incorporating qualitative data into decisions Building relationships Building hardiness in students	
EQ component	Building an atmosphere of emotional safety Demonstrating empathy	

In this chapter, we explore the interdependency of logic *and* values by exploring the delicate balance between fairness and consistency. From there, we explain the balance between the logic and values poles, establish an emotional intelligence connection for this lens, and explain how you can best leverage the priorities inherent in this lens.

129

The Interdependency Between Logic **and** *Values*

What does it mean to be fair? Which of these definitions sits well with you?

- ◆ Fairness means consistently enforcing rules and specifying prescribed disciplinary measures.

- ◆ Fairness means adjusting rules and specifying disciplinary measures after considering individual circumstances, community values, and whether modifications to the stated course of action are warranted.

The first one sounds so simple and easy to work with, doesn't it? But let's look at a very sticky case where *everyone* was right.

> You're a high school senior, a decent student with just a few tardies on your record. You have an after-school job on the clean-up crew of a local grocery store—cutting up boxes, tossing overripe produce, and sweeping floors. After work, you set your box cutter in a cup holder in your car and forget all about it.
>
> The next morning at school, you're called to the principal's office and told that you've violated the school's zero-tolerance weapons policy. A security guard spotted the box cutter through the car window. You're immediately suspended and face expulsion. You know better than to make things worse by arguing, but all you can think of is, "You've got to be kidding!"

Thus, went Tony Richards's morning in September 2008. Charlie Kyte, director of the Minnesota Association of School Administrators, gave an astute summary of the dilemma embedded in this incident:

> While schools have zero-tolerance policies, you must also allow judgment to come into play. The board's gotta look at this and say, "Hmmm, did this kid really create a horrible act?" The second thing they have to ask themselves is, by giving a less rigorous punishment, are they also opening the door to kids thinking they can get away with this stuff? (Simons, 2008)

School administrators recommended expulsion to the school board. The incident sparked quick reaction from students, parents, and the *Star Tribune* ("Think Before You Expel," 2008) editors, who wrote:

> School violence is a growing issue that needs to be taken seriously. But school officials must determine whether a transgression actually posed a threat to students and teachers or was merely a case of

forgetfulness. Intent must play a part in the enforcement of a policy so Draconian. . . .

No one would argue against the need for a firm weapons policy. But school officials and school board members must not allow the letter of the law to substitute for judgment and discernment.

A week later, the school board voted to record the incident as an expulsion, but allowed the student to return to school on probation for the next six weeks, with the stern warning that any additional infraction could mean expulsion. If the decision sounds like doublespeak, that just points out the dilemmas embedded in most zero-tolerance policies. Still, there are questions.

How do you stay consistent?

Should you be consistent?

Because the long-term consequences of the prescribed punishment so clearly didn't fit the crime, this incident is useful for making the case for making exceptions. However, uneven enforcement of any policy, even with the best of intentions, soon brings on valid cries of "Unfair!" from students, staff, parents, or all of the above.

A Real World of Rules With Exceptions

Figure 10.1 maps the interdependency between the logic and values poles.

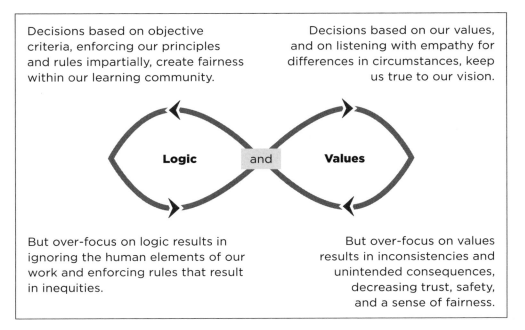

Decisions based on objective criteria, enforcing our principles and rules impartially, create fairness within our learning community.

Decisions based on our values, and on listening with empathy for differences in circumstances, keep us true to our vision.

Logic and **Values**

But over-focus on logic results in ignoring the human elements of our work and enforcing rules that result in inequities.

But over-focus on values results in inconsistencies and unintended consequences, decreasing trust, safety, and a sense of fairness.

Figure 10.1: The logic *and* values loop.

Think for a moment about the kinds of criteria on which decisions are based in your community. What might you add to the list in each category in table 10.2?

Table 10.2: Common Decision-Making Criteria

Objective Criteria	Subjective Criteria
Scores on true-false, multiple-choice, and short-answer assessments	Scores on essays, projects, and other open-ended student work
Articulated rules and clear policies	Alignment with values
Measurable criteria, such as cost and time commitments	Analysis to account for individual circumstances
Decision by lottery or other fair contests	Surveys of engagement, opinions, and satisfaction
Assessment of student academic growth through testing	Assessment of student academic growth through teacher observation

Remember that everything on the left actually has a subjective base—who designed and chose the assessments, set the rules, and selected the criteria? Even if those who did these things did so logically, human judgment was still involved.

Everything in the subjective category of table 10.2 involves rational criteria. One can be rational without being logical. Consider, for example, the huge role of the social environment, emotions, safety, and intrinsic motivation on student outcomes—not taking these factors into account often results in decisions not working out as predicted. You've seen this happen, whether it's an evidence-based reading program with texts that somehow fail to kindle a love of reading, or a discipline strategy that, in practice, conflicts with stated school values.

Have you heard the phrase, "Measure what you treasure"? If we value hardiness, self-motivation, perseverance, collaboration skills, and other soft skills in teachers and students, have we found robust ways to measure and include growth in these areas as part of our decision metrics? It is tougher, and we haven't necessarily practiced enough to consistently use good measures for things such as the effectiveness of an anti-bullying program or to accurately assess whether teaching students about growth mindset improves achievement.

Thus, this lens encompasses more than discipline. Learning communities benefit from the proper weighing of logic *and* values when making curriculum decisions, choosing mentoring programs, considering incentive programs for teachers or students, and just about any other decision a leader can make. It isn't either values or logic, it's both.

Margaret Wheatley and Myron Kellner-Rogers (1999) suggest thinking of measurement in terms of feedback: How can we create measures that serve the same purpose as feedback in a system? I often hear variations of, "How can we create learning experiences that give students the same kind of feedback they receive as they play and replay video games?" Wheatley and Kellner-Rogers (1999) suggest asking these questions about what we measure.

- **Who gets to create the measures?** They point out that the measurements need to be meaningful to those who are being measured.

- **How will we measure our measures?** Are you looking for unintended consequences resulting from your measurements? How will you know if they need to be updated to fit new contexts or circumstances?

- **Are we designing measures that are permeable rather than rigid?** Do your measures have the effect of putting blinders on a horse? Or, do they inspire new ways of looking at things or seeking answers in different places?

- **Will these measures create information that increases our capacity to develop, to grow into the purpose of this organization?** Note, for example, that SMART goals—strategic and specific, measurable, attainable, results oriented, and time bound (Conzemius & O'Neill, 2014)—can limit creativity and learning. Additionally, if people sense they are falling short, they are four times as likely to lie about their progress (Sytch, 2015).

- **What measures will inform us about critical capacities: commitment, learning, teamwork, quality, and innovation?** Again, we need to measure what we truly treasure, even if it is more difficult than finding discrete, objective measures.

Thinking about different measures can entirely change the questions we're asking. For example, one school staff began with a logic-oriented question of "What consequences would decrease the number of students being tardy to class?" As they discussed ideas, someone brought up, "What if we looked at this from the other end—from our values around student motivation and creating lifelong learners? What do we need to do so that students *want* to be in class on time? Not pizza parties but motivation connected with our other values?"

Someone told of a teacher she knew who started each tenth-grade language arts class with a short read-aloud passage from a high-interest book. Another teacher questioned if that took time away from the curriculum.

She answered that where other teachers routinely lost five minutes at the start of class due to a stream of interruptions from late students, this teacher finds every student in the room, before the bell, quiet and eager to hear what happens next in the story. With this example, the discussion turned to other possibilities such as beginning class with a learning tip of the day, or a game show–style review activity, or a stump-the-teacher contest. Although some still asked for consequences, both logic *and* values factored into the policies they considered.

As you work to leverage this very difficult dilemma—think back to the safety and humanity issues in the box-cutter incident—here are two embedded interdependencies to ponder: (1) justice and mercy and (2) individual and community.

Justice and Mercy

Fictional tales are rich with examples of justice and mercy and can allow for deep discussions of the difference between what people deserve as punishment and what might help them grow and change. For example, in *Touching Spirit Bear* (Mikaelsen, 2001), a teen who is himself a victim of parental abuse attacks and severely injures another student. Instead of turning the teen over to the juvenile justice system, both sides agree to try a mediator-facilitated circle of justice. Yes, the teen deserves punishment, but will he get the help he needs in detention facilities? Yet simply granting forgiveness and setting him free is obviously not the answer, either. The group decides to give the teen a tough second chance—they sentence him to a spirit quest on an island. Read the book before deciding on the appropriateness of the merits of their choice, but can you see how they are holding the boy accountable while offering him a chance to grow?

The box cutter case illustrates how a school board struggled with the justice embedded in zero tolerance and found a way to show mercy through probation.

Regarding the adults in a learning community, pointing out unacceptable behavior to a staff member and providing a way to make amends or develop the skills needed to stop the behavior show justice and mercy. Granted, some violations require removal, yet mercy might involve confidentiality or other considerations.

ASK YOURSELF

Are zero-tolerance policies adhered to in your learning community? Might any result in inequities?

Individual and Community

The kinds of decisions we're talking about affect not just the individuals but also the community in which they are being made. For example, Tim Arnold, a management consultant, helped found Southridge Homeless Shelter in St. Catharines, Ontario. The shelter's mission statement includes several key interdependencies such as those we are exploring in these pages. Justice and mercy often inform decisions regarding what a resident needs *and* the potential impact on community.

For example, while they run a dry shelter and there are clear guidelines around substance abuse, what happens to violators depends on who else is in residence and whether the shelter's drug culture seems healthy or unhealthy. If the violator is the only current resident with substance abuse issues, they lean toward mercy, along with getting the person the help he or she needs. However, if other people are struggling to remain sober, they focus on community needs over those of the individual and enforce the stated policies by asking the violator to leave while also making suggestions for getting help.

There *is* consistency; the consistency, though, exists in acknowledgement of a complex community with multiple competing priorities they need to consider.

Jennifer Garvey Berger (2012) points out that holding these kinds of tensions requires leaders to be at a high stage of adult development. They truly understand that both sides can be right—and need each other to find the whole truth.

ASK YOURSELF

How are circumstances taken into account in your learning community? Do community members struggle to consider circumstances without meeting the needs of individuals at the expense of community or vice versa?

The EQ Connection

The key EQ areas for this lens are building an atmosphere of emotional safety and demonstrating empathy. The following are a few key points regarding empathy that apply to this chapter.

◆ Remember that empathy is more than knowing how the other person feels; it's also understanding the root sources of those feelings. Without that deep understanding, it is very difficult to effectively engage with objective and subjective criteria in decision making. For example, understanding why the teen in *Touching Spirit Bear* (Mikaelsen, 2001) was so full of anger was crucial to navigating the need for both justice and mercy in a decision-making process.

◆ Even if you think you understand where another person is coming from, he or she may need to be heard. What open-ended questions can you ask—listening while working to understand the emotions involved and their ramifications—with the goal of suspending your own feelings and suppositions? Try, "So, tell me what happened?" instead of "Why did you do that?" Or, "What plan are you thinking might help you avoid this?" rather than "Here's what you should do. . . ."

The following are a few key points on building an atmosphere of emotional safety that apply to this chapter.

◆ Part of making decisions using both logic *and* values is ensuring that decisions are seen as fair. If they aren't, cries of "That isn't fair!" will soon echo from students and staff. Although issues of confidentiality can block full explanations, being open about the competing interdependencies, as in the case of the Southridge Homeless Shelter, can allow others to understand the reasoning.

◆ When others call for uniform enforcement of rules, point out how this can lead to unintended consequences, from the near-expulsion consequences in the box-cutter incident to lying about SMART goals to lack of equity in decisions. Thinking across both ends of the spectrum takes far more effort but eventually builds the trust and safety necessary to move forward as a true learning community.

Priorities Inherent in the Logic and *Values Lens*

Table 10.3 highlights the priorities connected with this lens. Which of these resonate more with you? Which may be more key to your current leadership goals?

In the next two sections, we'll look at strategies to increase your use of both the logic pole and your use of the values pole. Remember that it may take at least six tries using a strategy before you feel comfortable or see results.

Table 10.3: Priorities Connected to Logic *and* Values

Logic Priorities	Values Priorities
Fair-Mindedness	**Empathy**
I believe in calmness and objectivity, using consistent standards so that my decisions and actions are fair, just, and effective.	I believe in stepping into the shoes of others and understanding their experiences, values, and points of view.

Five Ways to Increase Your Use of the Logic Pole

To strengthen your use of the logic pole, use the following five strategies.

1. **Use logic tools:** If logic isn't a strong suit, practice using if–then question stems and matrices for decisions. Many people with a values-based decision-making style find it easier to consider logical criteria if they make a matrix; if–then thinking or considering precedents may be as important as how individuals are affected. Figure 10.2 shows a sample matrix.

Decision: _Changing Staff Meeting Timing_

Options	Cost	Precedents to consider	Potential unintended consequences
Before work	Union contract considerations		Meetings cut short before decisions made
Rotating schedule	Potential substitute teachers?		Uneven attendance
Lunch meetings	Catered lunch	Will food always be provided?	Needed break time taken away; less energy for work

Figure 10.2: A matrix for making decisions more logical.

Other generic logical criteria that might be used include the following.

- Time involved
- Consistency with policies
- Space limitations

- Past performance information

- Data from student achievement, progress toward goals, and so on

- Survey data

2. **Re-evaluate a values decision:** Choose a decision you weren't particularly happy with. Were there unintended consequences? What precedents might you have set? Reconsider the decision using these questions. What elements of decisions might you be glossing over?

3. **Work on objectivity:** If you naturally empathize with people, learn to ask yourself: What would someone unfamiliar with this situation observe? How might an objective person counter my concerns? Would any actions I might take that come from empathizing actually be harmful in the long run? (Think in terms of enabling behaviors.)

4. **Find a precedent partner:** Who in your learning community is excellent at thinking of unintended consequences and the precedents you might be setting? Work with him or her to adjust your ideas to minimize these concerns.

5. **Work on the view from 30,000 feet:** David Rock (2006) suggests identifying which way of thinking you are engaging in. Whether you (or members of your team) more naturally focus on values or on logic, you (or the team) may habitually default to certain levels of thinking, whether appropriate or not. The levels are the following.

   - *Vision thinking*—Understanding your high-level goal for any decision—for example, the high-level goal for discipline of fostering student responsibility through leveraging justice and mercy; this is at the heart of success for any decision, conversation, or project.

   - *Planning thinking*—Identifying how you will get to the goal, before setting all the details

   - *Details thinking*—Making a plan for action; the problem comes when we move to details before ensuring we're headed in the right direction.

   - *Problem thinking*—Focusing on blame and what went wrong; again, some of this is helpful, but contrast this with, say, focusing on solutions and the energy that can come from that.

   - *Drama thinking*—Acknowledging emotions and conflicts may be unavoidable and necessary for sorting out how to avoid issues in the future; getting stuck here means emotions have taken over, and no one is moving forward.

The view from thirty thousand feet means you're aware of the level of thinking going on within your team and are working to move to the appropriate level. If you favor empathy and values, watch how long you stay with drama, as you might be concentrating too much on the relationship aspects in isolation from the bigger picture.

Five Ways to Increase Your Use of the Values Pole

To strengthen your use of the values pole, use the following five strategies.

1. **List the stakeholders:** Many people with a logical decision-making style find it easier to consider values-based criteria if they make a matrix; the most logical choice may not be acceptable to some, or it might clash with individual or team values. Figure 10.3 illustrates a simple example.

Decision: *Changing Staff Meeting Timing*

My task: Suggest time slots that raise the least number of concerns over the following constituencies.

Constituency	Values to consider	Their top concerns	Questions they might raise
Employees with young children	*Work–life balance*	*Whether day care can accommodate suggested meeting time*	*Can we keep options within normal hours?* *If not, can we always meet the same day?*
Hourly employees	*Fairness*	*Whether meetings require extra trips to work*	*Can we call into meetings?* *Who must attend?*
Parents	*Equity*	*Their day care needs if we do late-start meetings*	*Are students losing learning time?*

Figure 10.3: A matrix for using values in making decisions.

*Visit **go.SolutionTree.com/leadership** for a free reproducible version of this figure.*

As you choose criteria for your matrix, the goal is stepping into the shoes of each constituency to consider how each choice might affect them. Another way to approach this is to list how choices might affect each group, as shown in figure 10.4 (page 140).

	Morning meetings	Lunch with refreshments	Rotating schedule
Workers with young children	May not have day care coverage	Lunch helps staff recharge for the afternoon.	Some day cares aren't flexible.
Hourly employees	May object if they have afternoon shifts	They aren't compensated for lunch; pay issue?	Sometimes may be very inconvenient; virtual meeting solution?

Figure 10.4: Using empathy to consider how choices affect specific groups.

2. **Re-evaluate a logic decision:** Choose a decision you weren't particularly happy with. Whose needs did you not consider? How did it mesh with stated learning community values? Where did emotions or unrecognized needs of students or staff result in the decision not playing out as expected? What elements of decisions might you have glossed over?

3. **Find a values partner:** Identify someone who can brainstorm how decisions fit or go counter to stated values. Ask him or her how you can better explain or perhaps even dismiss choices after considering values. Your partner might also help point out when values are in conflict with each other or when a value is missing. For example, an over-focus on preparing students for career or college can result in a lack of emphasis on social and emotional learning, or leadership skills, or self-efficacy, or something else that is key to student success, if that thing isn't also part of the community's values.

4. **Balance self-fulfillment and empathy:** In yourself and in those around you, watch whether personal hard work and accomplishment are blocking empathy. The "I pulled myself up by my bootstraps and so can they" or "I overcame the same hardship" and other similar beliefs in self-reliance are correlated on some measures of emotional intelligence with low empathy. Step into their shoes and really delve into why they may not have the same resources, resilience, or support that you had.

5. **Read the research:** Before dismissing any subjective criteria as too soft to count or to use reliably, check the research. We now know that good teacher-student relationships have as much or more impact on student learning (Hattie, 2012) as many so-called hard instructional strategies. Collective

teacher efficacy is, again, one of the highest-impact strategies for student success (DeWitt, 2017). Student engagement (not entertainment) measurements correlate with school success (Gallup, 2016). They aren't fluff. Pick a measure you aren't comfortable with, and head to a research database. If you no longer have access to a university online database, chances are your local library card comes with access to Academic Search Premier (https://bit .ly/2xL5rLD) and other sources of research—and the librarians are equipped to do a search for you as well.

ASK YOURSELF

This lens is about getting the best of the objectivity of logic and subjectivity of values in decisions in your learning community. Do you tend to favor one over the other? How well are you balancing logic *and* values?

CHAPTER 11

Getting Results *and* Building Trust

In education, we often talk about the importance of outcomes. Did an initiative lead to higher grades or test scores? Did a new conflict-resolution practice result in fewer discipline problems? However, planning that focuses on measurable results is only half of the picture. The other half is working to build trust among members of your team, ensuring that they know they are valued for who they are rather than only for what they accomplish. This lens is about using the priorities in table 11.1 to move toward organizational success *and* a culture of collective efficacy.

Table 11.1: The Outcomes *and* People Lens Domain

Lens 8	Outcomes *and* People	
Priorities	Results Measurability	Trust Appreciation
Common initiatives, issues, or leadership responsibilities that involve this lens	Using data Increasing student achievement Teacher-evaluation systems Building relationships Supporting teacher growth	
EQ component	Experiencing self-fulfillment Employing interpersonal skills: giving feedback	

In this chapter, we explore the interdependency of outcomes *and* people by looking at an example of how a real leader and her team recognized the importance of reaching important outcomes without losing sight of the people involved. From there, we explain the balance between the outcomes and people poles, establish an emotional intelligence connection for this lens, and explain how you can best leverage the priorities inherent in this lens.

Real Results From Real Teams

Jennifer Abrams, an education and communications consultant, recognized early on when she transitioned from teacher to new teacher coach that educators often either mishandle or avoid needed conversations regarding performance or professional growth. She says, "I watched administrators provide feedback to teachers, especially new ones, that either wasn't humane or wasn't growth-producing. You can be caring *and* hold people accountable" (J. Abrams, personal communication, September 11, 2018).

All too often, Jennifer sees a similar pattern play out. At the start, administrators or team leaders have a clear picture in their heads of what they hope to change—the results they hope to see.

Formally or informally, they set up how they will measure progress. Perhaps they're targeting classroom management and decide to count how many students each teacher is sending to the principal's office. Or, they refer to set criteria in a teacher evaluation system. Or, they're counting the number of *high-yield strategies* or *differentiation techniques* or some proxy for *student engagement*.

I italicized those terms because this is often where Jennifer finds the root causes of communication problems. The school leaders will tell her that some teachers just aren't on board or refuse to take feedback. But when Jennifer talks to the teachers, they tell her, "I'm not sure what I'm supposed to do." She relates:

> I talk about having clarifying conversations before having hard conversations. For example, a group of new teachers was told, "You need to engage students more." No one explained what, in the eyes of leadership, engagement looked like, nor did they provide any suggestions or strategies. The administrators labeled them "difficult to work with" when they reacted sensitively to feedback that they hadn't made progress.
>
> How can you hold people accountable if you haven't clarified the outcomes you're looking for? A common picture of what student engagement looks like actually takes the sting out of critique since you're looking at objective data. During one workshop, a school leader got what I was saying, and told me, "I've been yelling at staff to do high-yield strategies. But the last professional development we offered on the topic was four years ago, and half of the staff is new. (J. Abrams, personal communication, September 11, 2018)

Do you know what you expect of people? Do they have a clear understanding that matches yours? These form the foundation of effective, growth-oriented feedback.

Frequently, leaders haven't broken apart the outcomes they are after in a way that fosters growth. Jennifer gave me another example:

> Two leaders were trying to help teachers with classroom management. Upset that too many students were being sent to the office, all their feedback and suggestions—what I call hard conversations—revolved around not sending students to the office. When I asked, "But isn't the goal better classroom management? What strategies are you suggesting?" their only response was, "Better discipline." They couldn't dissect what that meant in order to offer student-engagement strategies, or transition tips, or seating options, or suggestions on ensuring lessons were pitched right. They hadn't deconstructed what they were asking for—I see this again and again. (J. Abrams, personal communication, September 11, 2018)

There are at least three ways that this leadership lens can quickly get out of balance.

1. In the interest of being supportive, leaders avoid giving feedback because they don't know how to do it in a growth-oriented way. Perhaps their protocols focus too much on "letting wisdom emerge from the teacher," and they don't have strategies to give necessary suggestions when a teacher lacks experience in a given area. Or, they are afraid of teachers seeing them as harsh or critical.

2. In the interest of holding teachers accountable, feedback is direct, but too harsh to promote growth.

3. Leaders aren't clear about expectations, so purpose, methodology, or feedback are too vague to be effective.

All three approaches to leadership can result in ineffective feedback that doesn't support professional growth and can lead to loss of safety and trust.

With these examples in mind, consider how you think people on your team, or in your building, would rate the statements in figure 11.1 (page 146)? Try rating each one on your own. Then, ask someone else on your team to do the same—choose someone whose people skills are a little different from yours. Or, survey your staff with a free, online tool for anonymous surveys such as SurveyMonkey (www.surveymonkey .com). Compare your answers. Where do you have the pulse of the team? Where are you off base?

Score each of the following: (1) seldom, (2) sometimes, (3) often, or (4) frequently.	
We invest sufficient time in building good relationships among the adults in this building or on this team.	
Teams have excellent collaboration skills.	
Our leaders are good listeners—they take time to understand our concerns, needs, and triumphs.	
People feel safe and supported here—they admit mistakes and ask for help to improve practice.	
Performance feedback from leadership is valuable, helpful, and supportive.	
Our leader is aware of each team's atmosphere and provides the necessary support to improve trust or collaborative practices.	
We know how to engage in difficult conversations both productively and respectfully.	

Figure 11.1: Gauging the conditions for collective teacher efficacy.

*Visit **go.SolutionTree.com/leadership** for a free reproducible version of this figure.*

Collectively, if your staff give high ratings to statements like these, chances are you've created the circumstances for collective teacher efficacy—see chapter 3 (page 33) to review key leadership contributions to this powerful influence on student learning. However, can you hear some leaders—and politicians and members of the business community and parents—saying, "Adults should know how to collaborate, and schools shouldn't have to waste time and resources teaching staff how. If we're really going to move this school forward, we need to hold people accountable for meeting goals. Are students learning? Is teaching improving?" They're over-focused on the outcomes pole, forgetting that it takes time to build collective teacher efficacy.

The Measure of Outcomes and People

Figure 11.2 summarizes the ongoing interdependencies between the outcomes and people poles.

Is there any doubt that these poles are interdependent? What purpose do schools have, after all, if students don't grow academically? Likewise, teachers are motivated—they feel that sense of efficacy—when their efforts bring about student learning. But if we don't take care to build trust and relationships, teachers don't feel safe or supported and eventually become less effective.

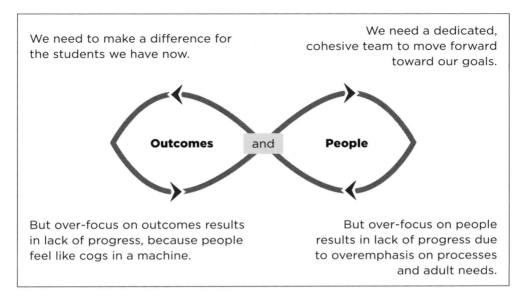

We need to make a difference for the students we have now.

We need a dedicated, cohesive team to move forward toward our goals.

Outcomes and **People**

But over-focus on outcomes results in lack of progress, because people feel like cogs in a machine.

But over-focus on people results in lack of progress due to overemphasis on processes and adult needs.

Figure 11.2: The outcomes *and* people loop.

There is no perfect amount of time to spend on building relationships, nor is there a perfect data set or accountability system to guarantee performance. Given the emphasis on data-based decisions and teacher evaluations, you are probably aware of how well you are working with the outcomes pole. The survey in figure 11.1 can help you gauge how well you're doing on the people pole. I often see leaders rely on formal performance reviews and data dives (for example, analyzing student assessments) to derive action steps for getting results; and yes, these are useful, just as team building or professional development on collaboration can improve trust. However, *every* leadership interaction—day in and day out—can help or hinder striking a successful balance within this ongoing paradigm.

Consider the following two key interdependencies between two equally valuable leadership roles: (1) conditional respect and unconditional respect and (2) clear expectations and clear support. One is about holding people accountable for progress toward goals, and the other is about building a culture of collective efficacy. How might the interdependencies affect your goals and initiatives?

Conditional Respect and Unconditional Respect

Every person in a learning community needs to feel that they belong—in fact, that atmosphere of safety and belonging is the number-one predictor of team effectiveness (Coyle, 2018). Unconditional respect allows everyone to feel that they are part of a loving family.

Remember from chapter 3 (page 35) that Felps et al. (2006) report three things that effective leaders do to create this sense of belonging.

1. They listen intently in conversation while ensuring that no critique comes from others. People feel safe sharing problems and mistakes.

2. They give individual attention so each person feels unique and valued.

3. They make it clear that relationships matter and are ongoing.

This by no means implies that anything goes. Similar to how a parent might say to a child, "I love you, but that behavior is unacceptable," a leader can say, "I value you, *and* I expect you to grow as a professional." Unconditional acceptance makes it possible to accept critique that is skillfully given, matches expectations, and leads to growth.

ASK YOURSELF

Is it easier for you to see what people need to do to improve or to see their general value to your learning community? How do you show appreciation for each staff or team member? How do you help them grow?

Clear Expectations and Clear Support

It is those clear expectations that are highlighted in the second interdependency—if we are holding people accountable, we also need to support them in helping them grow, and be specific about the help they can receive as well as the expectations for improvement. Like Jennifer, over and over I've seen leaders critique teachers when expectations are too general or lack any actual strategies for improvement.

Chapter 13 (page 167) delves more deeply into how to set clear expectations while allowing for the kind of autonomy that leads to innovation and motivation; here we are talking about clarity that actually *neutralizes* critique.

For example, at one school I filmed my work with a group of students as they learned to engage in collaborative problem solving. From the films, teachers identified specific strategies I used over the course of three problems to improve how students listened to each other and engaged with the work. We developed a common language around beginning with reflection time for every student, creating and using a common work-space for the group, and employing teacher moves that ensure that everyone's voice was heard. Through watching how I had to scramble to get all of that going, the teachers learned that no one expected them to run perfect groups the first time around!

ASK YOURSELF

Would others say your expectations are clear? Are you also clear on what support teachers can request as they work to grow professionally?

The EQ Connection

Crucial for this lens is competency in the EQ areas of experiencing self-fulfillment and the interpersonal skill of giving feedback in ways that build emotional safety. The following are a few key points regarding self-fulfillment that apply to this chapter.

◆ Self-actualization and self-respect come from reaching both personal and professional goals. Effective leaders should feel a sense of pride and accomplishment in what their team is accomplishing—this is why this EQ competency is tied to the outcomes lens. However, the danger lies in becoming so wrapped up in driving toward goals that you lose sight of the people who are making that progress possible.

◆ Ensuring that everyone on the team feels a sense of accomplishment connected with the stated results you are seeking is also crucial—this EQ component is about more than just the leader. However, remember that people may be motivated by different measures of progress on different fronts. Margaret Wheatley (2017) points out that data have assumed an almost cult-like status, but we may not be measuring what is most important, nor probing for the reasons behind the numbers: "The sophisticated analytics, the charts, graphs, and dashboards, are not giving us information. They're submerging us with data. It is only information that makes a difference" (p. 121).

Are you getting the information you need about student motivation, student self-efficacy, student relationships, student curiosity, and other factors besides academics that may be key to motivating some of your staff?

The following are a few key points on the interpersonal skill of giving feedback that apply to this chapter.

◆ Remember that clear expectations serve to depersonalize feedback. For example, if in professional development, teachers have learned about activating prior knowledge, and they understand when, how, and why to use strategies, feedback can focus on progress toward those shared understandings.

◆ Jennifer Garvey Berger and Keith Johnston (2015) provide an excellent technique for ensuring that feedback is growth-producing: Consider each session where you are providing feedback as a learning opportunity for you as well as for the teacher or staff member. They suggest asking some key questions of yourself before and during sessions:

- What if this person weren't a problem for me to solve, but a key knowledge holder for me to understand?

- What is it this person knows about the situation that could shift or change my mind and how might I find this out?

- How could I learn something here? (Berger & Johnston, 2015, p. 65)

Priorities Inherent in the Outcomes and *People Lens*

Table 11.2 highlights the priorities connected with this lens. Which of these resonate more with you? Which of these may be more key to your current leadership goals?

Table 11.2: Priorities Connected to Outcomes *and* People

Outcomes Priorities	People Priorities
Results	**Trust**
Meeting or exceeding our stated goals is at the top of my priority list.	I am committed to creating an environment where people can count on the integrity of myself and others, and on our reliability, vulnerability, compassion, strength, and support.
Measurability	**Appreciation**
Because we only pay attention to what we measure, I want to ensure we are using helpful data, both soft and hard, to assess progress toward goals.	I want to create an atmosphere where people demonstrate respect for each other, regardless of expertise.

In the next two sections, we'll look at strategies to increase your use of both the outcomes pole and your use of the people pole. Remember that it may take at least six tries using a strategy before you feel comfortable or see results.

Five Ways to Increase Your Use of the Outcomes Pole

To strengthen your use of the outcomes pole, use the following five strategies.

1. **Clear expectations:** You've seen how crucial it is to make clear to people what you are holding them accountable for in order to reach outcomes and build trust, but let someone else be the judge of how clear you actually are. Ask if your goals, expectations of teachers, or suggestions for implementation can translate into actionable steps. Have you quantified any important expectations such as the frequency with which staff should use a strategy or how long it generally takes to reach proficiency in using the strategy? For example, some experts in implementing high-level student discussions estimate it takes six weeks for teachers and students to regularly engage in these kinds of discussions (Herbel-Eisenmann & Cirillo, 2009). If you provide expectations and ask people to explain them back to you, do you agree with what they say? Have you listed support resources—options for learning teams, coaching, video or other online resources, books, and so on?

2. **Measure the soft stuff:** Reread the Margaret Wheatley (2017) quote in this chapter's The EQ Connection (page 149), and think about what your school or team is tracking. Have adults built relationships with every student in the school? Do students see reading as a viable choice for a leisure activity? Do people willingly share dilemmas or mistakes? Do teachers believe that professional development is addressing their needs? What else might you track that would not only enhance your ability to course-correct as you strive for outcomes but would also build trust and show appreciation of your staff?

3. **Check reality:** Do a reality check on whether your team is truly on track to meet goals. Consider factors such as the following.

    *   Organizational capacity to provide coaching and other forms of support

    *   Time

    *   Equipment

    *   Current policies and goals

    If expectations aren't realistic, what can you change? Think about this in the context of the preceding factors. Think logically: "If we don't _____, then _____ will happen." Or, "If we _____, will we be setting a wise or unwise precedent for _____?"

4. **Work on purpose:** If your school's mission, vision, and values don't have you leaping out of bed in the morning, how can you find that connection? Is the mission too generic? Is it unreachable? Is it uninspiring? Does it need reshaping? Do outside forces impose it? Or, do you need to reconsider your own vision as a leader in order to reconnect with the work of your learning community? Driving for results you believe in is far more motivating than simply driving for stated goals.

   You may wish to back up and consider what you hope to accomplish as a leader. Once you can sum up that hope in a short statement, use the list of leadership priorities in chapter 1 (pages 16–18) to brainstorm just three that are key to what you hope to accomplish. Use the process in chapter 16 (page 209) to own your vision of leadership.

5. **Practice learning-mode feedback:** Revisit the different questions you can ask during coaching or feedback sessions to ensure you are learning even as you encourage professional growth in others. This takes practice. Before a session, consider doing a quickwrite on the following questions.

   • What were my expectations? If I ask, what will the other person say my expectations were? How might I be clearer?

   • What did I not understand about what others might experience as they worked toward our stated goal? Does anything need to change—the goal, the timing, support, or something else?

   After the session, reflect on what you learned. What will you carry forward into your next feedback session? How does this affect where and how you set expectations?

Five Ways to Increase Your Use of the People Pole

To strengthen your use of the people pole, use the following five strategies.

1. **Analyze what isn't going well:** Choose a meeting, relationship, or project where you were dissatisfied with the results. List what role you played and what you might have done more effectively. Ignore all external factors and instead concentrate on the impact of your ideas and actions. Where were you to blame? What will you start doing differently?

2. **Practice appreciation and acknowledgement:** Many educators enter the field because they want to have a positive impact on the lives of others, and they need to hear that they are doing so to stay motivated. Make sure that

people know you value their role in team success. Write notes that make specific mention of employees' ideas, efforts, or skills; let your leadership team know of individual accomplishments; and talk about other contributors out loud in meetings as appropriate. Although not everyone is comfortable with public praise, almost everyone wants to hear that their efforts are noticed and make a difference.

3. **Be vulnerable:** Admitting your own mistakes is perhaps the quickest path to ensuring that others feel free to admit theirs. The goal isn't disclosure as much as setting the tone of, "I know I can improve here and would like to draw on the collective wisdom of the team to do so." You might do this by doing some of the following.

   - Share stories of your own growth experiences as a classroom teacher and what you learned from them.

   - State your own development goals as a leader and the kinds of feedback that would help you grow.

   - Be clear about the portions of what you are asking that are predictable and where you are uncertain of what might happen.

   - Lay out a goal or problem. Ask team members, "What do you think we should do?" and avoid voicing your own ideas until you have heard from everyone.

4. **Study a case:** With the goal of providing better support, step into the shoes of an employee who is not doing well. Plan a conversation using these strategies.

   - Be specific regarding expectations that aren't being met. Don't say, "You're not working up to speed," but rather, "Your contributions to the last two projects were late, whereas everyone else met the deadlines." Instead of, "Your work quality is poor," quantify with, "I had to spend three hours revising your last report, compared with less than twenty minutes for the others I received."

   - List your assumptions on why this employee is falling short of expectations. Again, try to be specific. Then, brainstorm other possible explanations, including the need for skill development, external factors such as problems at home, and miscommunicated instructions or expectations.

   - Talk with the employee, remaining nonthreatening and calm. Emphasize that you aren't issuing performance warnings but instead working to understand what might be keeping him or her from working up to potential. Solicit specific reasons and possible solutions.

Frequently, when I'm asked to coach underperforming employees, they are lacking a very specific but learnable skill, or they have misunderstood their priorities. For example, as I used these conversation steps with a teacher whose performance had been rated unsatisfactory, she realized that she lacked lesson-planning skills. (Yes, she should have mastered these years before, but my only concern at that point was her classroom.) We spent a full day together on class time flow, planning lessons, and planning units. From then on, she had control of her class. What appeared to be incompetence was a lack of a specific skill that could be taught and learned.

5. **Test for trust:** If you didn't jump at the chance at the beginning of the chapter, try surveying your team or staff using the survey in figure 11.1 (page 146). What can you learn about the current atmosphere in your building? What can you improve? What actions might you take? This is especially important if being aware of others' emotions isn't one of your EQ strengths.

ASK YOURSELF

This lens helps you balance seeing measurable results of your school's initiatives with creating an environment for collective efficacy. Are you striking the right balance between outcomes *and* people?

CHAPTER 12

Effectively Using Positional Power *and* Sharing Power

School leaders often find themselves bestowed with wide-ranging powers to influence what their staff can do and how they do it (positional power), but the best leaders know when to share that power (collaborative power). This lens is about making good decisions using the priorities in table 12.1 to both use the authority you have because of the position you hold (the power to pole) *and* engage in shared, collaborative leadership (the power with pole).

Table 12.1: The Power To *and* Power With Lens Domain

Lens 9	Power To *and* Power With	
Priorities	Expertise	Openness
Common initiatives, issues, or leadership responsibilities that involve this lens	Instructional leadership Sharing leadership Strategic planning	
EQ component	Experiencing self-fulfillment Employing interpersonal skills: giving feedback	

In this chapter, we explore the interdependency of power to *and* power with by examining what it looks like when there is an imbalance in this dynamic. From there, we explain the balance between the power to and power with poles, establish an emotional intelligence connection for this lens, and explain how you can best leverage the priorities inherent in this lens.

The Importance of Knowledge From the Ground and From Above

What's to be done when students are simply way behind their peers? Most educators now agree that more-of-what-didn't-work-before remediation programs of the past result in tracking or disengagement, but seldom do students actually catch up (Hammond, 2015). Accelerating learning—helping them make more than a year's growth—is often touted as a solution. But how do you do that, especially if more than 20 percent of your students are below grade level, often seen as the threshold for effectiveness with many response to intervention (RTI) programs? It isn't easy, is it?

FURTHER DEVELOPMENT

RTI refers to a multitiered system of supports composed of instructional strategies, implementation tools, and other essential elements deployed through three tiers of intervention, extension, prevention, and enrichment (Buffum, Mattos, & Malone, 2018; Buffum, Mattos, & Weber, 2012).

I'd been working with mathematics teachers at a school for a couple of years and truly admired their dedication. They went out of their way to work with students individually. If one found a particularly good professional development workshop, say for teaching fractions or running small groups, most of the rest of the team would also go through the course. They kept in contact with researchers at a nearby university and willingly participated in studies that showed great promise for improving student outcomes.

Together, we spent a year identifying resources, instructional practices, and assessments to accelerate student learning on fractions, a pivotal content strand for success in algebra. The teachers had collaborated on plans for kicking off the new school year with lessons designed to bring all students to mastery of several big ideas before beginning the textbook fractions unit. They already knew that only about a third of the incoming sixth graders in their high-poverty school were at grade level, and this team of sixth- through eighth-grade teachers collaborated extensively to ensure that, at least for fractions, these students would catch up and master the sixth-grade materials.

Then, just before school began, a high-level leader from the district office announced that fractions instruction would start with the grade-level materials. Teachers were to accelerate, not remediate with content from the prior year. There were statements about not closing the achievement gap if you're backing up instead of moving ahead with growth mindsets. Any deviation from the strategic plan would be grounds for insubordination.

Some of the teachers from other schools who had also been engaged in research on fractions suggested some middle ground. There were rumors of screaming matches, but the policy held, and at the end of the fractions unit, only one-third of the students were at grade level. The remaining two-thirds were further behind than ever.

Note that the district leader was partially right—the more time spent on prior year concepts, the less time there would be for moving ahead on the current year's curriculum. At its best, power to allows leaders to get things done, and this leader was taking the vision toward the goal of avoiding harmful forms of remediation. However, that leader wasn't in the classrooms—his decisions lacked the real-time data the teachers were using in designing their interventions. Problems arose because he only held part of the truth. As we saw in chapter 2 (page 23), a growth mindset is only helpful if students have the knowledge and skills to make perseverance worthwhile. Power to— the power of his position—gave him the authority to issue the mandate. However, what if he'd partnered with the teachers who had been studying intently the very dilemma he was trying to fix? What if he'd reviewed with teachers the formative assessments they planned to use to pinpoint exactly which concepts to emphasize rather than demanding uniform implementation of a standardized curriculum?

Margaret Wheatley (2017), who has worked extensively with leaders in diverse industries and around the globe, states that the U.S. military was the first true learning organization she ever observed. The U.S. Army learned decades ago to trust the soldiers, who had real-time data, with decisions. Possession of information was more important than rank. Wheatley describes observing a mock battle with a commander. Computers notified soldiers and tanks when their mistakes made them casualties. Afterward, she listened in as soldiers and their captain debriefed the mock battle and discussed how to avoid repeating their mistakes. She reports:

> Later, sitting in the café with the colonel, I blurted out that I had never seen so much learning going on. I'd been in many organizations, in many different circumstances, but I'd never seen a leader even faintly enthusiastic, let alone rubbing his hands in glee, about the amount of learning he was witnessing with all the mistakes going on. And I'd never experienced the energy and focus at the back of that truck. I consolidated all these experiences to the colonel in one statement: "The Army is the first and only true learning organization I've ever seen." (Twenty-five years later, I've only encountered a few others and none come close). (Wheatley, 2017, p. 129)

She also reports:

> I was told that it took about fifteen years for soldiers to be able to speak truthfully in the presence of senior commanders. And it took even longer for senior commanders to appreciate the perspectives of those below them. What motivated everyone to learn how to think well together was the shared imperative of learning. It's better to learn than be dead. (Wheatley, 2017, p. 197)

Why bring up the Army when we fight enough battles over education as it is? Because we need models of true learning organizations, and this example clearly illustrates both power to (setting vision, conducting training, determining tactical decisions, and more) *and* power with (sharing power with everyone to achieve success). Are you positioned to learn and adjust plans by sharing power?

Real Results From Real Teams

Figure 12.1 illustrates the interdependencies between the power to and power with poles.

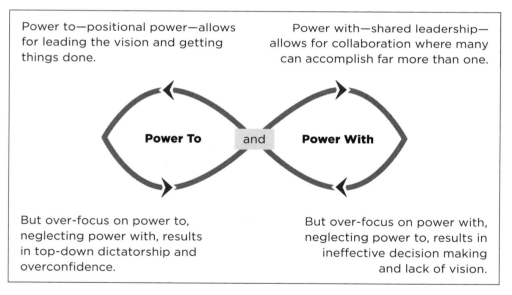

Power to—positional power—allows for leading the vision and getting things done.

Power with—shared leadership—allows for collaboration where many can accomplish far more than one.

Power To   and   **Power With**

But over-focus on power to, neglecting power with, results in top-down dictatorship and overconfidence.

But over-focus on power with, neglecting power to, results in ineffective decision making and lack of vision.

Figure 12.1: The power to *and* power with loop.

In some organizations and cultures, positional power has gotten a bad name, and is generally associated with power over and resulting abuses of power. In education, we've all seen examples of new leaders who come in with their own agendas, pushing changes to make names for themselves. As pushback to these examples, in Australia especially, I've heard school leaders say that they don't identify themselves as school principals so that no one will think they're putting themselves above everyone else. Collaborative power is seen as the answer.

Yet organizations have found uneven results with so-called leaderless organizations or teams (Gelles, 2015). Problems arise when no one has or assumes direct responsibility for outcomes. It turns out the "The Buck Stops Here!" sign President Harry Truman kept in the Oval Office (Federal Reformatory, n.d.) represents prescient wisdom that is critical for accountability. Somehow, group responsibility doesn't work as well in many situations. Consider how in the army example, the captain of a squadron, and the colonel, and the general, have ultimate responsibility even as there is shared responsibility.

When does positional power seem like the right emphasis to you, and indeed is effective, and when might collaborative power work better in moving toward goals? Consider the themes in table 12.2.

Table 12.2: Benefits of Positional Power and Collaborative Power

Power To (Positional Power)	Power With (Collaborative Power)
Guiding the creation of an organizational vision and values (or preserving a current, effective one)	Ensuring that everyone has a motivating connection with the vision
Ensuring that decisions are being made that continue to move the team or school toward its vision, while using its values	Using inclusive processes to make decisions aligned with vision and values
Being responsible for plans, agendas, and goals, both short term *and* long term	Collaborating with those who are working daily in the areas that decisions will affect
Setting clear expectations about goals and anything that needs to be implemented with fidelity while nurturing an atmosphere of trust, where people willingly share mistakes for continuous learning for everyone	Working together to agree on what needs standardization and where autonomy might be granted, as well as on assessing how realistic expectations are
Finding and dedicating resources to an effort and becoming a champion for doing more of what is working	Sharing triumphs and struggles in an atmosphere of trust and continuous learning for everyone so that best practices spread and resources go to doing more of what is working well

In our opening scenario, think how differently student outcomes might have been if the district leader had gotten the balance right by:

- Using *power to* set the vision of establishing a growth mindset in students, using assessments to pinpoint conceptual understanding of fractions, and starting instruction from there with the goal of teaching to mastery of concepts embedded in grade-level standards

- Using *power with* teacher leaders, forming a team of in-the-trenches teachers already engaged in research on this dilemma or already succeeding at accelerating students who were below grade-level standards in fractions

- Using *power with* the teacher leaders, planning professional development to roll out this nuanced approach to remediating (for which the definition is to address a problem) while setting students up to move ahead at a faster pace

- Using *power with* all teachers by giving them time to ask questions, setting up clear channels for addressing their concerns, and scheduling sessions where teachers can bring examples of student work or assessment data to get help in implementing the new strategies

- Using *power to* set clear expectations that all teachers will follow the new approach and what it will look like in their classrooms, while also making clear that because the proficiency levels of students differ from building to building, the pacing may be different; however, decisions to add time to any strand of the unit are to be backed up by student data from new, quick assessments of conceptual understanding that the implementation team develops.

Here are two interdependencies to keep in mind as you work to get the most out of positional power (power to) and collaborative power (power with): (1) effective leaders and effective participants and (2) self-regard and humility.

Effective Leaders and Effective Participants

Remember Wheatley's (2017) comment that it took fifteen years for troops to learn to speak up, and longer for leaders to learn to listen to troops? Think of how the priorities that are core to this lens—expertise and openness—play into this dilemma. Are there areas where your expertise is deep enough that you aren't inclined to engage in collaboration? Who else might have equal expertise, formed in different ways from yours, that might lead to different, enriching ideas? Are you open to them? Leaders need to develop skills and confidence to act on power to when their expertise warrants it and to collaborate with openness to learning when others have different, valuable information.

Likewise, participants need the skills to engage in collaboration—we aren't born knowing how to listen, share ideas, build on the thoughts of others, recognize our biases and entertain other perspectives, and slow down processes to ensure that not just decisions are made, but that ways to build consensus and buy-in are chosen. If everything has been top-down, it seldom works to call a meeting and expect instant teamwork.

ASK YOURSELF

Look back through the paragraphs in this section. Which capacities do you need to develop? What do team members need?

Self-Regard and Humility

Think about this interdependency both inwardly and outwardly. Leaders need enough self-regard to believe in their own ability to lead. Who wants to work for someone who is waiting to fail once again? However, check how you attribute your success. How often do you stop to think who else is contributing to making your plans become reality? Think specifically about who keeps what on track or helps others collaborate or encourages everyone when progress is slow. It's a tricky thing to be aware of your own strengths and contributions as well as those of others.

Also, be aware of how others view you. Do they see you as competent and humble? The power to *and* power with lens represents a significant tool for accurately displaying both competency and humility.

ASK YOURSELF

Who can give you honest feedback as to whether you have the right balance of acknowledging the contributions of others while also displaying confidence and pride in your contributions?

The EQ Connection

The key EQ areas for this lens are experiencing self-fulfillment and employing the interpersonal skill of giving feedback. The following are a few key points regarding self-fulfillment that apply to this chapter.

- Power To has the very positive aspect of allowing you to lead others toward a vision you strongly believe in. What motivates you to take on leadership responsibilities? What do you hope to bring into reality? Leadership isn't easy, and recognizing that positional power can further what you feel called to do can keep you going when things get tough.

- Take a look at your school or team's plan. Is your attitude more on the side of "If we accomplish this, I'll be positioned to take a bigger leadership role," or is it, "If we accomplish this, we will really see improved learning outcomes for students and staff"? There is some room for both, as long as the decisions you are making include the priorities of both self-fulfillment and humility.

- As you enter new leadership positions, how do you evaluate the strategies, initiatives, curriculum, and other agenda items of the prior leader? Look back at Tim Brown's story in chapter 4 (page 50) on leadership *and* listening— before introducing anything on your own agenda, what might you learn from listening to what is valued in your new learning community?

The following are a couple key points on giving feedback that apply to this chapter.

- Remember to use sessions where you are giving feedback as opportunities to learn—as give and take. Revisit the advice of Berger and Johnston (2015) who suggest two key questions to foster this mindset:
    - What if this person weren't a problem for me to solve, but a key knowledge holder for me to understand?
    - What is it this person knows about this situation that could shift or change my mind and how might I find this out? (p. 65)

    They point out that in any complex, fast-changing environment, everyone needs to be learning, every day. Thinking of feedback as give and take lets you be open to how others' experiences, perspectives, and ideas might influence your next steps, much as the army is constantly learning from those at the front line.

- What about receiving feedback on your own performance? Formal perform-ance reviews may not even touch on the kinds of things these Twelve Lenses of Leadership are asking you to work on. Further, are you truly open or do you tend to assume you're being misunderstood? Remember that many leaders seldom receive any accurate feedback. Robert Witherspoon and Randall White (1997) list four blocks to feedback.

- People in power struggle to find good sources of criticism.
- Most leaders value being seen as competent; for many, accepting criticism threatens that competency.
- The nature of leadership thwarts introspection.
- Many leaders believe their edge—such as being overly assertive, critical, or outspoken—brought success and hesitate to change.

What might be blocking you from receiving accurate feedback? Who might give you the kind of feedback you need to hear?

Priorities Inherent in the Power To and Power With Lens

Table 12.3 highlights the priorities connected with this lens. Which of these resonate more with you? Which of these may be more key to your current leadership goals?

Table 12.3: Priorities Connected to Power To *and* Power With

Power To Priorities	Power With Priorities
Expertise	**Openness**
I model respect of competency, thinking highly of demonstrated skills, knowledge, work, and results.	I seek and ponder contrary data, new perspectives, and other points of view before reaching conclusions.

In the next two sections, we'll look at strategies to increase your use of both the power to pole and your use of the power with pole. Remember that it may take at least six tries using a strategy before you feel comfortable or see results.

Five Ways to Increase Your Use of the Power To Pole

To strengthen your use of the power to pole, use the following five strategies.

1. **Clarify your why:** Think of power to as your motivation for wanting to lead in the first place. What would you like to have influence over as a leader? What would look different in classrooms if you could successfully set direction and guide others in getting there? What would look different among your staff, on your team, or in education in general?

2. **Dismiss *power over* for *power to*:** Write down your negative thoughts about leaders and power. Then look through them. How many highlight abuses by leaders who are wielding power for their own purposes rather than using power for accomplishing things that align with the vision and values of the organization? Some people find that they need to write a formal description of an ideal leader before they can see themselves as ethical leaders wielding power to. Consider making a list, completing the prompt, "With positional power, I could . . . ."

3. **Dismiss aggressiveness for assertiveness:** Similarly, you might be worried, especially if you are female, about being taken as aggressive or pushy even when you are simply carrying out your leadership responsibilities. Be clear on the difference—aggressiveness is about making people do what you want, while assertiveness is expressing wants clearly and setting limits in ways that respect yourself and others.

4. **Demonstrate authority:** Authority doesn't mean turning into a dictator. It means that when something warrants your positional power, ensure that you present yourself as one worthy of being followed. Do away with tentative language such as, "So I'm thinking . . ." or "I'm sure you've already thought of this, but . . . ." These phrases have their place—such as being willing to be vulnerable when acknowledging your own mistakes—but not when you are delivering a message of confidence.

5. **Use your job description:** In what areas or for what purposes are you expected to take the lead? What are you directly responsible for accomplishing? Think of these areas in terms of power to, and then step up to the challenge.

Five Ways to Increase Your Use of the Power With Pole

To strengthen your use of the power with pole, use the following five strategies.

1. **Clarify your who:** Who does what you can't do? Who has knowledge that would take too much effort for you to master to the same extent? Who easily builds bridges, already did something you want to accomplish, or loves to do something you prefer to avoid? Invite them into collaboration.

2. **Dismiss inefficiency for shared ownership:** If you frequently act alone because of fears over the inefficiencies of making decisions with others, reframe the pain or roadblocks involved as pathways to creating shared ownership.

3. **Appoint a leader—delegate:** If you are forming a collaborative team for an effort, remove yourself from the temptation of being too directive by delegating leadership to someone else. Yes, you can still make expectations clear, but if you form a committee to get creative with the school day schedule, put someone else in charge of the final project. Leave the final crafting of professional development in the hands of the committee. Let others set curriculum review criteria for your perusal. Formally give up ownership, while maintaining final approval of, and responsibility for, outcomes.

4. **Invest in collaboration:** If working collaboratively with a leadership team is difficult, consider hiring an outside facilitator. Look for someone who understands how to help a group work toward a common purpose, recognizes and appreciates each member's differing strengths and needs, and establishes good working protocols.

5. **Use the think, pair, share strategy:** One of the easiest protocols to help leaders learn to listen and participants to learn to share is the simple Think, Pair, Share strategy. Put out a question for everyone to answer and ask everyone to quickwrite for a few minutes about their thoughts, questions, responses, concerns, and so on. Then have them discuss their writings with one other person in the group and, as they do so, identify what they want to share with the entire group. Then, provide time for everyone to share their ideas. Have someone scribe the ideas for display on a screen or whiteboard. Go last in sharing so your views don't persuade the group. Be ready to point out how your ideas are changing based on what you heard from others.

ASK YOURSELF

This lens is about taking clear leadership when warranted and sharing leadership to maximize the benefits of collaboration and shared leadership. How well are you balancing power to *and* power with?

Having Clarity on What and Why *and* Having Flexibility on How

Any policy, initiative, or practice requires clarity—clarity of time, clarity of method, and so on. But leaders sometimes get so caught up on process that they fail to focus on what matters most—ensuring that outcomes are actually aligning with stated goals. This is why it's just as important to ensure you maintain flexibility, no matter the clarity of the plan, to allow smart people to produce their best work. This lens is about using the priorities in table 13.1 to set a vision that is clear to everyone *and* leave room for creativity, innovation, and individuality in how they get there.

Table 13.1: The Clarity *and* Flexibility Lens Domain

Lens 10	Clarity *and* Flexibility	
Priorities	Organization Accountability	Originality Autonomy
Common initiatives, issues, or leadership responsibilities that involve this lens	Planning strategically and implementing initiatives Setting clear expectations and providing feedback Being flexible	
EQ component	Building an atmosphere of emotional safety	

In this chapter, we explore the interdependency of clarity *and* flexibility by looking at an example of a situation where a good strategy might not work for every situation, thus showing the importance of flexibility. From there, we explain the balance between the clarity and flexibility poles, establish an emotional intelligence connection for this lens, and explain how you can best leverage the priorities inherent in this lens.

When Successful Ideas Aren't Universal

Picture a group of middle school teachers and administrators participating in a classroom walkthrough before the school day begins. One of the top priorities in the school plan is improving teacher organizational strategies to eliminate certain kinds of disciplinary issues before they arise. Each teacher has a clipboard and an observation sheet with the group's agreed-upon focus of identifying best practices in how rooms are arranged to facilitate classroom management (figure 13.1).

Peer Classroom Observation Sheet

Observation Objective: Identifying effective classroom and instructional organization strategies

Prompts for maintaining focus on factual evidence:

• I saw or noticed . . .

• I wondered about . . .

• I counted . . .

Write a summary of your observations and questions to share with the teacher whose classroom you observed.

Figure 13.1: Peer classroom observation sheet.

Now imagine you are one of the teachers participating in this exercise. The second classroom you visit simply amazes you. A chart on the whiteboard with *Class Contest* at the top shows tally marks for each section the teacher has on criteria, such as all students have pens or pencils, all students are on time, all discussion groups return organized supplies, and so on. Five cups, one for each section, hold popsicle sticks with each student's name on one. A stack of bins on the side of the room indicates where each class is to turn in homework, and there's more.

The teacher next to you, one of those creative colleagues who is always coming up with new ideas for his classes, says, "I've heard she takes care of the contest in less than a minute by saying, 'On one, show me your pencils . . . five . . . four . . .

three . . . two . . . one,' and they all hold them up. The students even help each other out, sharing, so the class can get a high score. I need to start using her system."

You've worked with this teacher, though, and you know he tends to jump around in agendas, add ideas spontaneously to lesson plans, and pull the right item out of a backpack jammed full of papers, books, journals, and student work. You say, "I'm curious . . . if you ran that contest, how many days would go by before you'd forget to do it in one of your sections?"

"Um, probably two," he says, laughing, "and I can just hear one of the girls in the front row saying, 'You forgot!' or 'You're not doing it right!' But shouldn't I *train* myself to do this, since her classroom runs more smoothly than mine?"

Ideally, following such a walkthrough, the observers would discuss all the strategies they saw for organizing classroom processes, and they would identify which had been effective for teachers who weren't necessarily naturally organized themselves.

The school's goal might also be stated as improving classroom management by first managing physical space and student supplies to minimize transition time and disruptions. You can see, though, how forcing every teacher to use the same strategies wouldn't be helpful. So many strategies—whether we are talking about building relationships, managing supplies, facilitating learning, or giving directions—are not in your power to uniformly implement throughout a building. How they play out in reality depends on the strengths of the teachers as well as the mix of students in the classroom.

When I participated in conducting a walkthrough like this in real life, we were collaborating to identify possibilities that clearly aligned with the community goal. Those involved helped to define the characteristics of such practices so they could communicate them to the rest of the staff. Teachers could then choose among the strategy options or compare their own ideas to the expectations on the list. We also made sure they knew they could ask questions for further clarity.

Thus, the fuzzy manage-your-classrooms scenario that Jennifer Abrams talked about in chapter 11 (page 144) becomes clarity *and* flexibility.

Flexible, Yet Not Fuzzy, Clarity

Perhaps the example in the preceding section seems simple—of course teachers need to organize their classrooms in different ways—but managing this interdependency in other areas is far more difficult.

For example, as you work to articulate a coordinated horizontal and vertical curriculum—what students do and learn at each grade level and how it relates to other grade levels—clarity is needed for capturing the information in a manner that is uniform enough to be useful. An anything-goes mentality in unit planning can quickly become useless to anyone but the person who created the unit. However, I've seen unit-planning forms that are so rigid, detailed, and time consuming that teachers, out of self-preservation, collaborate on ways to get around the rules. Further, the eyes of your most creative teachers generally gloss over when they have too much structure. They may fail to note the stated clear expectations because of their natural drive to put their own twist on the unit.

Figure 13.2 illustrates the interdependency between the clarity and flexibility poles.

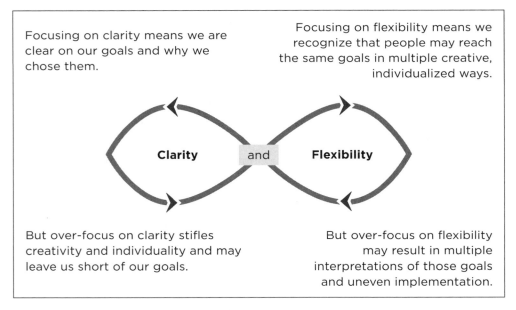

Focusing on clarity means we are clear on our goals and why we chose them.

Focusing on flexibility means we recognize that people may reach the same goals in multiple creative, individualized ways.

Clarity and **Flexibility**

But over-focus on clarity stifles creativity and individuality and may leave us short of our goals.

But over-focus on flexibility may result in multiple interpretations of those goals and uneven implementation.

Figure 13.2: The clarity *and* flexibility loop.

Ideally, you get the best of both worlds when expectations are clear about what everyone is supposed to do and what everyone can do differently, but doing so requires acknowledging that adults react to fuzzy expectations in two different ways.

1. Some immediately note what they don't understand and work to get the clarity they need. Their motto is, "Why start if I might waste time by moving in the wrong direction?" Sometimes they even start asking questions before you've finished explaining expectations, because they have a built-in radar

for noting when something is missing from their informational needs. It's easy to misjudge this as needy.

2. Others honestly don't recognize the ambiguities in what is being asked and unconsciously fill in the blanks with their own ideas and understanding. If the leader assumes that they deviated on purpose, it's easy to misjudge these people as rebels when, in truth, they'd received a fuzzy plan.

The trick to this lens, then, is being clear about both where fidelity is required and where flexibility exists. Then, everyone in your learning community can indeed move toward common goals with maximum innovation along the way. At its heart, it requires a different approach to planning, which involves making best use of some of the other lenses in this book. Here's how a plan that is loose or tight or one that is clear or flexible might come into being through these other lenses.

1. **Power to *and* power with:** The leader, upholding the learning community vision, chooses a goal or area of need and assembles a collaborative team whose members are interested in this area and have diverse experiences or skills related to this area.

2. **Reality *and* vision:** Together, the team articulates the goal, understanding its short-term and long-term time and other resource requirements, to ensure that what they are proposing is realistic.

3. **Breadth *and* depth:** The team considers how this goal aligns with other initiatives. Is there synergy, allowing space for this undertaking to reach a level of mastery?

4. **Clarity *and* flexibility:** Together team members set up the plan and do the following.

    *   Articulate the criteria for successful implementation. (Clarity)

    *   Provide a timeline for implementation. (Clarity)

    *   Communicate what will be covered in professional development or via other available support. (Clarity)

    *   Allow time for teachers to plan for how they will meet the success criteria by asking them how and when the criteria fit with their curriculum and how and why their plans might be different from the stated timeline. (Flexibility)

    *   Ask teachers to set dates for when they will provide evidence of progress toward goals; in other words, instead of micromanaging

mini-deadlines, set the expectation for teachers to pinpoint projected progress points and, at each one, seek feedback. (Flexibility)

- Make plans to check teachers' overall progress toward goals by asking when and how they will re-evaluate their overall plan for an initiative or goal, check that their plan is on track, and plan for flexing their schedule. (Flexibility)

Note that this step also allows for balancing outcomes *and* people. Yes, you are ensuring that people are striving toward the right results, but you are building the conditions for collective teacher efficacy. After all, if teachers are allowed to flex so they can put their strengths and beliefs into action, while still aligning with learning community goals, motivation rises via autonomy, mastery, and purpose (Pink, 2009).

If you do this right, instead of a static plan that sits on a shelf, you'll have a dynamic plan—a plan full of indicators that help you discern when something is going well, when someone needs extra support, when it's time to celebrate a milestone, when it's time to reallocate resources, and so on. This contrasts with a linear action plan that often only communicates, "We're behind!" or that ignores crevices that start to open during implementation.

Keep in mind that the following two ideas can help leverage the delicate interdependency between clarity *and* flexibility: (1) fidelity and innovation and (2) community goals and individual goals.

Fidelity and Innovation

Some strategies and initiatives leaders simply must implement with fidelity—where solid research backs up certain processes and protocols, and where planning is necessary to realize the results these strategies aim to achieve. An example of this is guided inquiry. In a meta-analysis of 360 studies, Louis Alfieri, Patricia Brooks, Naomi Aldrich, and Harriet Tenenbaum (2011) conclude that direct instruction outperforms unassisted discovery learning (a common interpretation of inquiry where teachers absent themselves from the process).

However, what the researchers call enhanced discovery learning outperforms direct instruction. Fidelity is required in planning and implementation to ensure that students have necessary background knowledge, which may include direct instruction. Teachers are to interact with students frequently and ask students to explain their reasoning as they choose strategies. Preplanning often involves forming questions to ask students that will prompt their thinking rather than provide answers. Teachers also need to identify when suggestions or examples might be needed to keep students on track with the core purposes of the lesson.

As teachers move from direct instruction to more inquiry-based teaching, fidelity to these planning considerations brings success. Organizers that help them cover all of these areas are often useful. However, there will always be teachers who see such organizers and automatically think of other ways to do things. To address this, ask questions like, "How would you like to change this?" Often, they decide to try it with fidelity at least once. Or, they are clear about the changes they would make. If the goals will still be met with the changes, what better way to foster creativity and innovation than to let teachers try out such ideas as they are teaching?

ASK YOURSELF

How do you separate what must be done with fidelity and where originality will produce better results?

Community Goals and Individual Goals

Let's say you have a schoolwide goal of increasing the time students spend reading texts of their own choosing—reading for the enjoyment of reading. Aspects of how to get there might be clear, such as professional development on introducing student book talks in the classroom and helping students find the perfect books. But having teachers consider their own strengths, motivations, needs, or struggles with the schoolwide goal, and then identifying a personal goal that aligns with it, can add to the entire learning community. For such a reading initiative, teachers might set goals for one or more of the following.

◆ Read a certain number of books for the grade level they teach that are a bit outside of their normal interests; this ensures they'll have more suggestions for students with varied tastes in reading materials.

◆ Find more culturally diverse texts for the school.

◆ Increase the size of their classroom libraries by visiting the public library, estate sales, or other low-cost options.

◆ Take the lead in enrolling the school in the Teacher's Choice Award program (www.uft.org/teaching/teachers-choice) to receive more books for the library.

- ◆ Organize and train volunteers to help students find the right book.

- ◆ Form a private online book club for students at a site such as Goodreads (www.goodreads.com).

What other possibilities can you think of? Giving teachers time to brainstorm together and flesh out their ideas leads to better articulation of the *why* and *how* that are key to reaching these goals. However, beware of too much emphasis on the kinds of measurements and accountability factors that might incent teachers to set less challenging or risky goals.

Also note that, while it is easy to say, "Please pursue your own goals for your classrooms, professional learning, licensing requirements, or students," it is harder to ensure that you have left enough time and energy for them to do so. Are you flexible enough with professional development or team time that there is room for the kinds of individual thinking, brainstorming, and peer coaching that will set everyone up for success?

ASK YOURSELF

When do you have teachers set individual goals that relate to the community goals? Do they tend to set stretch goals that indicate a safe-to-fail atmosphere, or do they play it safe?

The EQ Connection

The key EQ area for this lens is building an atmosphere of emotional safety. The following are a few key points regarding this area that apply to this chapter.

- ◆ The best way to be sure that your goals and expectations are clear and will guide your learning community toward its vision is to create space for questions, concerns, and suggestions. If trust is present, members of the learning community know that the goals are attainable and that you will support them. Then, questions and concerns align with ensuring that each person feels equipped to move forward. If you are still working on building this atmosphere where people are valued for who they are and know they will have support, consider the size of what you are asking. What smaller, short-term yet high-impact part of it might you pursue to build everyone's confidence and trust in you as a leader?

◆ When trust and safety are present, people can aim higher than they can if they fear being shamed or penalized for failure. Remember that fears about failing to reach SMART goals prompt a four-fold increase in lying about results (Sytch, 2015). That sort of fear does no one any good. Of course, we don't want preventable, epic fails when teachers are working with students, but normalizing that it may take five to six tries before teachers and students are used to a strategy—or that aiming for success with 90 percent of your students but only succeeding with 80 percent is a good start—builds the right kind of atmosphere.

Priorities Inherent in the Clarity and Flexibility Lens

Table 13.2 highlights the priorities connected with this lens. Which of these resonate more with you? Which of these may be more key to your current leadership goals?

Table 13.2: Priorities Connected to Clarity *and* Flexibility

Clarity Priorities	Flexibility Priorities
Organization	**Originality**
I emphasize thinking through project or systems processes and needs and expectations to create workable plans and practices.	I value tapping our imaginations, connecting ideas in unusual ways, using artistic skills, or using other tools to find unique pathways.
Accountability	**Autonomy**
I establish realistic expectations and responsibility for outcomes, striving for clarity regarding what is and isn't under our control.	I foster teams where each member can be effective when thinking and acting independently.

In the next two sections, we'll look at strategies to increase your use of both the clarity pole and your use of the flexibility pole. Remember that it may take at least six tries using a strategy before you feel comfortable or see results.

Five Ways to Increase Your Use of the Clarity Pole

To strengthen your use of the clarity pole, use the following five strategies.

1. **Clarify the why:** Everyone in a learning community has a better chance of moving toward the vision when they understand and connect with the *why* of the vision at a personal level. One strategy for ensuring this is guiding

the way people talk about the goals. Kerry Patterson, Joseph Grenny, David Maxfield, Ron McMillan, and Al Switzler (2011) say:

> Stop obsessing over the unpleasant aspects of what you're required to do, and focus your attention on the values you're supporting. The words you use to describe what you're doing profoundly affect your experience of the crucial moment. For instance, when sticking to a lower–calorie diet, don't undermine your own motivation by describing your choices as "starving" or "going without." You're doing far more than manipulating calories. You're becoming healthy; you're sticking to your promise; you're sacrificing so that you'll be mobile when playing with your grandkids. This difference in description may sound small, but words matter. They focus the brain on either the positive or negative aspects of what you're doing. (p. 57)

What reframing ideas related to your school's goals might have a similar effect? For example, instead of talking about "filling out unit plans," are your teachers hearing language like "making it easier to share great lessons" or "dividing and conquering our workload"?

2. **Consult your opposite:** One of my colleagues is a master at finding new voices to inform our work and keep us flexible. However, she relies on me to determine when it's time to stop gathering information and make some decisions. Understanding each other's strengths and needs makes this a successful alliance. Who might provide some balance for your flexibility? Who might find the holes in your expectations or point out where there is too much flexibility to ensure a common vision?

3. **Review a past plan:** Take a look at a past effort where goals were set without clear paths for reaching them, whether by you or by others. Recall what went well. What fell short? Why? Where might clarity have helped?

4. **Review your message:** Do you need to pass your next message about vision, goals, strategies, plans, or initiatives past someone else? Who can help you see what you don't see as far as whether you are demanding uniformity or keeping things too loose?

5. **Build together:** One of the school principals I worked with asked her staff to work in groups to list the questions they had about a new initiative. The administrative team came up with three questions. The teaching teams came up with between sixteen and twenty-two questions. The principal highlighted this discrepancy as an example of why he needs the teaching

teams to speak up; he found all those additional questions important, worthy of answers, and simply not on his radar without their help.

Note that this exercise also demonstrates a level of leadership vulnerability that leads to trust.

Five Ways to Increase Your Use of the Flexibility Pole

To strengthen your use of the flexibility pole, use the following five strategies.

1. **Let others in sooner:** Many introverted leaders like to have their plans set before sharing; they need to know what they're thinking before talking about it. Yet this can result in others seeing them as not getting things done. Ask for advice earlier with phrases such as, "This is a preliminary idea," "How might you proceed?" and "What questions do you have?" This also demonstrates a willingness to be vulnerable to making mistakes, a quality that you seek to foster in others.

2. **Use SayDoCo:** Alan Fine (2010) provides a framework for flexible clarity. He asks people to:

   • *Say* what they will do

   • *Do* what they say

   • *Co*mmunicate if they find they can't stick to a plan, including a new timeline

   The last step is key. This framework helps everyone understand that when you ask for plans, they are approximations and not certainties. It leaves room for optimism, changing circumstances, and accountability. Of course, if trust isn't present, people are afraid to communicate that the initial timeline was too aggressive and only later on do you find out that the plan isn't working.

3. **Plan goals, but leave processes open:** Think through the end results you need. What do people need to know? You can leave processes open yet show films of exemplary classrooms, display work from students in schools like yours, or have everyone try a few different strategies before deciding on which one they will use. Ask for people to revoice the expectations and regularly discuss how they can get there.

4. **Remember the motivating power of autonomy:** Charles Duhigg (2016) points out that "a prerequisite to motivation is believing we have authority over our actions and surroundings. To motivate ourselves, we must feel like we are in control" (p. 22). Babies want to hold their own spoons even

if it means they eat a bit less. Nursing home residents who fight against rules thrive more than those who don't. And in all the years in between, we are motivated by having some autonomy. Every time you are tempted to prescribe best practices or what seems like the best schedule or some other certainty, back up and ask, "Where can I add some autonomy for others?"

5. **Experiment with no plan:** Ask your team what should be on the agenda for your next time together. Or, have someone else set the whole agenda. What necessary things happen that you hadn't thought about? What are you learning about your need for control?

ASK YOURSELF

This lens is about setting the course toward organizational goals and vision while allowing for individual pathways of originality and creativity. How well are you balancing clarity *and* flexibility?

CHAPTER 14

Planning for the Predictable *and* Embracing the Possible

What is under your control? What isn't? Just about every educator has, at least once, poured maximum effort into changing a classroom practice or adopting a new curriculum or rolling out performance assessments or building an effective team atmosphere—you fill in the blank—only to learn that something outside of their control has turned their efforts into a waste of time. For this reason, leaders are often wary of the unknown, and it is indeed important to provide your staff and school with stability, but it is just as important to take into account the possibility of the unforeseen as you plan. This lens is about using the priorities in table 14.1 to ensure that you plan for what is predictable *and* allow for what is possible.

Table 14.1: The Predictability *and* Possibility Lens Domain

Lens 11	Predictability *and* Possibility	
Priorities	Dependability	Complexity
Common initiatives, issues, or leadership responsibilities that involve this lens	Strategic planning Professional development	
EQ component	Recognizing your own emotional state Being aware of others' emotions	

In this chapter, we explore the interdependency of predictability *and* possibility with an ideal example of a community working together to improve learning; we then demonstrate how even well-intentioned initiatives can go awry. From there, we explain the balance between the predictability and possibility poles, establish an emotional intelligence connection for this lens, and explain how you can best lever-age the priorities inherent in this lens.

The Possible and the Probable

The small town of Austin, Minnesota, is an exemplary of how businesses, community, and schools can work together. A key player is the Hormel Foundation, the legacy of the family that started Hormel—yes, the Spam people. The Hormel Company, a Fortune 500 firm, knows that it can't attract world-class business executives and scientists to its headquarters unless the schools can deliver a world-class education. The Hormel Foundation (n.d.) has supported initiatives in gifted education, revamping of science labs, technology, and more.

John Alberts, executive director of Educational Services for Austin, has headed up the planning for many of these efforts. When his team received a new grant for technology, John surmised:

> At that particular moment in time, we knew intuitively by observing other schools that it's not about the technology. Implementations elsewhere didn't look the way we wanted to look. We partnered with Learning Technologies Media Lab because they started with the question we wanted to start with. Not, "What should we buy?" but "What do we want learning to look like, and what do we want to see happen with kids?"
>
> We spent the first year anchoring back to what we know, what we're good at, and what we want learning to look like here. The statements we generated about learning—all of them could be implemented without technology. Our external partner recognized how education can be transformative but also knew the limits of technology. From there it blossomed out. (J. Alberts, personal communication, May 21, 2018)

One way to frame their approach is that they started with what is predictable. Constants in teaching and learning include the following.

- Teachers need to prioritize both building relationships and academics.
- We can cultivate curiosity and creativity in students, and indeed must do so, even as we help them acquire knowledge.
- Students learn best when they have some autonomy over what and how they are learning.

On the other hand, technology is quite unpredictable, isn't it? We've seen exponential increases in the capacity of handheld devices in the past few years—and even most experts failed to predict how smartphones would revolutionize connectivity so soon after their appearance. As soon as a school gets a document camera in every classroom, they're made obsolete by a new tablet app or a better platform for sharing documents. Or, you fund a high-tech whiteboard in every room and observe that some staff members use it just like their old one, or like a projection screen, or even just for displaying artwork. What you thought would improve student learning instead unpredictably fosters poorer concentration habits, less collaboration, and other unintended consequences, or has no impact at all.

We naturally plan for changes based on what we know—we of course want to adopt best practices, research-based initiatives, and what has worked elsewhere. But just like in the stock market, past performance in schools, especially ones outside your learning community, may predict general patterns for schools everywhere, but is not a reliable predictor of the individual performance at your school. Teaching and learning involve complex systems of adults, students, families, politics, news events, and more—all of which makes choosing solutions with linear rationale ("This worked before, so it will work again" or "This worked there, so it will work here") fraught with peril. Berger and Johnston (2015) put it this way:

> Complexity is about getting our heads around what is possible (because anything could happen) rather than what is probably going to happen (which is determined from what has happened before).
>
> This shift—from trying to get your head around what is most likely to trying to get your head around what is in the field of possibilities—is much bigger than it sounds. As research has shown in study after study, our brains just don't like this. Our general pattern is to prune and simplify. We need to work at it if we are going to create new patterns of behavior for thinking and acting in this new world. We need to talk to one another differently, gather information differently, build strategies and plans for the future in new ways. (pp. 11–12)

In a sense, the interdependency of the predictability and possibility poles is continuity *and* change (chapter 8, page 101) on steroids. The big difference, though, is using this tension to develop criteria for decisions so that you notice when you are relying on predictions in instances where they are useless.

John points out that leaders work to solve problems people actually have and avoid generating ideas when looking for a solution. In his case, technology wasn't the answer but simply one of the options. At each phase of planning, John and his team asked if possibilities other than technology provided a better match with their clearly articulated vision of learning in Austin Public Schools.

As the team developed their technology strategy, they identified some other elements they felt they could predict. John is clear about the necessity of long-term focus:

> Where we are now was years in the making. Today we've recognized the fact that as we move the work ahead, we need ground-level support. So, we have technology coaches in every building to work with teachers at their level to use technology to improve instruction. We didn't start with that, but we involved the teachers in how they wanted to see learning happen, and they asked for coaching. Systemwide, we set things up to get the feedback we need to make it all happen and to make adjustments. (J. Alberts, personal communication, May 21, 2018)

Another predictable factor that John invests in, which applies to nearly every change in the district, is the crucial role of every school principal involved. That person must believe in and uphold the district vision. John knows they may have fears similar to those their teachers experience:

> Principals are thinking, "You mean I'm going to be leading a building that is tech-infused when I didn't teach that way? I never had to create classes on the web like that!"
>
> We keep the principals involved, helping them see that it is impossible to be an expert in everything—and that they don't have to be. (J. Alberts, personal communication, May 21, 2018)

To help their principals learn to work with possibilities, Austin Public Schools invested in training in improvisational theater. Once a month for a year, they attended workshops conducted by Brave New Workshop, a Minneapolis-based company. John reflects that, for the first three months, he thought they were going to kill him, but then he started hearing the language, and he realized his own development involved thinking about resistance as deriving from understandable fear and helping switch that fear to discovery. The improvisation tools helped them think differently and improved their capacity to embrace change and thus support their teachers.

A third predictable factor in John's thinking is the need for empathy:

> How do I understand the needs of the people I'm serving? Too often, not enough time goes to carefully considering the point of view of people affected by change. Assumptions are made without

knowing. If you begin there, with the pain point or problem—whatever you want to call it—you'll find more than fear. (J. Alberts, personal communication, May 21, 2018)

John is echoing the emphasis of chapter 10 (page 129) on using both logic *and* values in decision making. However, the goal of the kind of empathy mapping he describes ensures that the way initiatives proceed helps connect teachers and administrators with the overall vision. They collectively ask the question, "What mindset shift will help everyone embrace their common vision of what learning looks like in Austin?"

In Austin, the initiative started with talking about learning instead of about technology. They discussed human-centered design instead of focusing on innovation. They took time to delve into empathy instead of focusing on resistance by starting with the central tenet and going on from there.

Realize that working with predictability *and* possibility requires complex, not linear, thinking. It is systems-based, and there are tools you can use to improve your thinking when planning new initiatives through the predictability *and* possibility lens. In the following sections, we examine two of them.

Continuous-Improvement Cycle

To help leaders develop systems thinking skills, Austin Public Schools has invested in the strategic planning and institutional change models developed by the Baldrige Institute (Baldrige Performance Excellence Program, 2017a, 2017b). These research-based trainings and tools, including ones tailored to education, promote systems thinking rather than a reactive approach to planning. They use the analogy of moving from simply putting out fires to preventing fires to explain their approach, as shown in table 14.2.

Table 14.2: The Baldrige Performance Excellence Program

The Fire Hose Analogy	Steps Toward Mature Organizational Strategic and Operational Goals
1. Reacting to a problem—putting out the fire	At this stage, an organization has poorly defined goals; activities mainly solve immediate problems rather than using proven processes.
2. General improvement—installing more fire hoses	Some strategies and goals and some repeatable processes are in place.

continued →

3. Systematic improvement— noting fire-vulnerable areas and installing smoke and heat detectors	Processes align with key strategies and goals, and the organization shares and re-evaluates them periodically.
4. Strategic improvement— system-wide heat sensors and sprinkler system	The organization coordinates goals, processes, measures, and change efforts across all units. Efficiencies come from evaluating and uniformly implementing what is working. Innovation and improvement come through clarity of goals and constant reevaluation of what is and isn't working.
5. Organization-wide improvement—all locations are using fire-resistant materials and other prevention techniques	

Source: Adapted from Baldrige Performance Excellence Program, 2017a, 2017b.

This continuous-improvement cycle differs from linear strategic planning by requiring the kind of analysis up front that Austin Public Schools illustrated by defining what learning should look like before buying technology. They aim to avoid installing those proverbial fire extinguishers and hoses without first taking a preventative approach to fire safety. How well-aligned are your planning processes, active goals, measurement systems, and periodic evaluation and adjustments of your plan?

Scenario Planning

Another tool for systems thinking is *scenario planning,* a discipline that helps you unearth possibilities, both positive and frightening. Whereas most strategic planning focuses on honing the best assumptions, scenario planning begins by asking critical questions that unearth different plausible sets of assumptions. Then, the leadership team considers large projects in the context of each of these scenarios about the future. It measures plans in terms of how well they fare in very different future scenarios, not just in what the stakeholders assume to be the most likely future.

Daniel Rasmus (Goral, 2012), who has written on using this tool in higher education, says:

> Scenarios help organizations navigate the future by putting a name on uncertainty. It cannot be stated too emphatically that people easily ignore what can't be known, or apply a biased value and pretend they know what the future will bring. Scenario planning forces organizations to confront what they can't know, put a name on it, and then think about the implications for their institution. . . . If you don't put a name on uncertainty, people will have their own lists that cast doubt and foster misunderstanding. By making uncertainty

explicit, organizations can make better decisions because they share
a well-documented, and common view of the world and the forces
at play in it. (p. 69)

He points out that known uncertainties one can address through scenario planning include curriculum (for example, Will the Common Core survive?), pedagogy
(determining the right mix of direct instruction, guided inquiry, and so on), funding
levels and sources, and public trust of public education. How might you benefit from
formally evaluating plans under different scenarios that consider these factors?

Note that each of these thinking strategies requires substantial investment in
professional development and implementation, but how many strategic change initiatives fail because of lack of one or both of these? Think about leveraging the
short-term and long-term needs of your community. Systems thinking about change
through techniques such as these doesn't place us above the fallout of unforeseen
events, but it makes us more resilient when they happen because our core purpose
is more universal.

Effective Plans for a Complex, Unpredictable World

Figure 14.1 maps the interdependency between the predictability and possibility poles.

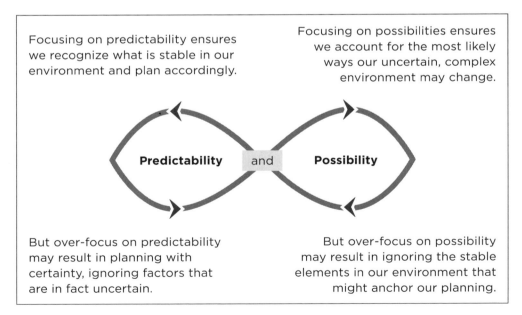

Figure 14.1: The predictability *and* possibility loop.

Take a moment to bring to mind some current and past initiatives you've been
involved with. Then, add a few entries to the lists in figure 14.2 (page 186).

Factors that interfered with initiatives achieving predicted results	Possibilities we didn't think about until we were well into implementing an initiative	Initiatives where we chose perfectly and got the results we expected

Figure 14.2: Assessing past initiatives.

*Visit **go.SolutionTree.com/leadership** for a free reproducible version of this figure.*

If you were starting a new initiative tomorrow, would you feel safer relying on probability of success, even though it might not actually be predictable, or on your analysis of the potential of several possibilities? Ideally, you could find that central tenet that John spoke of, something along the lines of "What learning looks like" or "Understand the problems people are trying to solve." Here are two interdependencies that can help you navigate what may seem like pure guesswork: (1) top-down and bottom-up and (2) internal controls and external forces.

Top-Down and Bottom-Up

Austin Public Schools has all the positive traits of a learning organization that Margaret Wheatley (2017) recognized in the army (see page 157). Leaders solicit feedback and work to listen to everyone. One tool Austin Public Schools uses is crowdsourcing ideas with eight other districts. Teachers—and everyone else—can submit ideas to their online *Thoughtluck* and then vote on which they would most like to see become reality. The top vote-getters are workshopped through an agreed-upon, human-centered design process and then microtested—the group considers how the idea might be best implemented given the capacities and potential concerns of those involved, and a few educators try it before rolling out the idea districtwide.

John's team also uses Thoughtluck to see where ideas are coming from and which buildings are voting for which ideas—teachers submitted over thirteen thousand votes on various ideas in 2017. In reviewing the resulting data, a building principal noted strong support at her site for an idea that wasn't chosen for district focus. She decided to support its development for her school, but still within the framework of the district vision.

Thus, although an overall vision came from the top, every level contributed input to flesh it out, and everyone continues to support and carry it out. The teachers in the classrooms have detailed knowledge of what is happening, what is changing, and what might be possible. Make use of it!

ASK YOURSELF

How do you gather and use front-line information in planning?

Internal Controls and External Forces

Human beings aren't the rational, economically-driven creatures that many predictions assume them to be. Human systems are even messier. A key piece of handling this interdependency is identifying what you can and can't control. Note that understanding and articulating what is under everyone's control also foster being dependable—a key factor in others seeing you as someone they want to follow.

Sometimes your learning community has the capacity for more control than people recognize. For example, a teaching team told me, "We can't control whether parents are completing student homework for them." Together, we brainstormed several strategies, such as having students explain mathematics problems where the handwriting didn't match the student's penmanship, or changing how the team graded homework, or working with the school principal from the first open house of the school year to help parents see homework in a different light.

Sometimes the learning community has less capacity to control a situation; unfortunately, on several occasions the schools I've been working with have been seriously affected by violence—against a student, in the community, or involving parents. Or, there's an external change in curriculum, standards, testing, or other factors just as we are close to completing our work on the status quo. You can't plan for every contingency. That's the realm of anxiety. To deal with this, consider how schools regularly plan for helping students with emotional distress. Or consider how, when we work with concepts such as power standards, we are using a strategy to cope with ever-changing external standards. When we have a vibrant, shared vision of what learning looks like, we can stay the course through all kinds of external disruptions.

ASK YOURSELF

Do people in your learning community spend more time discussing what you can control or what is outside of your control?

The EQ Connection

The key EQ areas for this lens are recognizing your own emotional state and being aware of others' emotions. The following are a few key points regarding recognizing your own emotional state that apply to this chapter.

♦   How do you react to taking risks? Nardi (2011) finds clear differences in how much people with different personalities activate the area of the brain that involves taking calculated financial or strategic risks. Recognizing your own fearlessness or anxiety can be important in empathizing with others and to ensuring that you aren't overly confident when playing with possibilities.

♦   How comfortable are you with complexity? If you long for linear solutions, lack of workable ones can foster a sense of loss or frustration. Ask yourself: "Am I hoping the facts will add up to a clear choice?" "Am I hoping that one solution will solve several problems or solve a problem for all staff or all students?" or, "Do I struggle to see the viewpoints of others?"

The following are a few key points on being aware of others' emotions that apply to this chapter.

♦   Remember how John reframed resistance as fear before understanding how to help his principals? Where do you need to, as Covey et al. (1994) put it, seek first to understand and then to be understood? This often involves using empathy which, as I wrote in chapter 3 (page 33), involves understanding not just what people are feeling, but the root cause.

♦   If intense reactions to events, proposed changes, or other happenings often surprise you, ask yourself, "Why am I so unaware of what is going on?" "To whom should I be listening?" "From whom should I be seeking feedback?" "What do I need to observe?" "Who can help me understand what people are experiencing?" "Who might I run proposed changes by to help me consider other viewpoints?"

Priorities Inherent in the Predictability and Possibility Lens

Table 14.3 highlights the priorities connected with this lens. Which of these resonate more with you? Which may be more key to your current leadership goals?

Table 14.3: Priorities Connected to Predictability *and* Possibility

Predictability Priorities	Possibility Priorities
Dependability	**Complexity**
I want to be known as trustworthy and reliable when carrying out the charges I have been given.	I recognize when linear solutions are inadequate and plan for uncertainty, paradoxes, multiple scenarios, and volatility.

Being seen as trustworthy comes from carrying out what you say you will do. That is fine unless you've advocated a simple solution when the problem is complex. How do you incorporate both of these priorities into your leadership work?

In the next two sections, we'll look at strategies to increase your use of both the predictability pole and your use of the possibility pole. Remember that it may take at least six tries using a strategy before you feel comfortable or see results.

Five Ways to Increase Your Use of the Predictability Pole

To strengthen your use of the predictability pole, use the following five strategies.

1. **Look for the big idea:** Back up from the problem you think you are solving to see if a bigger dilemma is at play. For example, "What mathematics curriculum meets our model of learning?" may not be a good question if the real dilemma is "How do we increase teacher knowledge of mathematics, so they can support guided-inquiry methods of learning?"

    You've seen other big ideas in this chapter. Use them to identify what is predictable in a world where past experience may or may not predict future results.

2. **Slow down:** Although we urgently want to ensure that our current students receive the best education possible, several of the examples in this book illustrate how slowing down actually allows for acceleration of improved teaching and learning. How might spending extra time defining values or engaging in improvisation training, or bringing in an external partner, bring about a better understanding of your needs?

3. **Check assumptions:** If you love new ideas, complexity, and change, you might also be prone to making big assumptions about what needs fixing, where people are struggling, or the priorities others have. Review your channels for hearing other voices, receiving feedback, and allowing concerns to be voiced. How can you be sure you are solving real problems rather than coming up with ideas in need of a problem?

4. **Make your best bet:** Sometimes, you do need a quick decision or a sure-fire, short-term win to generate buy-in or enthusiasm. In this scenario, predictability is an excellent strategy. What is most likely to have the impact you desire? Go for it!

5. **Brush up on logic:** A majority of us think we're being logical when we're actually being persuasive. Logic ensures that our conclusions flow from our assumptions. Try this exercise (Nardi, 2011).

    a. Ask a perplexing question about recent events, such as, "With today's technology, how can you crash a cruise ship into a dock?" (Check the video on YouTube if you haven't heard of this incident.)

    b. Brainstorm three possible explanations.

    c. Pick two explanations and rephrase them: The more (or less) _____ happens, then the more (or less) _____ happens.

    d. Try both explanations in three alternative contexts (school, work, and home) to see how well the explanations hold up.

    e. State the best-fit principle. (What is empirically true? Simple? Just? Relevant?)

    f. Apply your best-fit principle to a current problem to derive a policy solution.

Five Ways to Increase Your Use of the Possibility Pole

To strengthen your use of the possibility pole, use the following five strategies.

1. **Intentionally delay closure:** When a solution seems obvious, slow down. Put the idea in a folder and lock it away in a drawer for a week. Then, revisit it with an eye to what has happened in the meantime or whomever else you might contact for new information. Revisiting often brings a fresh perspective as to what other possibilities exist or what opportunities or threats you haven't yet considered. Do this with presentations, projects, and proposals, as well as with plans.

2. **Ask different questions:** Some leaders feel uncomfortable asking questions that they don't know the answers to, but that of course is the heart of delving into possibilities. The following are some questions you might pose to your team to seek out new possibilities.

   - "What are the connections to larger issues or other people?"
   - "What possible solutions or ways to approach the problem can you list?"
   - "What insights and hunches do you have?"
   - "What is this problem analogous to?"
   - "What other directions can you explore?"
   - "What other possibilities might there be if there were no restrictions?"
   - "What do the data imply?"
   - "What theories address this kind of problem?"

3. **Think with complexity:** Revisit the previous sections on systems thinking: Continuous-Improvement Cycle and Scenario Planning. These tools are designed to help us move away from dangerous applications of linear-problem and linear-solution thinking. A good guide to scenario planning is *Scenarios: The Art of Strategic Conversation* by Kees van der Heijden (2005). A web search for *Baldrige Performance Excellence Program* also leads to several informative resources. The point is not to endorse a specific perfect tool; instead, investigate one or the other. Compare their ideas to how your learning community currently functions. Consider asking questions such as the following.

   - "How often do we make decisions with a complexity view rather than in isolation from other parts of our system?"
   - "How often do we solve a presenting problem before looking for underlying causes or long-term rather than short-term fixes?"
   - "How often have our strategic goals created new problems via the lenses listed in this book? For example, when have we focused on uniform implementation of rules only to find that certain policies then create inequities?"
   - "When have we ignored fears or uncertainties, only to have those unnamed fears turn into resistance? How do we fail to anticipate obstacles we could surmise with proper attention? How do we otherwise impede progress?"

4. **Seek other perspectives:** Look both within and without your learning community. Ask a leader from a content area or grade level seemingly unrelated to your dilemma. Check with people in your community engaged in related businesses or nonprofits—scientists, booksellers, fitness center owners, mathematics tutors, and more. Ask parents. Ask students. See what faith communities have to say. Network to see how leaders in all these areas have increased their skills in dealing with uncertainty.

5. **Think in systems:** Besides the Twelve Lenses of Leadership that make up this book's core chapters, each chapter mentions two other ongoing interdependencies that promote systems thinking. Go back through these pages and consider which ones relate to the issues at hand. Remember that each involves a system—applying a linear solution will simply result in a new set of problems when you have such polarities. Keep the following principles in mind.

   • When people are arguing over who is right on any of these, help them articulate what they value about their own positions and what they fear about other positions. No single position offers a complete perspective. Each only holds part of the truth, and people need other perspectives.

   • You can't solve these dilemmas once and for all. The downside of one pole is often seen as a problem with the upside of the other pole as a solution. The upside of one pole is not a final solution. It is a natural self-correction in the ongoing oscillation between the two poles. Seeing one upside as a solution leads to it being called a mistake later on.

   • Avoid dismissing the fears the other side will bring about resistance; they hold part of the truth.

   • We hold so tightly to our own position that we often fail to see its downside.

   • Most of the pendulum swings in education policy result from linear solutions when these interdependencies or polarities are in play. Examples include how mathematics is taught, the ebbs and flows of standardized curriculum and testing, a focus on teacher accountability or on supporting teachers, and so on. We can stop the swings if we slow down enough to notice the recurring patterns, name the paradoxes or polarities involved, and work to get the upside of both poles.

ASK YOURSELF

This lens is about planning for what is predictable while allowing for what is possible. How well are you balancing the things you can depend on *and* embracing complexity?

CHAPTER 15

Making Measurable Whole-Child Achievement Progress *and* Finding Purpose

In education we focus a lot on achievement—achieving goals, closing the achievement gap, achievement in the community—and these are critical aspects of ensuring our students succeed in school and in their lives beyond school. Realize, though, that real achievement only happens when leaders also create for their staff engagement through purpose. This lens is about using the priorities in table 15.1 to find the right balance between moving forward toward your learning community's goals and ensuring members of the community continue to enjoy their work and find fulfillment.

Table 15.1: The Goal Orientation *and* Engagement Lens Domain

Lens 12	Goal Orientation *and* Engagement	
Priorities	Achievement Perseverance	Enjoyment Fulfillment
Common initiatives, issues, or leadership responsibilities that involve this lens	Work–life balance Creating lifelong learners Staff retention	
EQ component	Experiencing self-fulfillment Employing interpersonal skills: modeling balance	

The lens for this chapter works a bit differently from those of the other lens-focused chapters. We begin examining the interdependency of goal orientation *and* engagement with a self-examination of the predominant atmosphere of your school—is it a campfire or a pressure cooker? From there, we explain the balance between the goal orientation and engagement poles, explore a key truth to neuroscience, and then establish six related strategies that lie at the core of your development with this lens.

Of Campfires and Pressure Cookers

Is your school more like a campfire or a pressure cooker?

To me, campfires are welcoming sources of light and warmth—waiting to cook your meal or toast your marshmallow and illuminating evenings of story and song. Feed it with the right amount of wood, and you have a cozy haven. Toss in an extra log or two and there's no danger, although you might wait for the flames to die down a bit before roasting that sausage.

With pressure cookers, on the other hand—the old-fashioned ones that Grandma used—just a bit more water making steam or a tad too much pressure, and *bam*! Hope no one was standing nearby!

Is your school's atmosphere more like a campfire or a pressure cooker? What about your own stress level? Remember that stress tolerance is a component of EQ on formal instruments and that leaders who score really high on this metric are often unaware of the stress in those around them. Similarly, an overstressed leader can lead to an overstressed staff.

Perhaps you feel that you're both thriving at work and thriving in the rest of your life—you have time for good relationships and for taking care of yourself, and you're finding fulfillment at work. That is fantastic, for as a school leader, one of your responsibilities is modeling that living a balanced life is possible. In a review of other studies, Karen Edge (2014) summarizes the following.

- When leaders make work–life balance a priority, employees feel supported in doing the same.

- When leaders are stressed and exhibit poor habits of self-care, employees report more stress and poorer self-care.

So, campfire or pressure cooker?

Schools have never been overfunded, and educators have never had too little to do; but with funding cuts, unfunded mandates, shifts in society, and changes in technology, more and more educators are just a step away from burnout. The last *MetLife Survey of the American Teacher* (Markow & Pieters, 2012) shows that the percentage of teachers satisfied with their jobs dropped from 59 percent in 2009 to 44 percent in 2011. The percentage of teachers planning to leave the profession increased from 17 percent to 29 percent. Further, only about 45 percent were optimistic that student achievement levels would improve over the five years following the study. That means they lack efficacy—that sense that what they are doing will bear fruit. This makes it difficult, day in and day out, to find the kind of fulfillment that fuels efforts just as wood fuels a fire. Instead, they want out of the pressure-cooker atmosphere.

Yes, we want to lead schools where every student is experiencing academic, social, and emotional success—but both students and adults also need to enter the building eagerly, anticipating engagement and fulfillment, rather than with burnout and discouragement. Teachers and students alike should be able to both reach their destinations and enjoy their learning journeys.

Engaging Journeys and Goal-Oriented Destinations

Figure 15.1 maps the interdependencies between the goal orientation and engagement poles.

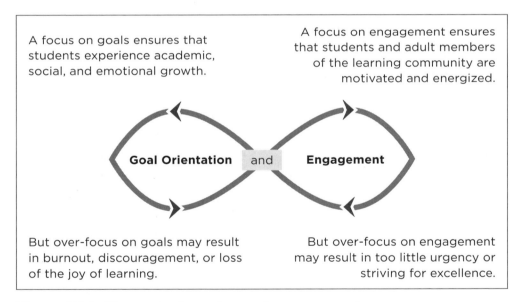

A focus on goals ensures that students experience academic, social, and emotional growth.

A focus on engagement ensures that students and adult members of the learning community are motivated and energized.

Goal Orientation and **Engagement**

But over-focus on goals may result in burnout, discouragement, or loss of the joy of learning.

But over-focus on engagement may result in too little urgency or striving for excellence.

Figure 15.1: The goal orientation *and* engagement loop.

Helping organizations find the right balance in this loop has become a top priority for my colleague, Ann Holm, and me. In 2015, I was simultaneously working with two pressure-cooker organizations, a nonprofit and a university system. "Do more with less" was the mantra at both, thanks to staff reductions, but what they hadn't noticed was that while they were all getting used to swimming in a less-crowded pot, changes in the workplace had turned up the temperature, and the pot was boiling.

Do you know the fable that if you put a frog in a pot of boiling water, it'll leap right out? It's not true (Fallows, 2006), but it goes that if the water is warm, that an amphibian will swim around happily even as you turn up the temperature until it's too late.

That's what happened to these organizations, with technology and other changes in workplace norms. Think about the following and ask yourself, "How was this going to solve our problems, and what have been the unintended consequences?"

- Smartphones
- Online-meeting platforms
- Shared calendars
- High-speed internet at home
- Data-management systems
- Web-based learning

The two organizations I was working with had adopted all of these, and staff found themselves at the office no matter where they were. Their exhaustion spilled over into their work with me. It seemed like every email started with "I'm sorry this is late" and every meeting with "Sorry I'm late."

So, I had back-to-back meetings with the leadership teams at both organizations, and I decided to give them a survey that Ann and I were developing. How much did they know about how their brains truly work? After all, you've surely heard it said that we are human beings, not human doings? We have limits. In both organizations, over 70 percent of the employees who took the survey had bandwidth scores below what we considered a level at which they could be energized, efficient, effective, and engaged. We then went through two rounds of improving, testing, and revising the survey to the point where we now have a valid Brain Energy and Bandwidth Survey that helps organizations pinpoint where their norms and policies are interfering with employees' ability to do the work. It also helps individuals reassess their personal approaches to health habits, technology, and other areas to make the most of what we know about the brain.

This is where we're going to break with our format a bit. Instead of exploring two major interdependencies associated with this lens, we're going to focus on a key neuroscience truth and some strategies you can use to put it to work for you.

A Key Neuroscience Truth

Our brains are rewiring to deal with the constant stimulation, interruption, and task-switching that technology is driving. But our brains haven't *evolved*. It takes generations upon generations for human systems to adapt to major changes. What we're experiencing is suboptimal use of our neuropathways, with activities driving us that we aren't wired to handle. This explains much of the stress and lack of time so many people feel (Medina, 2008).

As you work through the next sections, think about how you handle your brain energy—and that of those around you. Your brain demands energy; just the prefrontal cortex, the home of executive function, uses up to 20 percent of your body's available glucose (Schwartz, Gomes, & McCarthy, 2011). What is crucial to understand, though, is that you have only a finite amount of brain fuel available for the following.

- ◆ Using your collaborative leadership skills

- ◆ Engaging in strategic thinking and other complex tasks

- ◆ Exercising willpower to persevere

- ◆ Staying calm and exercising emotional intelligence skills

- ◆ Avoiding poor dietary habits

- ◆ Following through on an exercise plan

- ◆ Slowing down and avoiding impulsive decisions and actions

Use up that limited fuel doing any of these and you simply don't have it available for others. Consider how you're less patient after a long day at work, or how a cookie seems like a solution after a hard conversation. These feelings are not unique to you, and you can use awareness of them to improve your daily life.

Bandwidth helps us exercise more control and recognize more quickly when we're headed in the wrong direction. Let's look at the six main areas our research indicates you need to handle well if your brain is indeed to be at its best for you as a leader—and if those you lead are going to be truly engaged: (1) fueling our brain, (2) focusing through mental habits, (3) filtering through possibilities, (4) balancing priorities, (5) staying connected, and (6) making time work for you.

Before we dig in, note that managers often say, "I can't control the health habits of my staff or their use of social media or . . . ." However, that's not the full story. For example, the full Brain Energy and Bandwidth Survey also has measures of employee engagement and of whether the workplace supports habits that foster good brain energy and bandwidth. The biggest predictor of employee engagement? Workplace support—the area that leaders *do* control.

FURTHER DEVELOPMENT

The Brain Energy and Bandwidth Survey calculates your score for the six factors that make up the next six sections of the chapter, providing an overall bandwidth score. There are also questions on personal effectiveness and engagement, and a section on whether the workplace supports good bandwidth habits. It has statistical validation and is proving to be a useful tool for coaching conversations and leadership collaboration on improving workplace norms. If you would like to experience the survey, contact me through my website (www.janekise.com/contact-me).

Fueling Our Brain

You've heard it before: exercise, sleep, and diet. Your body is an organic system that requires attention to physical, emotional, spiritual, and mental needs and habits. Here are some of the most useful tips to keep in mind and pass on to others.

◆ Know that exercise—even a short walk around the block—is the most effective way to increase your willpower. If you want to avoid the donut, display more patience, persevere on a tough assignment, or gear up for a stop at the gym, get up from your seat and move.

◆ Ensure that everyone knows the dangers of sitting too much. Our bodies were meant to be active; some research indicates that sitting all day decreases the impact of regular exercise. Encourage stretch breaks, standing desks, walking meetings, and other strategies to break up sedentary lifestyles. This includes students, who, if you don't plan for movement, will move and interact when you least want them to.

◆ Sleep is a biological need. The average adult needs seven hours per night, but you may need less or more. Indicators of insufficient sleep include being overly irritable or moody, craving junk food or caffeine, and struggling to stay alert. If you wake up to the alarm and simply don't feel rested, your body is craving more sleep.

◆ Some people wonder if they can compensate for Monday–Friday early rising by sleeping in on the weekends. The answer is yes—sleep is like a bank in that a large deposit can make up for a deficit (Harvard Health Publishing, 2007), and people who engage in this pattern seem to be as healthy as those who regularly get up rested, with no alarm. However, that doesn't mean you're not still operating at a deficit during the week, and you certainly can't let yourself be sleep-deprived for the entire nine months of the school year and make it up over the summer. Long periods of truly not getting enough sleep affect your health in other ways. Note that this isn't the same as insomnia; if you struggle to fall asleep but still feel rested, you're fine. Similarly, there are sleep disorders that cause fatigue regardless of your volume of sleep (Lichstein, Means, Noe, & Aquillard, 1997).

◆ The world is full of contradictory dietary information, but a few things stand out. You're better off getting your vitamins from real food, although supplements can be beneficial. That means eat your fruits and vegetables. You need protein—and leaner cuts of meat or plant sources are for the most part better than fattier sources. Consume white flour and sugar in moderation— the way they produce a flash of glucose in our systems simply isn't helpful. If you know you aren't eating well, keep searching until you find a source of advice and social support for improving your diet that works for you. Your brain depends on it.

◆ Caffeine and alcohol are fine in moderation, according to research (American Cancer Society, 2018, 2019). Ask yourself, *Am I enjoying these or dependent on these?* This is tricky with caffeine since skipping it produces headaches for most people. Remember, though, that after two p.m., a walk rather than a cup of coffee is a better way to refuel. Similarly, addiction to wine is becoming a major health issue for working women, with its social acceptance and the habit of a rather large glass after work every day. Many reputable cancer research websites are suggesting no more than two to four drinks per week (American Cancer Society, 2019; breastcancer.org, 2019).

Think through anything you can do as a leader to model and encourage good habits in your workplace, from fridges where people can store healthy foods to legitimizing a short walk during lunch to providing information on sleep and associated conditions that impact fatigue.

Focusing Through Mental Habits

More and more people are reporting that they are losing their ability to focus. Manoush Zomorodi (2017), a National Public Radio reporter, started the Bored and Brilliant project when she noted uncomfortable changes in personal habits. She struggled to concentrate while reading longer, complex books that she used to read with ease; and she knew she was wasting time on her phone, filling every spare minute with her favorite game or checking email—time that used to go to productive daydreaming about stories and ideas and plans and her infant son's needs. She started an online podcast experiment consisting of seven challenges, and twenty thousand listeners quickly signed up; she wasn't the only one concerned about losing her ability to mentally focus.

Here are a few key concepts about what your brain needs in order to focus when it's really necessary.

- Multitasking is a myth. Your prefrontal cortex has to task-switch, stopping one activity and rerouting activity to the part of the brain needed for the next. It can take up to 50 percent longer to complete tasks if you are task-switching. And no, the digital generation is not better at this. In fact, analysis of our bandwidth survey data revealed that trying to multitask frustrates them even more than their elders.

- All of us need focused time for complex tasks—uninterrupted blocks of at least forty-five minutes. When we are interrupted, it takes as long as twenty-five minutes to return to the level of concentration we had. How can you find those blocks of time so that you can complete work more efficiently?

  When a group of school leaders shared ideas in a workshop I facilitated on bandwidth, suggestions included giving each administrator one day a week with no responsibilities for student discipline, leaving school grounds for a nearby coffee shop when a crucial deadline required complex thinking, and allocating time on the calendar for concentration that is as essential as meetings. Get creative; focusing means being more effective and efficient.

- A major block to focus is email. How often do you check yours? One of the Bored and Brilliant project challenges (www.wnyc.org/series/bored-and-brilliant) records how often you do—and people averaged eighty times a day (Zomorodi, 2017)! Cut back to once an hour, and you'll still be as responsive as anyone can reasonably expect.

- The idea of cognitive steps is a useful tool for staying focused. For example, if your phone is on your desk, and you are only a finger touch away from checking your email, there are no cognitive steps involved. If, when you need to concentrate, you place your phone in airplane mode, put it in your briefcase, and move the briefcase across the room, three cognitive steps stand between you and your email.

◆ Read up on power naps. You will get a legitimate boost from a twenty-minute nap in the afternoon, when your circadian rhythm causes a drop in body temperature that brings on drowsiness (National Sleep Foundation, n.d.). I use a phone app called Power Nap (https://apple.co/2x7aeUl) that gently wakes me up before I descend into deep sleep. Trying to power through that feeling of drowsiness usually means getting less done in an hour than if you took the nap and worked the other forty minutes. Naps mean mental sharpness and efficiency.

◆ Research also supports making a habit of some reflective practice—meditation, yoga, or journaling (Davidson & Begley, 2012). Don't have time? Remember, this is about fueling your brain so that you can be the leader you need to be!

Filtering Through Possibilities

Worldwide connectivity means we have access to endless information all the time. How do you ensure that you are finding the information you need without getting lost in endless web searches or cat videos or research-turned-shopping expeditions or other traps of the Information Age?

◆ In *The Paradox of Choice*, Barry Schwartz (2004) demonstrates how *maximizers*, who want to ensure that they have made the absolutely best choice, are less happy with their decisions than *satisficers*, who search for what is good enough given the importance of the decision. Satisficers are aware that too many choices lead to discontent—think of the frustration of trying to sift through two dozen different cuts or fabrics of jeans to find the perfect fit, or the perfect cereal in the breakfast aisle. How do you limit your choices to save brain energy for other things? Do you use news filters to find key stories? Do you stick to the same menu item at a restaurant or coffee shop? Do you read what your book club selects instead of looking for something at random? Limiting choices in a few areas of life lets you avoid decision fatigue. For example, note that people who are buying cars are more likely to say "yes" to expensive options if those are offered at the end of a long list of other decisions rather than first thing!

- Be wary of how the internet is set up to keep you searching rather than guide you in filtering. Clickbait, hits, and users are, after all, the language of the web and of drug addiction. Zomorodi (2017) describes a conversation with Tristan Harris, who is involved in technology design:

> The most important thing to acknowledge is that it's an unfair fight. On one side is a human being who's just trying to get on with her prefrontal cortex, which is a million years old and in charge of regulating attention. That's up against a thousand engineers on the other side of the screen, whose daily job is to break that and keep you scrolling on the infinite feed. (p. 92)

Think about how you, as a leader, can ensure that information isn't overwhelming your staff. Can a data coach filter down data to what are most useful to the end users? Without taking away autonomy, are there ways to share book suggestions, mathematics problems, apps, or even recipes for quick, healthy lunches? Are you giving too many choices when you provide ideas on how to implement what teachers learned during professional development?

Balancing Priorities

A factor analysis of all the items on our bandwidth survey shows relationships between maintaining healthy relationships (work, home, and social), activities for rest and relaxation, and taking care of yourself when ill. We call it balancing priorities.

- Does your learning community encourage people to stay home when they are ill? Or, is there a martyrdom attitude that results in people spreading germs? Yes, sick days and substitutes are inconvenient, but again, our bodies demand rest to recover, and spreading sickness isn't helpful in the community.

- Patience and presence outside of work are two crucial life-quality indicators. When you are with friends or family, are you present with them? Or is your mind still back at school? Being fully present, not just present, matters. Far too many people use up their brain energy at work, leaving them with little patience for family members. Would others say you are easily irritated before and after work? How can you ensure that your personal life benefits from bandwidth? Note that problems such as road rage also come from too little bandwidth.

- What do you do for rest? We all need a pastime, hobby, or other activity that lets our brains relax. Television—not binge-watching—fits in this category, as do beach reads such as the latest thriller or fantasy bestseller. If you relax while cooking, listening to music, or playing games, these might suffice as well. Just make sure that you turn off your "I must be productive all the time" messages, and give your brain a break.

◆ Finally, does your learning community make time for maintaining relationships with one another? Matthew Lieberman (2013) points out that we are social creatures, wired to live in groups to survive the threats of saber-toothed tigers and take advantage of division of labor. Without the time to develop good relationships, our minds default to, "Who is in favor?" "Who might be blamed?" "Who likes me?" "Who is or isn't looking out for us?" "Are things fair?" Review chapter 11 (page 143) on getting results while building a team for ideas on ensuring that people have the relationships at work that they need.

Staying Connected

Even though we have 24–7 connectivity, people feel lonelier and more isolated than ever—and our bandwidth survey data indicate that Millennials and Generation X colleagues feel even more disconnected than older generations.

◆ Social media both connects and isolates us. By now you've probably heard that people can get caught up in comparing their current level of happiness to the posts they see from friends on vacation, out for dinner, celebrating life highlights, and so on. They're more miserable after being on social media. Be aware of your moods before and after checking Facebook, Twitter, Instagram, or your other favorite sites. How can you make social media work for you, and how can you disconnect from it if it's a net negative to your state of mind?

◆ How do you handle staying connected at home? Several studies show that when phones are on the table, close acquaintances report less empathy in their conversations than device-free conversations with strangers (Misra et al., 2014). Again, do your workplace norms allow for personal space or are availability expectations interfering with effectiveness and engagement?

◆ In general, be realistic about your device habits. The National Safety Council (2012) finds that making phone calls, even with hands-free devices, mimics the effects of driving under the influence of alcohol. Texting while driving, forbidden in many states, is a factor in way too many fatal crashes, and, our phones serve as mindless entertainment when we could be reading, creatively daydreaming, chatting with real people, enjoying the natural sites around us instead of taking pictures of it, and more.

How does your learning community support good technology habits?

Making Time Work for You

Remember that as a school leader, whether you are making time work for you influences whether others in your learning community also feel empowered to work toward life balance. Again, human beings have absolute limits on what they can do. Research shows how when you *know* you're short of a key resource—time, money, relationship quality, health, safety, and so on—bandwidth goes down (Mullainathan & Shafir, 2013). We lose executive function and have less control over where our attention is directed. These scarcities cause tunnel vision—we focus on the scarcity at hand rather than our true priorities. This is why you can be in a reasonably important meeting, but if you need to meet a crucial report deadline in a few hours, your mind keeps defaulting to that report rather than the meeting discussion.

Our bandwidth survey asks whether people feel things are unintentionally falling off their plates. We make two key suggestions for lessening the impact of so much to do, so little time.

1. Limit distractions. Turn off email notifications and every other notification that you possibly can to make the most of the time you have. Remember the idea of cognitive steps and how even placing your phone across the room can help you concentrate.

2. Plan for the inevitable delays life brings your way and insist that your team members begin to do so as well. Traffic delays happen, meetings run over, you get stopped in the hallways, mini-crises arise. Instead of running perpetually behind, schedule time in between meetings and other events. Use the time wisely—one of the leaders we coached started blocking out fifteen minutes in between meetings with her team members so she could complete any promised actions and then refocus to be absolutely fresh for each subsequent person.

Note that this whole chapter is on ensuring you take care of yourself so that you can care for others—and so that others feel empowered to take care of themselves. It's also about the EQ skill of demonstrating empathy. If you do have a high stress tolerance, are you truly listening to how striving for excellence may be causing undue stress, leading to low bandwidth, issues of scarcity, impatience, ill health, and more?

Priorities Inherent in the Goal Orientation and Engagement Lens

Table 15.2 highlights the priorities connected with this lens. Which of these resonate more with you? Which of these may be more key to your current leadership goals?

Table 15.2: Priorities Connected to Goal Orientation *and* Engagement

Goal-Orientation Priorities	Engagement Priorities
Achievement	**Enjoyment**
I believe in setting worthy goals, planning for how to reach them, and then doing so.	I want to create a work environment that is inspiring, congenial, and playful, where people can find fun, humor, and purpose.
Perseverance	**Fulfillment**
I want to model and encourage others in sustaining momentum and having fortitude while making tangible progress.	I want to concentrate my efforts on the dreams and endeavors that bring meaning and purpose to myself and to those I lead.

Because this entire chapter contains our best efforts to help people fuel their brains, focus their attention, and filter information so that they can be energized, efficient, effective, and engaged, there is no last set of Five Ways to . . . sections. Instead, do the following.

1. Look back through the sections of this chapter that describe the six factors that contribute to bandwidth.

2. Ponder which ones might be easy and difficult for people in your learning community—adults and students.

3. Think about how you as a leader can model and make changes that can increase this vital resource for all.

Reaching goals depends on you taking these steps.

ASK YOURSELF

This lens is about moving forward toward your learning community's goals while members of the community continue to enjoy their work and find fulfillment. How well are you balancing goal orientation *and* engagement?

CHAPTER 16

Focusing on Your Priorities

"Wait, this is *practical*."

"Wait, you can do this *again and again*."

Whenever I train others to use the tools in this book to coach leaders, those are their most common reactions; and my coaching clients tell me all the practical ways they're using the process and ask to go through it again and again for new goals or roles.

Now that you've progressed to this final chapter, I am hoping that you see this book as a resource, not a one-and-done read. Let's make sure the value of the Priority Focus process I laid out in chapter 1 (page 14) is clear by walking through how it fits with research on effective leadership development and by working through your own leadership goal.

A Goal That Guides Development

A priority focus is different from SMART goals or an action plan; it is designed to remind you day in and day out of your priorities, as well as to let you quickly assess whether you are on track for reaching your goal. Figure 16.1 (page 210) illustrates a sample focus from my own goals for ensuring that the sessions I facilitate are focused and actionable. Note that I started working on this goal after asking a colleague, "What do you think is the one big thing I should work on?" She related how my sessions were always seamless and attendees left thinking they had everything they needed to implement whatever I was teaching about all by themselves. Then she added, "But they don't. You just make the complex sound easy. You need to provide less in order to ensure they walk away and *do*. Narrow your focus to make room for being explicit about one or two particular aspects they can do immediately. And, perhaps, be explicit about what might be difficult without more support or training or study."

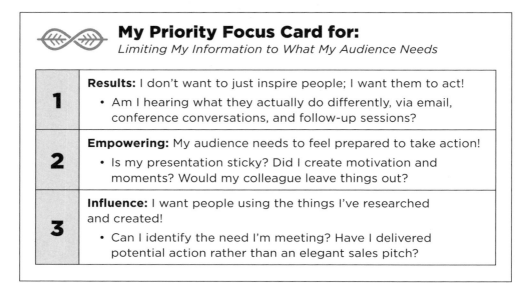

Figure 16.1: Sample priority focus card.

Creating and using a focus like this incorporates the five components of worthwhile leadership development that I introduced in chapter 1 (page 11). Let's revisit these in the context of the goals inherent in your priority focus.

1. **The skills and dispositions you need depend on your context:** Note that your goal isn't coming from a list of five things to do as a new leader or essential tasks at the start of the school year or other standardized views of what leaders should do. Instead, as you focus your priorities, you'll be considering what you naturally pay attention to and your EQ skills with regard to a specific goal, chosen using the criteria on page 16 (Choosing Your Priorities).

2. **Skill development happens not in isolation, but while working and reflecting on real responsibilities and issues:** Look back at page 16 for a list of ways you might find the right kinds of goals for this process. Avoid generalities like "Improve my visioning" in favor of more specific phrasing for your context such as, "Communicate a vision that gets my team to rise and shine." Or instead of "Improve my empathy skills," look for a specific application such as, "Understand the sources of excitement and concern regarding our new curriculum." Note that to determine my own priority focus, I asked a trusted colleague to tell me the "one big thing" she'd like to see me change for our work to be more effective.

3. **Leaders need to unearth and address mindsets:** If you haven't already done so, once you have the goal, choose ten priorities from the list in figure 1.1

(pages 16–18), keeping this prompt in mind: *Is this one of the ten priorities most crucial to meeting this particular goal?* Remember, use sticky flags rather than circling priorities so that the pages can act as an extension of your working memory.

Then, take a look at the lenses linked to your ten priorities (see figure 1.2, page 19). Which are the three most crucial interdependencies to consider as you pursue your goal? Questions to ask yourself include those listed after figure 1.2 and on the following list, which offers a slightly different way to decide.

- If I focus on the lenses my priorities indicate, am I overlooking any lens that is vital to success? Which three of these interdependencies are probably most important for this goal? Given the most important lenses, which priorities deserve the most focus?

- How do the lenses and priorities I'm choosing relate to my current EQ skills? You can find a summary of the EQ skills related to each lens in figure 3.6 (page 44–45). Will accomplishing this goal be natural for me? Will it be a stretch?

- Do I need to focus on my strengths, or in this case, will overusing my strengths lead to vulnerability in a key blind spot?

- Do I have a skill-development need that has to become a priority focus?

Using your answers to these questions, choose the three priorities most critical to the success of your goal. Consider the following.

- One way to think of these, whether they are easy or difficult for you, is to ask yourself, "If I don't focus on these three leadership priorities in this situation, might I greatly increase the risk of somehow derailing?"

- Sometimes leaders eliminate a priority that is so key to their leadership style that they believe they will follow through with it no matter what. Sometimes choosing priorities under *both* poles of a lens is key—and acknowledges the messy fact that leadership priorities can pull us in two directions at once!

Finally, read the chapters in this book for your chosen lenses to develop an understanding of the interdependencies involved and to select and act on ways to make better use of the skills each lens requires.

4. **Leaders need to measure whether they're developing:** You'll recall that the kinds of goals that work for this process aren't very amenable to SMART goals. Instead, you'll be working with *Why?* and *How will I know?* statements.

Kelly McGonigal (2015) points out that people are far more likely to reach their goals if they clearly articulate why the goal is important. So, for your three priorities, do the following.

a. Make sure each of the priorities you chose is personally meaningful to you. Note that at this point, some clients substitute words for the ones in my top forty list (pages 16–18). For example, a rather creative leader changed *Enjoyment* to *Dancing into my office*.

b. Use figure 16.2 to brainstorm your *Why?* and *How will I know?* statements. First, do a quickwrite that captures your ideas. Perhaps an analogy will come to mind that will increase the meaningfulness of the statement for you. When you've brainstormed the *Why?* using ten to fifteen words, create a statement or question that captures why that priority is so important to your goal. For example, for my *results* priority, my *Why?* is, "I don't want to just inspire people; I want them to act!"

c. Use the same process to capture, in ten to fifteen words, a reminder question or statement you can use to quickly assess whether you are on course with your goal. For example, my reminder for Results encourages me to reach out in some way to learn whether my presentation or workshop proved useful.

Then, create a priority focus card. Use the form in figure 16.3 (page 214) or create your own.

Sound simplistic? Most people find that this kind of focused document takes at least two hours to create. They then laminate it and post it prominently— by their computer, on a mirror, or wherever they might regularly reflect on whether they are being intentional.

5. **Set aside time for reflection:** Depending on your *How will I know?* prompts, you might look at your card daily or weekly, but at least once a month, take time for deeper reflection. The process of appreciative inquiry, which identifies and encourages doing more of what is working, is ideal for this purpose. For each of your priorities, ask yourself the following questions.

- On a scale of 1–10, how would you rate yourself on working with this priority? Why are you already at that point?

- How or where have you made progress since last time?

- What did you do of which you are particularly proud?

- How can you amplify what you are already doing?

Priority Focus Card Form

Name:	Date:
Leadership goal: *(five to seven words)*	

EXAMPLE

Lens number and name:	*Lens 5: Continuity and change*
Priority focus:	*Creativity with the known*
Why is this so important now? *(ten to fifteen words)*	*I need to dig deeper with what I've already created!*
How will I know if I'm maintaining this focus? *(ten to fifteen words)*	*Am I staying energized to develop, expand, and promote my existing tools and ideas that I truly believe can help others?*
Lens number and name:	
Priority focus:	
Why is this so important now?	
How will I know if I'm maintaining this focus?	
Lens number and name:	
Priority focus:	
Why is this so important now? *(ten to fifteen words)*	
How will I know if I'm maintaining this focus? *(ten to fifteen words)*	
Lens number and name:	
Priority focus:	
Why is this so important now?	
How will I know if I'm maintaining this focus?	

Source: © 2019 by Jane A. G. Kise.

Figure 16.2: Priority focus template.

*Visit **go.SolutionTree.com/leadership** for a free reproducible version of this figure.*

- What is the simplest action you can take to raise your rating by a point?
- Can you think of an even simpler action than that?

Take time to journal or record your thoughts with a voice memo app so that you can revisit your thoughts and use the last three questions to form new action steps. Then, act on what you've identified as your next actions.

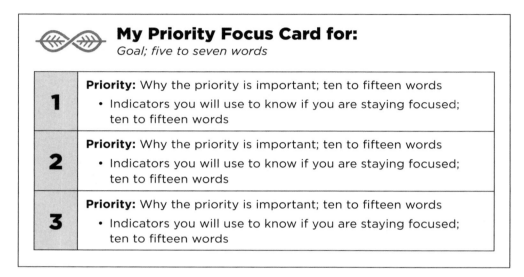

Source: © 2019 by Jane A. G. Kise.

Figure 16.3: Priority focus card.

*Visit **go.SolutionTree.com/leadership** for a free reproducible version of this figure.*

The Beginning of the End of the Beginning of the Journey

If you've followed through on this process, you now have a workable priority focus you can use to hold yourself accountable for developing as a holistic leader. If you found an accountability partner, you can start meeting regularly to encourage each other in your work as a school leader in a volatile, uncertain, complex, ambiguous world. If you reach your goal, you can choose another, sort your priorities, and develop a new priority focus.

Do this again and again. The best school leaders I've had the privilege to work with never stop working to improve their capacity to guide their learning community in helping every student succeed academically while also supporting their social, emotional, spiritual, and physical needs. May these pages help you reach your goals and enjoy the journey.

APPENDIX

Personality Type and the Lenses of Leadership

I've written extensively on personality type and leadership in other books. For *Holistic Leadership, Thriving Schools*, personality type serves as another way to identify your unconscious biases, as well as potential blind spots around the Twelve Lenses of Leadership. This appendix contains a brief description of the framework and its value for leadership development. If you are interested in learning more about this powerful tool for coaching and personal development, contact me through www .janekise.com/contact-me to receive a code that will give you one-time access to the TypeCoach Verifier. Through this interactive online experience (*not* an assessment or questionnaire) you will identify your four-letter personality type code and receive a six-page report about your type in education.

If you already know your four-letter type code, popularized through the MBTI®, you can use the chart at the end of this appendix (figure A.1, pages 219–220) as a further check for ensuring that you are focusing on the right priorities. As you do this, keep the following in mind.

- You may find that for a particular goal, all three of the priorities you selected via the process in chapter 16 (pages 209) align with your inborn personality preferences. That could mean, "Great! I was born to reach this goal!" Or, it could mean that you're unaware of competing priorities that are just as crucial to that goal and which are more natural for leaders with other preferences.

- You may find that all three of your priorities are outside of your preferences. Leaders I've coached where this is true have told me, "No wonder this is wearing me out!" Sometimes, they were aware they'd set a stretch goal and were embracing the challenge.

215

♦ More often, some priorities will match your preferences and some won't. Revisit what is on the other side of the proverbial coin in figure A.1 to ensure you're aware of your focus and what you may potentially be ignoring.

The personality type framework was first developed by Carl Jung ("Psychological Types," n.d.). The mother-daughter team of Katharine Briggs and Isabel Myers made his theory accessible and useful through the well-known Myers-Briggs Type Indicator (The Myers & Briggs Foundation, n.d.). The framework identifies four dichotomies that describe common differences in people.

1. **How we are energized (Extraversion and Introversion):** Those who prefer Extraversion are energized through action and interaction. Those who prefer Introversion are energized through solitude and reflection. Think how this colors our natural perceptions on classroom participation, collaboration and group work, silent reading, and more.

2. **The information we trust and notice first (Sensing and Intuition):** Those who prefer Sensing might also be described as detail-oriented, accurately drawing on past experiences and what their five senses tell them. They see the trees first. Those who prefer Intuition might be described as big-picture people, trusting the connections, themes, and analogies their minds devise. They see the forest first. In education, this preference pair has been demonstrated to affect how we learn to read and do mathematics, the test questions we write, our choice of content areas and university majors, and more (Kise, 2014).

3. **The criteria we use for decisions (Thinking and Feeling):** Those who prefer Thinking begin with objectivity and logic: if-then, pro-con reasoning and defining universal truths. Those with a preference for Feeling make decisions by stepping into the shoes of those involved to see how everyone will be affected and by weighing values. Misunderstandings and arguments about discipline, assessments, curriculum content, the importance of time for building classroom atmosphere, and more often stem from differences between the decision-making criteria Thinking and Feeling types use.

4. **How we approach life (Judging and Perceiving):** Those who like to plan their work and work their plan are Judging types who like closure and coming to judgments. (They are not more judgmental.) Those who prefer to keep options open longer in order to seek more information or perceptions are Perceiving types. (They are not more perceptive.) Our school

systems tend to overemphasize the norms of those who prefer Judging, with schedules, school bells, curriculum maps, and other structured plans. The valuable voices of Perceiving types are often missing from decisions.

A common misunderstanding about these types revolves around how they can be innate and yet not fixed. They are inborn preferences, but we can still choose how we act and can develop skills to move outside of our preferences as we mature. The framework of personality type points to patterns in human behavior, not what any individual will do at a given moment. It's about understanding one's own tendencies and the tendencies of others, because our personality preferences can feed our biases. The chart in figure A.1 shows the Twelve Lenses of Leadership and related type preferences. Leaders more naturally pay attention to the lens poles related to their preferences, although experience, training, collaborative partners, and other factors may bring balance.

Type	Extraversion	Introversion
Lens 1	**Leadership**	**Listening**
	Providing leadership while helping everyone learn to lead themselves	
Priorities	Influencing, Shepherding	Empowering, Connecting
Lens 2	**Breadth**	**Depth**
	Implementing needed initiatives and ensuring mastery of initiatives	
Priorities	Networking, Innovating	Legacy, Mastery
Lens 3	**Community**	**Individual**
	Building a collaborative culture while meeting individual needs	
Priorities	Relationships, Collaboration	Individuality, Personal development
Type	**SENSING**	**INTUITION**
Lens 4	**Reality**	**Vision**
	Accounting for very real barriers of time, resources, and so on, while leading toward a purposeful vision	
Priorities	Realism, Balance	Visioning, Optimism
Lens 5	**Continuity**	**Change**
	Building on current success while changing to meet the future	
Priorities	Experience, Creativity with the known	Challenge, Creativity with the new
Lens 6	**Short Term**	**Long Term**
	Addressing current needs while working toward systemic change	
Priorities	Efficiency	Adaptability

continued →

Type	THINKING	FEELING
Lens 7	**Logic**	**Values**
	Determining universal principles and rules and accounting for individual needs and perspectives	
Priorities	Fair-mindedness	Empathy
Lens 8	**Outcomes**	**People**
	Moving toward organizational success and creating a culture of collective efficacy	
Priorities	Results, Measurability	Trust, Appreciation
Lens 9	**Power To**	**Power With**
	Effectively using positional power while effectively sharing power	
Priorities	Expertise	Openness
Type	JUDGING	PERCEIVING
Lens 10	**Clarity**	**Flexibility**
	Clarifying expectations and remaining open to new processes and ideas	
Priorities	Organization, Accountability	Originality, Autonomy
Lens 11	**Predictability**	**Possibility**
	Setting goals and making plans while preparing for ever-changing environments and an uncertain future	
Priorities	Dependability	Complexity
Lens 12	**Goal orientation**	**Engagement**
	Making whole-child achievement progress while ensuring that adults and students have purpose	
Priorities	Achievement, Perseverance	Enjoyment, Fulfillment

Figure A.1: The type framework, Twelve Lenses of Leadership, and related priorities.

References and Resources

Active listening. (n.d.). In *Wikipedia*. Accessed at https://en.wikipedia.org/wiki/Active_listening on November 19, 2018.

Alfieri, L., Brooks, P. J., Aldrich, N. J., & Tenenbaum, H. R. (2011). Does discovery-based instruction enhance learning? *Journal of Educational Psychology, 103*(1), 1–18.

American Cancer Society. (2018). *Can coffee lower cancer risk?* Accessed at www.cancer.org/latest -news/can-coffee-lower-cancer-risk.html on February 19, 2019.

American Cancer Society. (2019). *Alcohol use and cancer.* Accessed at www.cancer.org/cancer /cancer-causes/diet-physical-activity/alcohol-use-and-cancer.html on February 19, 2019.

Association for Supervision and Curriculum Development. (n.d.). *Whole child.* Accessed at www .ascd.org/whole-child.aspx on October 18, 2017.

Association for Supervision and Curriculum Development. (2014). *Whole school, whole community, whole child: A collaborative approach to learning and health.* Accessed at www .ascd.org/ASCD/pdf/siteASCD/publications/wholechild/wscc-a-collaborative-approach.pdf on October 11, 2018.

Baldrige Performance Excellence Program. (2017a). *2017–2018 Baldrige graphics.* Accessed at www.nist.gov/baldrige/publications/baldrige-excellence-framework/baldrige-excellence -framework-graphics on September 21, 2018.

Baldrige Performance Excellence Program. (2017b). *From fighting fires to innovation: An analogy for learning* [Infographic]. Accessed at www.nist.gov/image/2017-2018-baldrige-framework -fighting-fires-innovationjpg on September 21, 2018.

Baumeister, R. F., & Tierney, J. (2011). *Willpower: Rediscovering the greatest human strength.* New York: Penguin.

Berger, J. G. (2012). *Changing on the job: Developing leaders for a complex world.* Stanford, CA: Stanford Business Books.

Berger, J. G., & Johnston, K. (2015). *Simple habits for complex times: Powerful practices for leaders.* Stanford, CA: Stanford Business Books.

Boaler, J., & Zoido, P. (2016). Why math education in the U.S. doesn't add up. *Scientific American Mind.* Accessed at www.scientificamerican.com/article/why-math-education-in -the-u-s-doesn-t-add-up on April 30, 2018.

breastcancer.org. (2019). *Drinking alcohol.* Accessed at www.breastcancerorg/risk/factors/alcohol on February 19, 2019.

Buffum, A., Mattos, M., & Malone J., (2018). *Taking action: A handbook for RTI at Work.* Bloomington, IN: Solution Tree Press.

Buffum, A., Mattos, M., & Weber, C. (2012). *Simplifying response to intervention: Four essential guiding principles.* Bloomington, IN: Solution Tree Press.

Carton, A. M., Murphy, C., & Clark, J. R. (2014). A (blurry) vision of the future: How leader rhetoric about ultimate goals influences performance. *Academy of Management Journal, 57*(6), 1544–1570.

Cherniss, C., Extein, M., Goleman, D., & Weissberg, R. P. (2006). Emotional intelligence: What does the research really indicate? *Educational Psychologist, 41*(4), 239–245.

Collins, J. (2001). *Good to great: Why some companies make the leap . . . and others don't.* New York: HarperBusiness.

Conzemius, A. E., & O'Neill, J. (2014). *The handbook for SMART school teams: Revitalizing best practices for collaboration* (2nd ed.). Bloomington, IN: Solution Tree Press.

Covey, S. R., Merrill, A. R., & Merrill, R. R. (1994). *First things first.* New York: Simon & Schuster.

Coyle, D. (2018). *The culture code: The secrets of highly successful groups.* New York: Bantam Books.

Dane, E., Rockmann, K. W., & Pratt, M. G. (2012). When should I trust my gut? Linking domain expertise to intuitive decision-making effectiveness. *Organizational Behavior and Human Decision Processes, 119*(2), 187–194.

Davidson, R., & Begley, S. (2012). *The emotional life of your brain: How its unique patterns affect the way you think, feel, and live—and how you can change them.* New York: Plume.

Dewey, J. (1990). *The School and Society and the Child and the Curriculum.* Chicago: University of Chicago Press.

DeWitt, P. M. (2017). *Collaborative leadership: Six influences that matter most.* Thousand Oaks, CA: Corwin Press.

Duhigg, C. (2016). *Smarter, faster, better: The secrets of being productive in life and business.* New York: Random House.

Dweck, C. S. (2006). *Mindset: The new psychology of success.* New York: Random House.

Dweck, C. S. (2015). Carol Dweck revisits the 'growth mindset.' *Education Week.* Accessed at www.edweek.org/ew/articles/2015/09/23/carol-dweck-revisits-the-growth-mindset.html on June 3, 2018.

Edge, K. (2014). A review of the empirical generations at work research: Implications for school leaders and future research. *School Leadership and Management, 34*(2), 136–155.

Fallows, J. (2006). *The boiled-frog myth: Stop the lying now!* Accessed at www.theatlantic.com /technology/archive/2006/09/the-boiled-frog-myth-stop-the-lying-now/7446/ on November, 28, 2018.

Federal Reformatory. (n.d.). *"The Buck Stops Here" desk sign.* Accessed at www.trumanlibrary.org /buckstop.htm on November 27, 2018.

Felps, W., Mitchell, T. R., & Byington, E. (2006). How, when, and why bad apples spoil the barrel: Negative group members and dysfunctional groups. *Research in Organizational Behavior, 27,* 175–222.

Fine, A. (2010). *You already know how to be great: A simple way to remove interference and unlock your greatest potential.* New York: Portfolio Penguin.

Freedman, M. (1992). Initiative fatigue. *Strategic Change: Briefings in Entrepreneurial Finance, 1*(2), 89–91.

Gallup. (2016). *2016 Gallup student poll snapshot report.* Accessed at http://news.gallup.com/reports/210995/6.aspx on March 21, 2018.

Gelles, D. (2015). *At Zappos, pushing shoes and a vision.* Accessed at www.nytimes.com/2015/07/19/business/at-zappos-selling-shoes-and-a-vision.html?_r=0 on February 18, 2019.

George, B. (2012). True north groups: A big idea for developing leaders. *Leader to Leader, 63,* 32–37.

Gerzema, J., & D'Antonio, M. (2013). *The Athena doctrine: How women (and the men who think like them) will rule the future.* San Francisco: Jossey-Bass.

Gilbert, E. (2015). *Big magic: Creative living beyond fear.* New York: Riverhead Books.

Glaser, J. (2005). *Leading through collaboration: Guiding groups to productive solutions.* Thousand Oaks, CA: Corwin Press.

Goleman, D., Boyatzis, R., & McKee, A. (2002). *Primal leadership: Realizing the power of emotional intelligence.* Boston: Harvard Business School Press.

Goral, T. (2012). Daniel Rasmus on the science of scenarios. *University Business, 15*(11), 68–69.

Grant, A. (2016). *Originals: How non-conformists move the world.* New York: Viking.

Gurdjian, P., Halbeisen, T., & Lane, K. (2014). Why leadership-development programs fail. *McKinsey Quarterly.* Accessed at www.mckinsey.com/global-themes/leadership/why-leadership-development-programs-fail on October 15, 2017.

Haidt, J. (2012). *The righteous mind: Why good people are divided by politics and religion.* New York: Pantheon Books.

Hall, G. E., & Hord, S. M. (2010). *Implementing change: Patterns, principles, and potholes* (3rd ed.). Boston: Allyn & Bacon.

Hammarskjold, D. (1964). *Markings.* New York: Knopf.

Hammond, Z. (2015). *Culturally responsive teaching and the brain: Promoting authentic engagement and rigor among culturally and linguistically diverse students.* Thousand Oaks, CA: Corwin Press.

Harvard Health Publishing. (2007). *Repaying your sleep debt: Why sleep is important to your health and how to repair sleep deprivation effects.* Accessed at www.health.harvard.edu/womens-health/repaying-your-sleep-debt on January 4, 2019.

Hattie, J. (2012). *Visible learning for teachers: Maximizing impact on learning.* New York: Routledge.

Heath, C., & Heath, D. (2010). *Switch: How to change things when change is hard.* New York: Broadway Books.

Herbel-Eisenmann, B., & Cirillo, M. (Eds.). (2009). *Promoting purposeful discourse: Teacher research in mathematics classrooms.* Reston, VA: National Council of Teachers of Mathematics.

Hord, S. M. (Ed.). (2004). *Learning together, leading together: Changing schools through professional learning communities.* New York: Teachers College Press.

The Hormel Foundation. (n.d.). *About the foundation.* Accessed at www.thehormelfoundation .com/pages/about-us/ on November 28, 2018.

Human Capital Institute. (2013). *Leadership and emotional intelligence: The keys to driving ROI and organizational performance.* White River Junction, VT: Author.

Jensen, E. (2005). *Teaching with the brain in mind* (2nd ed.). Alexandria, VA: Association for Supervision and Curriculum Development.

Johnson, B. (2012). *The polarity approach to continuity and transformation.* Sacramento, CA: Polarity Partnerships.

Kirby, L., & Kendall, B. (2008). *Type and culture: Using the MBTI instrument in international applications.* Palo Alto, CA: Consulting Psychologists Press.

Kise, J. A. G. (2014). *Unleashing the positive power of differences: Polarity thinking in our schools.* Thousand Oaks, CA: Corwin Press.

Kise, J. A. G. (2017). *Differentiated coaching: A framework for helping educators change* (2nd ed.). Thousand Oaks, CA: Corwin Press.

Kise, J. A. G., & Russell, B. (2008). *Differentiated school leadership: Effective collaboration, communication, and change through personality type.* Thousand Oaks, CA: Corwin Press.

Kotter, J. P. (1996). *Leading change.* Boston: Harvard Business School Press.

Kouzes, J. M., & Posner, B. Z. (2010). *The truth about leadership: The no-fads, heart-of-the-matter facts you need to know.* San Francisco: Jossey-Bass.

Kouzes, J. M., & Posner, B. Z. (2012). *The leadership challenge: How to make extraordinary things happen in organizations* (5th ed.). San Francisco: Jossey-Bass.

Lichstein, K. L., Means, M. K., Noe, S. L., & Aquillard, R. N. (1997). Fatigue and sleep disorders. *Behavior Research and Therapy, 35*(8), 733–740.

Lieberman, M. D. (2013). *Social: Why our brains are wired to connect.* New York: Crown.

Lyons, I. M., & Beilock, S. L. (2012). Mathematics anxiety: Separating the math from the anxiety. *Cerebral Cortex, 22*(9), 2102–2110.

MacKenzie, G. (1998). *Orbiting the giant hairball: A corporate fool's guide to surviving with grace.* New York: Viking.

Markow, D., & Pieters, A. (2012). *The MetLife Survey of the American Teacher: Teachers, parents and the economy.* New York: MetLife. Accessed at https://files.eric.ed.gov/fulltext/ED530021 .pdf on November 13, 2012.

Marzano, R. J. (2011). *The Marzano teacher evaluation model.* Englewood, CO: Marzano Research.

McFarland, A. S. (2006). Comment: Power—Over, To, and With. *City & Community, 5*(1), 39–41. Accessed at https://doi-org.ezproxy.hclib.org/10.1111/j.1540-6040.2006.00152.x on February 5, 2019.

McGonigal, K. (2015). *The upside of stress: Why stress is good for you, and how to get good at it*. New York: Penguin Random House.

McKeown, G. (2014). *Essentialism: The disciplined pursuit of less*. New York: Crown Business.

Medina, J. (2008). *Brain rules: 12 principles for surviving and thriving at work, home, and school*. Seattle, WA: Pear Press.

Meffert, H., Gazzola, V., den Boer, J. A., Bartels, A. A. J., & Keysers, C. (2013). Reduced spontaneous but relatively normal deliberate vicarious representations in psychopathy. *Brain, 136*(8), 2550–2562.

Mikaelsen, B. (2001). *Touching spirit bear*. New York: HarperCollins.

Misra, S., Cheng, L., Genevie, J., & Yuan, M. (2014). The iPhone effect: The quality of in-person social interactions in the presence of mobile devices. *Environment and Behavior, 48*(2), 275–298.

Mullainathan, S., & Shafir, E. (2013). *Scarcity: The new science of having less and how it defines our lives*. New York: Henry Holt.

The Myers & Briggs Foundation. (n.d.). *MBTI basics*. Accessed at www.myersbriggs.org/my-mbti-personality-type/mbti-basics on November 29, 2018.

Nardi, D. (2011). *Neuroscience of personality: Brain savvy insights for all types of people*. Los Angeles: Radiance House.

National Safety Council. (2012). *Understanding the distracted brain: Why driving while using hands-free cell phones is risky behavior*. Accessed at www.nsc.org/Portals/0/Documents/DistractedDrivingDocuments/Cognitive-Distraction-White-Paper.pdf on November 28, 2018.

National Sleep Foundation. (n.d.). *Sleep drive and your body clock*. Accessed at www.sleepfoundation.org/sleep-topics/sleep-drive-and-your-body-clock on November 28, 2018.

No Child Left Behind Act of 2001, Pub. L. 107–110, 20 U.S.C. § 6319 (2002).

Owen, H. (2008). *Open Space Technology: A user's guide* (3rd ed.). San Francisco: Berrett-Koehler.

Park, J., & Brannon, E. M. (2013). Training the approximate number system improves math proficiency. *Psychological Science, 24*(10), 2013–2019.

Patterson, K., Grenny, J., Maxfield, D., McMillan, R., & Switzler, A. (2011). *Change anything: The new science of personal success*. New York: Business Plus.

Pearman, R. R., Lombardo, M. M., & Eichinger, R. W. (2005). *You: Being more effective in your MBTI type*. Minneapolis, MN: Lominger.

Pink, D. H. (2009). *Drive: The surprising truth about what motivates us*. New York: Riverhead Books.

Psychological types. (n.d.). In *Wikipedia*. Accessed at https://en.wikipedia.org/wiki/Psychological_Types on November 29, 2018.

Putnam, R. D. (2000). *Bowling alone: The collapse and revival of American community*. New York: Simon & Schuster.

Resnick, L. B. (1999). Making America smarter. *Education Week Century Series, 18*(40), 38–40. Accessed at www.edweek.org/ew/articles/1999/06/16/40resnick.h18.html on December 26, 2018.

Rock, D. (2006). *Quiet leadership: Six steps to transforming performance at work.* New York: HarperCollins.

Rohr, R. (2013). *The naked now: Learning to see as the mystics see.* New York: Crossroad.

Saphier, J. (2005). Masters of motivation. In R. DuFour, R. Eaker, & R. DuFour (Eds.), *On common ground: The power of professional learning communities* (pp. 85–113). Bloomington, IN: Solution Tree Press.

Saphier, J., & D'Auria, J. (1993). *How to bring vision to school improvement: Through core outcomes, commitments and beliefs.* Acton, MA: Research for Better Teaching.

Schwartz, B. (2004). *The paradox of choice: Why more is less.* San Francisco: HarperCollins.

Schwartz, T., Gomes, J., & McCarthy, C. (2011). *The way we're working isn't working: The four forgotten needs that energize great performance.* New York: Free Press.

Simons, A. (2008, September 18). Box cutter was for work, but to school, it's a weapon. *Star Tribune*, p. 1A.

Skakon, J., Nielsen, K., Borg, V., & Guzman, J. (2010). Are leaders' well-being, behaviours and style associated with the affective well-being of their employees? A systematic review of three decades of research. *Work and Stress, 24*(2), 107–139.

Sun, J., & Leithwood, K. (2015). Leadership effects on student learning mediated by teacher emotions. *Societies, 5*(3), 566–582.

Sytch, M. (2015). *Limitations of SMART goals: Inspiring and motivating individuals* [Video file]. Accessed at www.coursera.org/lecture/motivate-people-teams/02-04-limitations-of-smart -goals-2g69s on October 9, 2018.

Tatum, B. D. (2017). *Why are all the black kids sitting together in the cafeteria? And other conversations about race* (20th anniversary ed.). New York: Basic Books.

Think before you expel: Anoka-Hennepin board should use judgment in box cutter case. (2008, September 22). *Star Tribune*, p. 8A. Accessed at www.startribune.com/think-before-you -expel/28672199 on November 27, 2018.

University of Pittsburgh. (n.d.). *Accountable Talk.* Accessed at http://iflpartner.pitt.edu/index.php /educator_resources/accountable_talk on November 26, 2018.

van der Heijden, K. (2005). *Scenarios: The art of strategic conversation.* New York: Wiley.

Wheatley, M. (2017). *Who do we choose to be? Facing reality, claiming leadership, restoring sanity.* Oakland, CA: Berrett-Koehler.

Wheatley, M., & Kellner-Rogers, M. (1999). What do we measure and why? Questions about the uses of measurement. *Journal for Strategic Performance Measurement.* Accessed at www .margaretwheatley.com/articles/whymeasure.html on October 11, 2018.

Witherspoon, R., & White, R. P. (1997). *Four essential ways that coaching can help executives.* Greensboro, NC: Center for Creative Leadership.

Zomorodi, M. (2017). *Bored and brilliant: How spacing out can unlock your most productive and creative self.* New York: St. Martin's Press.

Index

A

Abrams, J., 144–145
academic growth, 35
academic performance, 10
Academic Search Premier, 141
accomplishment, sense of, 149
accountability
    clarity and flexibility lens and, 167, 175
    outcomes and people lens and, 35
    polarity identification and, 28
    positional power and, 159
    reality pole and, 97
    support and, 148
Accountable Talk, 65, 69, 74
achievement, measurable whole-child
    about, 195–196
    engaging journeys and goal-oriented
        destinations and, 197–198
    neuroscience and, 199–200
achievement priorities, 195, 207
acknowledgement, practicing, 152–153
active listening
    EQ skills and, 43, 123–124
    leadership and listening lens and, 55–56
    listening pole and, 58
adaptability priorities, 115, 124
Advancement Via Individual Determination (AVID), 65
aggression, dismissing, 164
Alberts, J., 181–183, 186
Aldrich, N., 172
Alfieri, L., 172
appreciation, practicing, 152–153
appreciation priorities, 143, 150
Arnold, T., 135
assessments
    emotional self-awareness, 39
    relationship management, 43–44
    self-management of emotions, 40

social awareness of emotions, 42
Association for Supervision and Curriculum
    Development (ASCD), 4, 9, 72
assumptions, checking, 190
Athena Doctrine, The (Gerzema and D'Antonio), 36
atmosphere. *See also* emotional safety
    belonging and, 148
    campfires and pressure cookers and, 196–197
    emotional intelligence quotient (EQ) and, 35
    fixed and growth mindset classrooms and, 26
    relationship management and, 42–43
authority, demonstrating, 164. *See also* power to and
    power with lens
autonomy. *See also* community and individual lens
    about, 75–76
    breadth pole and, 72
    community and individual and, 76–78
    emotional intelligence quotient (EQ) and,
        81–82, 109
    flexibility pole and, 177–178
    individual pole and, 86
    priorities and, 167, 175

B

balance, 43, 87, 96, 145
Baldrige Institute, 183
Baldrige Performance Excellence Program, 183–184,
    191
bandwidth, 199–200, 206
Baumeister, R., 36
belonging, creating sense of, 148
Berger, J., 135, 150, 162, 181
biases
    holistic leadership and, 4
    leadership development and, 11–12
    listening and, 53
    personality types and, 217
blind spots, 4, 11–12, 217

Bored and Brilliant: How Spacing Out Can Unlock Your Most Productive and Creative Self (Zomorodi), 58, 202

both–and thinking
    about, 23–24
    identifying polarities and problems and, 28–29
    improving both–and thinking, 30
    polarities and, 24–28
    polarities, priorities, and emotional intelligence and, 29–30
    using, 5

bottom-up and top-down interdependencies, 186–187

Bowling Alone (Putnam), 71

Boyatzis, R., 46

brain energy, 199–200

Brain Energy and Bandwidth Survey, 198, 200

brain, fueling the, 199, 200–201

brainstorming, 73, 85

Brannon, E., 116

breadth and depth lens
    about, 61–62
    breadth and depth loop, 67
    breadth and necessary depth, 66–69
    clarity and flexibility lens and, 171
    EQ connection and, 69–70
    EQ skills and, 44
    increasing use of the breadth pole, 71–73
    increasing use of the depth pole, 73–74
    initiative fatigue and, 62–66
    personality types and, 219
    priorities and, 19, 70–71
    Twelve Lenses of Leadership and, 5

Briggs, K., 218

Brooks, P., 172

Brown, T., 50–52, 53, 54

buy-in, gauging, 57

Byington, E., 35

C

caring for others, 36

challenge priorities, 101, 110

change. *See also* continuity and change lens
    about, 101–102
    change pole and, 112–113
    continuity and, 105–108
    continuity pole and, 110–111
    resistance and fear and, 102–103

Child and the Curriculum, The (Dewey), 101

clarity, 163–164

clarity and flexibility lens
    about, 167
    clarity and flexibility loop, 170
    EQ connection and, 174–175
    EQ skills and, 45

flexible clarity, 169–174
    increasing use of the clarity pole, 175–177
    increasing use of the flexibility pole, 177–178
    personality types and, 220
    priorities and, 19, 175
    successful ideas and, 168–169
    Twelve Lenses of Leadership and, 5

classroom and student interdependencies, 80, 81

closure, delaying, 190

cognitive steps, 202–203

collaboration
    clarity pole and, 176–177
    community and individual lens and, 75, 83
    emotional intelligence quotient (EQ) and, 82
    flexibility pole and, 177
    individual pole and, 86
    interdependencies and, 23
    interpersonal skills and, 43
    possibility pole and, 192
    power with pole and, 165
    questions for, 70

collaborative learning communities. *See also* community and individual lens
    about, 75–76
    classroom and student and, 81
    collaboration meter, 79–81
    dilemma of community and individual and, 76–78
    standardization and customization and, 80–81

collaborative power
    about, 155
    knowledge from the ground up and, 156–158
    positional power and, 159
    real results from real teams and, 158–161

Collins, J., 111

community and individual interdependencies, 134, 135

community and individual lens
    about, 75–76
    collaboration and, 23
    collaboration meter, 79–81
    community and individual loop, 79
    dilemma of community and individual and, 76–78
    EQ connection and, 81–82
    EQ skills and, 44
    increasing use of the community pole, 83–84
    increasing use of the individual pole, 85–86
    personality types and, 219
    priorities and, 19, 83
    Twelve Lenses of Leadership and, 5

complexity priorities, 179, 189

confirmation biases, 12

connecting priorities, 49, 56

connections, maintaining, 199, 205

consensus, definition of, 40

consistency, 54. *See also* logic and values lens

constants, articulating, 111
constants in teaching, 180
context, 11
continuity and change lens
    about, 101–102
    continuity and change loop, 106
    deliberate continuity, constant change, 105–108
    EQ connection and, 108–110
    EQ skills and, 45
    increasing use of the change pole, 112–113
    increasing use of the continuity pole, 110–111
    personality types and, 219
    predictability and possibility lens and, 181
    priorities and, 19, 110
    resistance and fear and, 102–105
    Twelve Lenses of Leadership and, 5
continuous-improvement cycle, 183–184, 191
controls, internal, 187
core values, 123
Courageous Conversations, 88, 95
Covey, S., 122, 188
creativity
    change pole and, 112
    creativity and experience interdependencies, 107
    priorities and, 101, 110
    SMART goals and, 133
current success. See success
customization and standardization
    interdependencies, 80–81

D

Dane, E., 97
D'Antonio, M., 36
Dare 2 Be Real, 88
data-management systems, 198
decision making
    common decision-making criteria, 132
    empathy and, 136
    logic pole and, 137
    logical thinking and, 95
    thinking and feeling types and, 218
    values pole and, 139, 140
delegating, 165
dependability priorities, 179, 189
depth lens. See breadth and depth lens
development
    developmental focus, 13, 14–15
    leadership development, 11–13
    personal development priorities, 75, 83
    priority focus and, 209–212, 214
    short-term and long-term needs and, 119
    stages of adult development, 3
devices, use of, 56, 205

Dewey, J., 101
Differentiated Coaching (Kise), 80, 109
differentiated professional development, 80–81
direct instruction, 172–173
discovery learning, 172
divergence, planning for, 86
drama thinking, 138
Duffy, P., 88–90, 93, 94
Duhigg, C., 177
Dweck, C., 26–27, 29

E

Edge, K., 196
education and EQ, 34
effect size, 35
efficiency priorities, 115, 124
effort, 27–28
emotional intelligence
    about, 33–34
    brain energy and, 199
    improving emotional intelligence, 46–47
    polarities and priorities and, 29–30
emotional intelligence quotient (EQ)
    breadth and depth lens and, 61, 69–70
    clarity and flexibility lens and, 167, 174–175
    community and individual lens and, 75, 81–82
    continuity and change lens and, 101, 108–110
    EQ skills, 44–45
    goal orientation and engagement lens and, 195
    leadership and listening lens and, 49, 55–56
    logic and values lens and, 129, 135–136
    model for whole-child school leadership and, 38
    outcomes and people lens and, 143, 149–150
    power to and power with lens and, 155,
        162–163
    predictability and possibility lens and, 179, 188
    reality and vision lens and, 87, 94–95
    relationship management and, 42–44
    self-awareness of emotions and, 38–39
    self-management of emotions and, 39–40
    short-term and long-term lens and, 115, 123–124
    social awareness of emotions and, 41–42
    truths about, 34–37
Emotional Quotient-Inventory 2.0, 34
emotional safety
    clarity and flexibility lens and, 174–175
    continuity and change lens and, 108, 109–110
    logic and values lens and, 135, 136
    reality and vision lens and, 94–95
    respect and, 147
emotions
    awareness of, 38–39, 188
    self-management of emotions, 39–40

social awareness of emotions, 41–42, 55, 57
empathy
    digital devices and, 56, 206
    empathy mapping, 182–183
    EQ connection and, 55, 135–136, 188
    listening pole and, 58
    priorities and, 129, 137
    social awareness of emotions and, 41
    values pole and, 140
empowering priorities, 49, 56
engagement lens. *See* goal orientation and engagement lens
enjoyment priorities, 195, 207
enthusiasts, 72
excellence, pockets of, 54
executive functioning, 206
expectations, 150, 151. *See also* clarity and flexibility lens
expectations and support interdependencies, 147, 148–149
experience and creativity interdependencies, 107
experience priorities, 101, 110
expertise, 97
expertise priorities, 155, 163
experts, 84
extraversion, 53, 81, 218, 219

F
fair-mindedness, 129, 137
fairness, definition of, 130
fear and resistance, 102–105
feedback
    emotional intelligence quotient (EQ) and, 149–150, 162–163
    interpersonal skills and, 43
    logic and values lens and, 133
    outcomes and people lens and, 145
    outcomes pole and, 152
    reality pole and, 97
feeling types, 218, 220
Felps, W., 35, 148
fidelity and innovation interdependencies, 172–173
Fine, A., 177
fire hose analogy, 183–184
fixed mindset, 26–27
flexibility lens. *See* clarity and flexibility lens
focus
    focused attention, 56
    mental habits and, 199, 202–203
    over-focus, 4
fulfillment priorities, 195, 207

G
Galloway, A., 88–89
generalists, 67–68

George, B., 34
Gerzema, J., 36
Gilbert, E., 109, 113
Glaser, J., 40
goal orientation and engagement lens
    about, 195–196
    campfires and pressure cookers and, 196–197
    engaging journeys and goal-oriented destinations and, 197–198
    EQ skills and, 45
    filtering through possibilities and, 203–204
    focusing through mental habits and, 202–203
    fueling the brain and, 200–201
    goal orientation and engagement loop, 197
    making time work for you and, 206
    neuroscience and, 199–200
    personality types and, 220
    priorities and, 19, 204–205, 206–207
    staying connected and, 205
    Twelve Lenses of Leadership and, 5
    work-life balance and, 36
goals
    flexibility pole and, 177
    interdependencies and, 172, 173–174
    leadership development and, 12
    long-term pole and, 126–127
    priority focus and, 209–212, 214
    research on, 105
    self-fulfillment and, 149
    short-term pole and, 126
Goleman, D., 46
Good to Great (Collins), 111
Goodreads, 58, 174
Grant, A., 91, 112
Grenny, J., 176
group purpose, 35
growth mindset, 26–27

H
habits
    brain energy and, 199
    fueling our brains and, 200–201
    mental habits, 199, 202–203
    technology use and, 205
Haidt, J., 11–12
Harris, T., 204
Hattie, J., 35
Heath, C., 112
Heath, D., 112
hedgehog strategy, 111
hobbies, 204–205
holistic experiences, 1
holistic leadership, 3–4
Holm, A., 197–198
Hormel Foundation, 180

Human Capital Institute, 33
humility and self-regard interdependencies, 160, 161

I

images, using, 97–98
important and urgent interdependencies, 120, 122
impulses, 69, 199
inconsistencies, listening for, 54
incrementalism and urgency interdependencies, 92–93
independence
    emotional intelligence quotient (EQ) and, 82,
        94–95, 108, 123
    self-management and, 40
individual and community interdependencies, 134, 135
individual lens. *See* community and individual lens
individuality priorities, 75, 83
inefficiency and shared ownership, 164
influencing priorities, 49, 56
initiatives. *See also* breadth and depth lens
    about implementing initiatives, 61–62
    assessing past initiatives, 185–186
    clarity and flexibility lens and, 167
    community and individual lens and, 75
    continuity and change lens and, 101
    generalists and specialists and, 67–68
    goal orientation and engagement lens and, 195
    immense investment and, 63–65
    incrementalism and urgency and, 92–93
    initiative fatigue, 62–63
    leadership and listening lens and, 49
    logic and values lens and, 129
    outcomes and people lens and, 143
    power to and power with lens and, 155
    predictability and possibility lens and, 179, 183
    preparation and implementation and, 68–69
    reality and vision lens and, 87
    short-term and long-term lens and, 115
innovating priorities, 61, 71
innovation and fidelity interdependencies, 172–173
innovation and tradition interdependencies, 107, 108
inquiry-based teaching, 117, 172–173
Institute for Learning (IFL), 64, 65
instructional practices, 101
interdependencies
    breadth and depth lens and, 67–69
    clarity and flexibility lens and, 172–174
    collaboration and, 23
    community and individual lens and, 80–81
    continuity and change lens and, 107–108
    defining interdependencies, 31
    lenses and, 10
    logic and values and, 130–131
    logic and values lens and, 134–135
    outcomes and people lens and, 147–149
    power to and power with lens and, 160–161

    predictability and possibility lens and, 186–187
    reality and vision lens and, 92–94
    short-term and long-term lens and, 120–122
    short-term and long-term needs and, 119
    Twelve Lenses of Leadership and, 23
internal controls and external forces
    interdependencies, 186, 187
International Baccalaureate (IB), 64
internet, use of, 198, 204
interpersonal skills, 43. *See also* active listening; feedback
introversion types, 81, 218, 219
intuition types, 95, 218, 219

J

Johnson, B., 24–25, 26
Johnston, K., 150, 162, 181
judging types, 218, 220
Jung, C., 218
Jungian personality types, 18, 53, 84
justice and mercy interdependencies, 134

K

Kellner-Rogers, M., 133
Kise, J., 26, 80, 109
Kotter, J., 91
Kouzes, J., 57, 113
Kyte, C., 130

L

language
    authority and, 164
    frameworks and, 84
    independence and, 123
    reality and vision lens and, 93
leadership and listening lens
    about, 49–50
    EQ connection and, 55–56
    EQ skills and, 44
    example of leading while listening, 50–52
    increasing use of leadership pole, 56–57
    increasing use of listening pole, 57–58
    leadership and listening loop, 52
    leadership priorities, listening priorities, 52–55
    personality types and, 219
    priorities and, 19, 56
    Twelve Lenses of Leadership and, 5
leaders/leadership
    change and, 107
    components for leadership development, 11–13
    development focus and, 13, 14–15
    emotional intelligence quotient (EQ) and, 34–36
    holistic leadership, 3–4
    intentional leaders, 9–10
    leaders and participants interdependencies,
      160–161

leaders, students, and staff interdependencies, 92, 94
    priorities and, 13, 16–18
    priorities and lenses, aligning, 13, 18–21
    reflection and next steps, 21–22
    student achievement and, 106
    vision and, 91
    vulnerability and, 177
learning
    learning-mode feedback, 152
    models of learning, 157–158
    SMART goals and, 133
    web-based learning, 198
Learning Forward, 72
legacies, 127
legacy priorities, 61, 71
lens of educators/students, 2
lenses. See Twelve Lenses of Leadership; specific lenses
leverage, 25. See also specific lenses
Lieberman, M., 205
list of priorities, 16–18
listening lens. See leadership and listening lens
logic, brushing up on, 190
logic and values lens
    about, 129
    decision making and, 183
    EQ connection and, 135–136
    EQ skills and, 45
    increasing use of the logic pole, 137–139
    increasing use of the values pole, 139–141
    interdependencies between logic and values, 130–131
    logic and values loop, 131
    personality types and, 220
    priorities and, 19, 136–137
    rules with exceptions and, 131–135
    Twelve Lenses of Leadership and, 5
logic decisions, 140
logic tools, 137–138
long term, definition of, 120
long-term focus, 182
long-term lens. See short-term and long-term lens
long-term needs, 119, 185
long-term plan, 126–127

M

MacKenzie, G., 112
management, 106, 107
Markow, D., 196
Marzano, R., 73
mastery, 61, 71–73
mathematics, 117–119
Maxfield, D., 176
maximizers, 203
McGonigal, K., 212

McKee, A., 46
McKinsey and Company, 11–13
McMillan, R., 176
measures. See also achievement, measurable whole-child
    feedback and, 133
    measurability priorities, 143, 150
    measure of outcomes and people, 146–149
mental habits, 199, 202–203
Merrill, A., 122
Merrill, R., 122
messages, reviewing, 176
methodology, 145
MetLife Survey of the American Teacher (Markow and Pieters), 196
MHS Assessments, 34
micromanaging, 85
Middle Years Programme, 64
Mikaelsen, B., 134, 136
mindsets
    fixed and growth mindset, 26–27
    leadership development and, 11–12
    priority focus and, 211
Minnesota Association of School Administrators, 130
mission, definition of, 104
Mitchell, T., 35
models of learning, 157–158
motivation, 92
movies, using, 57, 58
multitasking, 202
Myers, I., 218
Myers-Briggs Type Indicator, 217, 218

N

Nardi, D., 55–56, 188
National Safety Council, 205
National Urban Alliance, 65
needs, 117–119, 185. See also short-term and long-term lens
networking priorities, 61, 71
networks, joining, 71–72
neuroscience truths, 199–200
No Child Left Behind Act (2002), 4
norms, 54–55
now and later interdependencies, 120, 121

O

objectivity. See also logic and values lens
    about, 129
    interdependencies between logic and values and, 130–131
    logic pole and, 138
    rules with exceptions and, 131–135
observations, peer classroom observation sheet, 168
online-meeting platforms, 198
Open Space Technology, 72

openness priorities, 155, 163

optimism, gauging, 98

optimism priorities, 87, 96

Orbiting the Giant Hairball (MacKenzie), 112

organization priorities, 167, 175

originality priorities, 167, 175

Originals (Grant), 91, 112

outcome biases, 12

outcomes and people lens

    about, 143

    accountability and, 35

    clarity and flexibility lens and, 172

    EQ connection and, 149–150

    EQ skills and, 45

    increasing use of the outcomes pole, 151–152

    increasing use of the people pole, 152–154

    measure of outcomes and people, 146–149

    outcomes and people loop, 147

    personality types and, 220

    priorities and, 19, 150

    real results from real teams, 144–146

    Twelve Lenses of Leadership and, 5

P

Paradox of Choice, The (Schwartz), 203

paraphrasing, 58

Park, J., 116

participants and leaders interdependencies, 160–161

partners. *See also* collaboration

    clarity pole and, 176

    possibility pole and, 192

    precedent partners, 138

    reality pole and, 97

    values partners, 140

Patterson, K., 176

peer classroom observation sheet, 168

people lens. *See* outcomes and people lens

perceiving types, 218, 220

perceptions, testing, 97

percolating, 51, 54, 57, 77

perseverance priorities, 195, 207

personal development priorities, 75, 83

personality type framework, 64, 218–220

perspectives, seeking other, 192

Pieters, A., 196

planning. *See also* predictability and possibility lens

    about planning for the predictable, 179–180

    change and, 181

    clarity and flexibility lens and, 171–172

    and a complex, unpredictable world, 185–187

    continuous-improvement cycle and, 183–184

    delays and, 206

    flexibility pole and, 178

    long and short of planning, 120–123

    long-term pole and, 126–127

    possible and the probable and, 180–185

    preplanning, 172

    reviewing past plans, 176

    scenario planning, 184–185

    short-term and long-term poles and, 124–125

    short-term pole and, 125

planning thinking, 138

polarities. *See also* interdependencies

    about, 24–25

    both–and thinking and, 25–26

    definition of, 23

    priorities and emotional intelligence and, 29–30

    problem-solution thinking and, 26–28

    unsolvable problems and, 28–29

Polarity Partnerships, 26

positional power

    about, 155

    collaborative power and, 159

    importance of knowledge from the ground up and, 156–158

    power to pole and, 164

    real results from real teams and, 158–161

Posner, B., 57, 113

possibilities, filtering, 199, 203–204

possibility lens. *See* predictability and possibility lens

power naps, 203

power to and power with lens

    about, 155

    clarity and flexibility lens and, 171

    EQ connection and, 162–163

    EQ skills and, 45

    importance of knowledge from the ground up and, 156–158

    increasing use of the power to pole, 163–164

    increasing use of the power with pole, 164–165

    personality types and, 220

    power to and power with loop, 158

    priorities and, 19, 163

    real results from real teams and, 158–161

    Twelve Lenses of Leadership and, 5

power, value of, 4

Pratt, M., 97

predictability and possibility lens

    about, 179–180

    effective plans for a complex, unpredictable world, 185–187

    EQ connection and, 188

    EQ skills and, 45

    increasing use of the possibility pole, 190–192

    increasing use of the predictability pole, 189–190

    personality types and, 220

    possible and the probable and, 180–185

    predictability and possibility loop, 185

    priorities and, 19, 189

    Twelve Lenses of Leadership and, 5

predictions, 126
Principles of Learning, 64, 65
priorities
     aligning with lenses, 13, 18–21
     balancing priorities, 199, 204–205
     breadth and depth lens and, 61, 70–71
     choosing priorities, 13, 16–18
     clarity and flexibility lens and, 167, 175
     community and individual lens and, 75, 83
     continuity and change lens and, 110
     goal orientation and engagement lens and, 195,
        206–207
     leadership and listening lens and, 49, 56
     leadership and listening priorities and, 52–55
     list of priorities, 16–18
     logic and values lens and, 129, 136–137
     outcomes and people lens and, 143, 150
     polarities and emotional intelligence and, 29–30
     power to and power with lens and, 155, 163
     predictability and possibility lens and, 189
     reality and vision lens and, 87, 95–96
     short-term and long-term lens and, 115, 124
     Twelve Lenses of Leadership and, 19
priority focus
     action plans and, 14
     goals that guide development and, 209–212, 214
     journey of, 214–215
     priority focus card, 212, 214
     priority focus template, 213
     sample priority focus, 210
     SMART goals and, 209
problem thinking, 138
problem-solution thinking, 26–28
processes, 177
professional development, differentiating, 80–81
protocols, 82, 95, 124–125
purpose. *See also* goal orientation and engagement
  lens
     breadth pole and, 72
     engaging journeys and goal-oriented
        destinations and, 197–198
     finding purpose, 195–196
     neuroscience and, 199–200
     outcomes and people lens and, 145
     outcomes pole and, 152
Putnam, R., 71

Q
questions, asking
     breadth pole and, 72
     change pole and, 112
     continuity pole and, 111
     micromanaging and, 85
     possibility pole and, 191
     short-term pole and, 126–127

working collaboratively and, 70

R
reactions, 69
readiness, 27–28
readiness and effort loop, 28
reading emotions, 57
realism priorities, 87, 96
reality and vision lens
     about, 87
     clarity and flexibility lens and, 171
     EQ connection and, 94–95
     EQ skills and, 44
     increasing use of the reality pole, 96–97
     increasing use of the vision pole, 97–98
     need to bring vision to reality, 90–94
     personality types and, 219
     priorities and, 19, 95–96
     reality and vision loop, 90
     Twelve Lenses of Leadership and, 5
     when vision meets reality, 88–90
reality check, 151
reflection, 13, 212
reflective practices, 203
relationships
     balancing priorities and, 204–205
     community and individual lens and, 75, 83
     community pole and, 84
     relationship management, 38, 42–44
research
     on bandwidth, 206
     on discovery learning, 172
     on number of goals, 105
     on willpower, 36–37
     values pole and, 140–141
resistance and fear, 102–105
Resnick, L., 26
respect interdependencies, 147–148
results. *See also* outcomes and people lens
     about getting results, 143
     about short-term results, 115
     and focus on tomorrow while thinking five
        years ahead, 116–119
     long and short of planning in schools and,
        120–123
     measure of outcomes and people and, 146–149
     outcomes and people lens and, 143, 150
     people pole and, 152
     real results from real teams and, 144–146
Richards, T., 130
risks, 188
Rock, D., 138–139
Rockmann, K., 97
Rohr, R., 11
role models, 73

routines, 111, 112

Russell, B.
    generalists and specialists and, 67–68
    ideal initiatives and immense investment and,
        63–65
    preparation and implementation and, 68–69
    testing depth before breadth and, 65–66

S

Saphier, J., 26

satisficers, 203

SayDoCo, 177

scenario planning, 126, 184–185, 191

Scenarios: The Art of Strategic Conversation (van der
    Heijden), 191

schools
    campfires and pressure cookers and, 196–197
    improvement and, 9
    student engagement and, 141

Schwartz, B., 203

scope of change, 93

self-actualization, 149

self-awareness, 38–39

self-care, 36, 196

self-control, 36

self-fulfillment, 38, 140, 149, 162

self-management, 38, 39–40

self-regard and humility interdependencies, 160, 161

self-respect, 149

sensing types, 218, 219

shared calendars, use of, 198

shared ownership, 164

shared responsibility, 159

shepherding, 49, 56

short-term and long-term lens
    about, 115
    EQ connection and, 123–124
    EQ skills and, 45
    focus on tomorrow while thinking five years
        ahead, 116–119
    increasing use of both poles, 124–125
    increasing use of long-term pole, 126–127
    increasing use of short-term pole, 125–126
    long and short of planning in schools and,
        120–123
    personality types and, 219
    priorities and, 19, 124
    short-term and long-term loop, 120
    Twelve Lenses of Leadership and, 5

short-term needs, 117–119, 185

sick days, 204

skills/skill development. *See also* active listening;
    feedback
    EQ skills, 44–45
    interpersonal skills, 43

leadership development and, 11
    priority focus and, 210
    soft skills and, 15, 29, 34

sleep, 200–201, 203

SMART goals, 12, 133, 175, 209

smartphones, use of, 56, 198

social awareness of emotions, 38, 41–42

social media, 205

soft data, 41, 55

soft skills, 15, 29, 34

specialists, 67–68

staff, students, and leaders interdependencies, 94

stakeholders, 139

standardization and customization
    interdependencies, 80–81

status quo, 89, 93

strategic thinking, 199

stress tolerance, 196–197

student achievement, 106

student and classroom interdependencies, 81

student engagement, 141

student success, 9, 141

student voice, 94

students, staff, and the leaders interdependencies, 92, 94

subjectivity. *See also* logic and values lens
    about, 129
    logic and values and, 130–131
    real world of rules with exceptions and, 131–135

success. *See also* continuity and change lens
    about, 101–102
    about long-term success, 115
    change pole and, 113
    when successful ideas are not universal, 168–169

support, 35, 153–154

support and expectations interdependencies, 147,
    148–149

SurveyMonkey, 145

surveys, 73

Switch: How to Change Things When Change Is Hard
    (Heath and Heath), 112

Switzler, A., 176

synergy, 72

systems thinking, 27, 183, 184, 192

T

Tatum, B., 88

teacher efficacy
    academic growth and, 77
    atmosphere and, 197
    clarity and flexibility lens and, 172
    emotional intelligence quotient (EQ) and, 34
    gauging the conditions for collective teacher
        efficacy, 146
    student success and, 141

Teacher's Choice Award program, 173

teacher-student relationships, 140

teaching, constants in, 180

teams, collaborative
  community pole and, 83–84
  emotional intelligence quotient (EQ) and, 82, 95
  vision pole and, 98

technology use
  empathy and, 56
  habits and, 205
  listening pole and, 58
  unpredictability of, 181

TED Talks, 71

Tenenbaum, H., 172

Think, Pair, Share strategy, 165

thinking
  levels of, 138–139
  personality types and, 218
  possibility pole and, 191
  problem-solution thinking, 26–28
  strategic thinking, 199
  systems and, 192
  Twelve Lenses of Leadership and, 220

Thoughtluck, 186

Tierney, J., 36

time
  complex tasks and, 202
  connections and, 58, 199
  making time work for you and, 199, 206
  predictability pole and, 189

to-do lists, 125

top-down and bottom-up interdependencies, 186–187

Touching Spirit Bear (Mikaelsen), 134, 136

tradition and innovation interdependencies, 107, 108

trust. *See also* outcomes and people lens
  about building trust, 143
  clarity and flexibility lens and, 174–175
  collaboration and, 177
  people pole and, 154
  predictability and possibility lens and, 189

Twelve Lenses of Leadership. *See also specific lenses*
  about, 5
  EQ skills and, 44–45
  interdependencies and, 23
  leadership responsibilities and, 10
  personality type framework and, 219–220
  polarities and, 25
  related priorities and, 19

TypeCoach, 20, 217

U

Unleashing the Power of Differences: Polarity Thinking in Our Schools (Kise), 26

urgency, 125–126

urgent and important interdependencies, 120, 122

U.S. Army, 157–158, 186

V

values. *See also* logic and values lens
  clarity pole and, 176
  core values, 123
  definition of, 104
  long-term pole and, 127
  vision and, 92

van der Heijden, K., 191

vision. *See also* clarity and flexibility lens; leadership and listening lens; reality and vision lens
  clarity pole and, 175–176
  definition of, 104
  personal vision, 98
  purpose and, 91
  values statements and, 92

vision thinking, 138

visionaries, 95

visioning, 87, 96

visioning day, 104

VUCA world, 1, 4, 30

vulnerability, 153

W

web-based learning, 198

"Were you ever a child?" 2–3, 5

Wheatley, M., 6, 133, 149, 157–158

White, R., 163

Whole Child Initiative, 4

whole-child approach to education, definition of, 9

whole-child leadership development process
  development focus, 13, 14–15
  priorities and, 13, 16–18
  priorities and lenses and, 13, 18–21

Why Are All the Black Kids Sitting Together in the Cafeteria? (Tatum), 88

willpower, 36–37, 199

Witherspoon, R., 163

work-life balance, 36, 196

Z

zero-tolerance policies, 130, 131, 134

Zomorodi, M., 202, 204

Step In, Step Up
Jane A. G. Kise and Barbara K. Watterston
Step In, Step Up guides current and aspiring women leaders in education through a twelve-week development journey. An assortment of activities, reflection prompts, and stories empowers readers to overcome gender barriers and engage in opportunities to learn, grow, and lead within their school communities.
BKF827

Creating a Coaching Culture for Professional Learning Communities
Jane A. G. Kise and Beth Russell
This practical resource provides activities designed to meet a wide variety of needs so you can choose the ones that fit your leadership style, the learning styles of team members, and the particular needs of the school.
BKF350

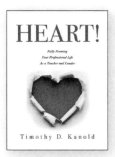

HEART!
Timothy D. Kanold
Explore the concept of a heartprint—the distinctive impression an educator's heart leaves on students and colleagues during his or her professional career. Use this resource to reflect on your professional journey and discover how to foster productive, heart-centered classrooms and schools.
BKF749

Transformative Teaching
Kathleen Kryza, MaryAnn Brittingham, and Alicia Duncan
Examine the most effective strategies for leading diverse students to develop the skills they need inside and outside the classroom. By understanding and exploring students' emotional, cultural, and academic needs, educators will be better prepared to help all students become lifelong learners.
BKF623

Solution Tree | Press *a division of* Solution Tree

Visit SolutionTree.com or call 800.733.6786 to order.

Wait! Your professional development journey doesn't have to end with the last pages of this book.

We realize improving student learning doesn't happen overnight. And your school or district shouldn't be left to puzzle out all the details of this process alone.

No matter where you are on the journey, we're committed to helping you get to the next stage.

Take advantage of everything from **custom workshops** to **keynote presentations** and **interactive web and video conferencing**. We can even help you develop an action plan tailored to fit your specific needs.

Let's get the conversation started.

Call 888.763.9045 today.

SolutionTree.com